NANI PALKHIVALA

Selected Writings

NANI PALKHIVALA

Selected Writings

Selected and Edited
by

L.M. Singhvi
M.R. Pai
S. Ramakrishnan

PENGUIN
VIKING
An imprint of Penguin Random House

VIKING

USA | Canada | UK | Ireland | Australia
New Zealand | India | South Africa | China | Singapore

Viking is part of the Penguin Random House group of companies whose addresses can be found at global.penguinrandomhouse.com

Published by Penguin Random House India Pvt. Ltd
4th Floor, Capital Tower 1, MG Road,
Gurugram 122 002, Haryana, India

First published in Viking by Penguin Books India/Bhavan's Book University 1999

10 9 8 7 6 5 4 3

ISBN 9780670888283

Typeset in *Nebraska* by SÜRYA, New Delhi
Printed at Replika Press Pvt. Ltd, India

www.penguin.co.in

Let noble thoughts come to us from every side

—*Rigveda 1-89-i*

CONTENTS

EDITOR'S NOTE

◆

NANI PALKHIVALA IS a living legend and has done India proud at home and abroad. His life and work are many splendoured, bearing the hallmark of integrity and verstality.

Early in his professional career and with the publication of his magnum opus on Income Tax, he came to be recognized for his preeminence as a great expert in the theory and practice of taxation. In later years, he became the most formidable critic of the fiscal policies of the Government. For years, he was the most articulate exponent of a new approach to taxation and economic reconstruction of India. Time has proved his perceptions and his prognoses to be prophetic.

An acknowledged leader of the Bar, his brilliant advocacy of issues of abiding public importance has had a creative impact on the exegesis and evolution of constitutional percepts and principles of India. To listen to his arguments in some of the landmark cases in the Supreme Court was to experience the spell of his magic persuasiveness as he would begin to unfold the vision of the Founding Fathers of the Constitution and to illumine the path of law.

Nani is a charismatic communicator and a great public educator. An orator *par excellence,* he knows that an orator's virtue is to speak the truth. He speaks the truth with transparent sincerity and conviction. In the inimitable words of Shakespeare, 'when he speaks, the air . . . is still, and the mute wonder lurketh in men's ears to steal his sweat and honey'd sentences.' What is more, he has shown a remarkable problem-solving capacity: 'Turn him to any cause of policy, the Gordian knot of it he will unloose'.

As India's Ambassador in the USA, he made a distinctive and memorable contribution in the domain of diplomacy and won many heartwarming accolades and citations.

Nani Palkhivala's books like *The Law and Practice of Income-tax, The Highest Taxed Nation, Constitution Defaced and Defiled, India's Priceless Heritage, Essential Unity of all Religions, We, the People* and *We, the Nation* have acquired the status of classics and have run into several editions. They bear eloquent testimony to his scholarship, his wit and wisdom, and his profound patriotism, intellectual depth, moral integrity, innate humanity and inborn humility.

The saga of Nani Palkhivala's life and work has an inspirational quality. Last year, during a convivial postprandial conversation at the elegant Palkhivala home in Bombay, I proposed quite spontaneously a publication of a select collection of his writings in the form of a Reader, which would convey the essence of his life and work. Shri S. Ramakrishnan, the Director General of Bharatiya Vidya Bhavan and General Editor of the Bhavan's Book University, who was present, promptly welcomed the idea.

My long friendship with Nani and his affection for me did not allow him to demur and dissent. There was grace in his humility as he yielded and gave his consent. And thus the idea of this book was launched. We then approached and coopted Shri M.R. Pai, who has had a long association with Nani.

Our three member Editorial Committee soon embarked upon the task of making a selection from his writings. This is our affectionate offering to Nani Ardeshir Palkhivala on the eightieth year of his Pilgrimage of Life. It has been a labour of love and an enriching experience for us. It is in the fitness of things that this volume is being jointly brought out by the Bhavan's Book University and Penguin Books India, both of which have earned a place of honour in the world of publishing.

We are in Nani Palkhivala's debt for agreeing to let us build one more bridge between him and the legion of his readers, admirers in India and abroad as also the younger generation through this Commemoration Volume. The credit for bringing the idea of this Commemoration Volume to fruition goes mainly to my two co-editors, Shri M.R. Pai, and Shri S. Ramakrishnan.

Guru Purnima Day,
28 July 1999

L.M. Singhvi

NANI ARDESHIR PALKHIVALA

A Profile

◆

IN 1972-73 THE full Bench of thirteen judges of the Supreme Court of India heard with rapt attention a handsome lawyer argue for five months before them that the Constitution of India, which guaranteed fundamental freedoms to the people, was supreme, and Parliament had no power to abridge those rights. The judges peppered him with questions. A jampacked court, corridors overflowing with members of the Bar and people who had come from far-away places just to hear the lawyer argue, was thrilled to hear him quote in reply chapter and verse from the U.S., Irish, Canadian, Australian and other democratic constitutions of the world.

Finally came the judgment in April 1973 in *Kesavananda Bharati v. State of Kerala,* popularly known as the *Fundamental Rights* case. The historic pronouncement was that though Parliament could amend the Constitution, it had no right to alter the basic structure of it.

The doyen of Indian journalists, Durga Das, congratulated the lawyer: 'You have salvaged something precious from the wreck of the constitutional structure which politicians have razed to the ground.' This 'something precious'—the sanctity of 'the basic structure' of the Constitution—saved India from going fully down the totalitarian way during the dark days of the Emergency (1975 -77) imposed by Mrs Indira Gandhi.

Soon after the proclamation of Emergency on 25 June 1975,

the Government of India sought to get the judgment reversed, in an atmosphere of covert terrorization of the judiciary, rigorous press censorship, and mass arrests without trial, so as to pave the way for suspension of fundamental freedoms and establishment of a totalitarian state. Once again, braving the rulers' wrath, this lawyer came to the defence of the citizen. His six-page propositions before the Supreme Court and arguments extending over two days were so convincing that the Bench was dissolved and the Court dropped the matter altogether. Commented a judge: 'Never before in the history of the Court has there been a performance like that. With his passionate plea for human freedoms and irrefutable logic, he convinced the Court that the earlier *Kesavananda Bharati* case judgment should not be reversed.'

This man, who saved the Indian Constitution for generations unborn, was Nani Ardeshir Palkhivala (popularly 'Nani'). His greatness as a lawyer is summed up in the words of Justice H.R. Khanna of the Supreme Court: 'If a count were to be made of the ten topmost lawyers of the world, I have no doubt that Mr Palkhivala's name would find a prominent mention therein'. The late Prime Minister Morarji Desai described him to Barun Gupta, the famous journalist, as 'the country's finest intellectual'.

Nani Palkhivala hails from a family whose ancestors could be traced to Hyderabad, Deccan. They were engaged in making palanquins or 'palkhis'. That is how 'Palkhivala' became a surname, rather rare among Parsis.

Born on 16 January 1920, of a respectable family with a thin purse but strong family values and faith in God, Palkhivala spent his childhood in Tardeo and Nana Chowk, Bombay (now Mumbai), with his parents, Sheherbanoo and Ardeshir, an older sister, Amy, and a younger brother, Behram. He adored his parents, and even in later years the mention of them brought tears to his eyes. Till they breathed their last, he took every conceivable care of their needs. Equally great was his reverence for his school teachers and college professors. He never forgot them throughout their lives and paid them respect and homage.

The main business of Palkhivala's father was running a laundry at Cumballa Hill, Bombay. He did his work so meticulously that some of the foreign residents, while departing for their native land, left their select costly garments with him to be washed and returned to them abroad, rather than getting the same washed in their own country. From him Palkhivala learnt to do work to perfection.

He met Nargesh Matbar as a student in St. Xavier's College, and married her in 1945. Though she too did her law degree, she never practised, but remained a devoted life partner, assisting him in his endeavours and shouldering the responsibilities of the household where hospitality is legendary.

'The child is father of the man.' Even as a small boy, Palkhivala was very studious and used to spend most of his time in reading. In the Matriculation he passed among the first fifty and stood first in English. Forgoing pleasures, and even some necessities of life, he would save almost every bit of money to buy secondhand books—then available at four annas a book. His favourite haunt was Popular Book Depot on Lamington Road, whose proprietor, the late Ganeshrao Bhatkal, allowed him full freedom to browse till the closing hours, an act of kindness which Palkhivala never forgot. Years later, while delivering the Ganesh Ramrao Bhatkal Memorial Lecture, appropriately on the subject 'Education and the Art of Reading', he began by saying that had Bhatkal been alive, he would have touched his feet as a mark of gratitude.

In addition to books, he had diverse interests right from his early days. He played the violin, was an expert at fretwork (the skill he put to liberal use in preparing gift items), studied palmistry, took part in elocution competitions at state and inter-state levels, did sketching and painting, and loved photography.

A man of many dimensions, he gave tuitions during his school and college days to lessen the load on his father, and started his career as a journalist on a monthly salary of Rs 15. His regular columns, 'Mild and bitter' and 'A handful of ashes', became popular with the public; and his articles on literary and other topics in different newspapers were a treat to read. His first article was published when he was thirteen.

Since his first love was literature, in which he has retained his interest throughout his life, at one time he had desired to be a college lecturer, but he lost the post to a lady because he did not have the teaching experience which she had. So worked destiny. And in later years he acknowledged his debt to the lady for what turned out to be a stroke of good fortune.

After he did his MA with Honours in English, his father wanted him to be a lawyer; while he, ironically, wanted to be a government servant, an ICS. The final examination was to be held in Delhi; but because of an epidemic there he was dissuaded from filing the application form for which a time had been set. After the period expired, the government announced the shifting of the venue from Delhi to Bombay because of the epidemic. Thus destiny worked once again. And in deference to his father's wishes he turned to law. He did his First LLB in 1943 and his Second LLB in 1944 from the Government Law College, both times standing First Class First. He passed the Advocate (Original Side) examination of the Bombay High Court in 1946, standing first in every individual paper.

He was a Professor of Law at the Government Law College, Bombay, and was appointed the Tagore Professor of Law at the Calcutta University. He delivered the prestigious Tagore Lectures without notes.

Palkhivala started his legal practice in the chambers of Sir Jamshedji Kanga, who had a formidable reputation for integrity, knowledge of taxation and other laws, and persuasive power. The young lawyer had a matchless meteoric rise at the Bar. His big break came only two years after starting practice, in a requisition case, *Rao v. Advani,* in which, in the face of all adverse High Court rulings, he convinced Justice N.H. Bhagwati of the Bombay High Court that a high prerogative writ was maintainable against the government. As a result of his tracing back the constitutional position for more than a hundred years, a writ of mandamus was issued against the state government in 1948, the first writ of its kind against any government in India.

Within four years of joining the Bar, he brought out *The Law and Practice of Income-tax* to which Sir Jamshedji agreed to lend his name.

He would charm the Court with his rhetoric and his highly intellectual and persuasive arguments. Some members of the Income-tax Appellate Tribunal said that they made it a point not to dictate the judgment soon after he presented his case, but they would let some days pass to break the spell he had cast.

His interest in economics and in the economic development of our country was the direct result of his work in the field of tax laws. He came to public attention through his Budget speeches. He first appeared on the platform of the Forum of Free Enterprise, in 1957, with his speech on the new pattern of taxation introduced at that time. In 1958 he gave his first public lecture on the Union Budget at Green's Hotel (where the Taj Intercontinental now stands). The yearly talks attracted continuously increasing numbers, and the Forum was forced to shift the venue to the larger Cowasji Jehangir Hall in 1965. The overflowing crowds proved the inadequacy even of this hall, and from the very next year, 1966, the meeting had to be shifted to the spacious Cricket Club of India East Lawns. As years passed, the Lawns too could not hold the swelling crowds, and in 1983 the Forum had to have recourse to the Brabourne Stadium itself. The galleries got speedily filled up and the entire ground in front of the stadium was packed with people, thousands of them standing all through the talk. They came not only from distant parts of Bombay but also from several other cities and states. Vijay Merchant, President of the Cricket Club of India, who welcomed the gathering in March 1983, remarked that 'Mr Palkhivala has brought the crowds back to the Brabourne Stadium', since test matches were no longer played at the stadium following the construction of another stadium nearby. The same sentiments were reflected in the welcome remarks of Bansi Mehta, Honorary Treasurer of the Club, at the meeting held in 1992 when he said: 'At least occasions like this means that good use is made of this vast expanse of beautiful ground. Today we partially redeem the dreams of those who created the stadium even if no cricket is played here any longer.' Lord Roll of Ipsden, who presided over the 1986 meeting, observed in his presidential address that nowhere in the world ('I repeat, nowhere in the world') would a Budget speech attract such an audience.

Foreigners who attended Palkhivala's speeches when they happened to be in Bombay at the time were amazed at his performance. Dr Willliam Emerson, a visitor from California, said that if such a speech were given in the USA, people would hold discussion sessions for days on the points made and newspapers would carry articles about them. An Australian once remarked: 'It was worth coming all the way from Australia only to listen to Nani Palkhivala's lecture. Never before in my life have I heard a lecture like this.' Mrs Clara Buck, a Hungarian from London, while being introduced to Palkhivala after one of his lectures, told him in almost identical words: 'It was worth coming all the way from England to hear you speak.'

The yearly meeting became a national event. As a President at one of the meetings remarked, 'There are two Budget speeches in the country, one by the Finance Minister in Parliament on the last day of February and the other by Nani Palkhivala to the public of this country.' In later years, bowing to public demand, he undertook a strenuous tour of Madras (now Chennai), Bangalore, Delhi, Calcutta, Ahmedabad, Hyderabad, Pune and other places to deliver Budget speeches. Audiences drawn from all walks of life considered this lecture an intellectual feast. Veerappa Moily, the then Chief Minister of Karnataka, while presiding over Palkhivala's talk in Bangalore in March 1993, remarked: 'Mr Palkhivala has been a consistent critic of the Budgets all these years. But the fact that he has welcomed the present and the previous two Union Budgets shows that it is not Mr Palkhivala but the Government which has changed its policies.' At a public meeting held in January 1997, at Bharatiya Vidya Bhavan, Prime Minister Deve Gowda, digressing from his prepared speech, addressed Mr Palkhivala and said, 'Sir, I used to be a listener of your speeches in Bangalore, and I respect you.'

His analysis of the Budget proposals in the Finance Bill and his skills as an orator par excellence made him a living legend, feared and respected by the government and adored by the public. He made his speeches replete with wit and humour, punctuated them with quotations from literature and references from history, and reeled off facts, figures and statistics to an incredible extent—without a scrap of paper before him. The late J.D. Choksi, presiding over one of his lectures, said he could not believe that such an accurate performance was possible; so at one such meeting he noted down all the facts and figures cited by Palkhivala and at home checked them with the Budget papers.

There was not a single mistake. Choksi added that if Palkhivala were to be the Finance Minister, he would deliver the entire Budget speech in Parliament from memory!

Palkhivala, who as a child suffered from a dreadful stammer, went on to become one of the world's great public speakers. His oratorical talents were not confined to legal and fiscal matters only. He addressed meetings of all sorts, of medical practitioners and journalists, of corporate managers, maritime engineers and trade union functionaries, of planters and farmers, the police and the armed forces. His subjects ranged sweepingly from the spiritual to the temporal, from yoga, religion and destiny to the stock exchange and road transport. When a freelance journalist, who was a lecturer in philosophy, was dismayed by the idea of having to interview this constitutional lawyer, he was put at ease by a friend who told him that 'there were few topics on which Palkhivala had not yet spoken'. He spoke on Sri Aurobindo and Adi Sankaracharya whose philosophy greatly inspired him. He has been most interested in the youth of India to whom the future of the country belongs, and he made it a point to accept invitations, even from far-flung places, to address students of various educational institutions. Several universities invited him to deliver convocation addresses. While in the USA as India's Ambassador, he delivered more than 170 speeches in different states, which included speeches at over fifty universities, sometimes giving three or four speeches a day at different places; and he had about eighty meetings with the media of different states, once giving seven interviews in a day. He was invited by the University of Waterloo, Canada, to deliver the 1984-85 Hagey Lectures, and by the Imperial College of Science, Technology and Medicine, London, to deliver the third GEC Lecture in 1992.

Just as his tax practice led him into economics, the requisition case of *Rao v. Advani* had got him interested and involved in constitutional law. Beginning with the *Golaknath* case in 1967, he fought a series of historic cases in the Supreme Court to defend the rights of citizens and the sanctity of the Constitution. The cases pertaining to bank nationalization, the Privy Purses, arbitrary restrictions on newspapers, and the rights of minorities to run educational institutions of their choice, and a number of other well-known cases culminating in the *Fundamental Rights (Kesavananda Bharati)* case, made him a national hero and brought him international fame. The Constitution was saved from total destruction. Referring to the string of cases, a Judge of the Supreme Court recently said at a public function: 'As far as law is concerned, Palkhivala is the all-time great in this country. Nobody can match him. If our Supreme Court is strong today, it is due to the work done by him. The *Kesavananda Bharati* case is the boon given by him to the Constitution. If the country remains a democracy, if it remains free, if our Constitution grows like a living tree, it is because of him. Who has done so much work in the field of law in any country?'

A touching testimony of the common man's gratitude to Palkhivala is the following letter to him in Hindi by a sepoy of the Supreme Court of India when the *Kesavananda Bharati* case was being argued:

> 'Respectful salutations to Shri Palkhivalasaheb,
>
> You are truly a great man. God, by His special grace, has given you enormous wisdom. You are the true friend of the common people and the poor of this country. By exerting yourself very much for the last few months, you are trying to get justice for the common people. You will definitely succeed in your efforts. Whatever new laws are made by our Government or plans are started, they have all proved useless. The common people are loaded with newer and newer taxes. But still the rulers do not understand the difficulties of the common people. I seek your pardon for writing this letter. I pray on behalf of the public of this country and myself to God that you win in your efforts. Otherwise, the people of this country will have to face very great difficulties. I pray to God to grant you great wisdom and to help you continue to seek justice for the people.'

Palkhivala's interest in the economic development of India led him into the corporate field. He joined the boards of the Reserve Bank of India, and several companies, both Indian and overseas, including the Industrial Credit and Investment Corporation of India Ltd; and later became the chairman of many of them. He was the Chairman of the Associated Cement Companies Ltd. for almost three decades. On 1 April 1961 he came into the Tata fold. In his association with the Tatas, he gave valuable advice on taxation, company law, and management matters. As Chairman, he successfully guided companies like Voltas Ltd., Tata Consultancy Services and Tata Exports Ltd (now renamed Tata International) and brought them to premier positions.

In a life packed with unremitting professional work, Palkhivala gave considerable time to public activities. The late A.D. Shroff, an eminent economist and industrialist, had founded the Forum of Free Enterprise in 1956 to protect private enterprise against the onslaught of state socialism which had become the dominant public policy after 1955. Palkhivala took over the mantle from the late Murarji Vaidya in 1968 as President of the Forum. Except for the period when he was Ambassador in the USA from September 1977 to July 1979, he led the movement with great commitment and dedication. He undertook country-wide tours to arouse public opinion on the economic freedoms and legal rights of citizens. The adoption of liberalization in 1991 can be said to be a vindication of his campaign, as it marked a U-turn in India's economic policies for which the Forum under his leadership was pleading.

As a tribute to Jayaprakash Narayan who played an outstanding role in regaining freedom for India after the nightmare of the Emergency, in June 1977 Palkhivala founded the Jayaprakash Institute of Human Freedoms. The purpose of the Institute is to strengthen the roots of Indian democracy and to carry on the epoch-making work of that great patriot. A sum of Rs 5,37,000, representing the entire profit from Palkhivala's seventh edition of *The Law and Practice of Income-tax,* was donated to this Institute.

Besides being India's Ambassador to the USA and its High Commissioner to the Bahamas, which posts he held concurrently, Palkhivala was a member of the First and Second Law Commissions, a member of the Senate of the University of Bombay, President of the Bombay Chamber of Commerce and Industry, and Chairman of the Maharashtra Economic Development Council, the Federation of Blood Banks' Association, the Leslie Sawhny Programme of Training for Democracy, the A.D. Shroff Memorial

Trust, the Lotus Trust, the Income-tax Appellate Tribunal Bar Association and the Auroville Committee of the Maharashtra State—to cite only a few areas in which he gave his best to the nation. He presented India's case in two disputes with Pakistan—first before the Special Tribunal in Geneva appointed by the UN to adjudicate upon Pakistan's claim to certain territories in Kutch, and next before the International Civil Aviation Organization at Montreal and later in appeal before the World Court at the Hague when Pakistan claimed the facility of overflying India. All arguments are read from written text before the World Court, because every word matters. Palkhivala is perhaps the solitary exception as he orally argued India's case from a carefully prepared text which was embedded in his phenomenal memory.

Palkhivala, totally wedded to ethical and spiritual values, has been closely associated with the Bharatiya Vidya Bhavan for nearly half a century now. He became Chairman of the Bhavan's Sardar Patel College of Engineering in 1982, and of its Arts, Science and Commerce College Committee in 1984. In 1985 he consented to be a trustee and member of the Central Executive Committee of the Bhavan, and in 1990 he was made Vice-President of the Bhavan worldwide.

The Bhavan's constitution was framed by its founder, K.M. Munshi, in 1937. In view of the phenomenal growth of the Bhavan in India and overseas, in 1986 Palkhivala was entrusted with the task of studying its constitution and suggesting additions and amendments to cope with the ever-changing scenario. He piloted the revision of the constitution with great vision and perception.

In 1984 the Bhavan's Sarva Dharma Maitri Prathistan was founded, the principal objective being to foster in India and overseas the message of interfaith fellowship. At the suggestion of Swamy Ranganathanandaji Maharaj, the present head of Ramakrishna Math and Mission, Palkhivala spontaneously agreed to be the Chairman of the Prathistan, and has been guiding its activities with great devotion.

In 1994 the Bhavan founded Sadachar Bharati to meaningfully observe the 125th birth anniversary of Mahatma Gandhi. On that occasion, over 250 high-ranking men from all walks of India's national life responded to the Bhavan's invitation. When Palkhivala saw the quality and earnestness of the participants, he was deeply moved. In his remarks, he observed that thought without concrete action is treachery and, among other things, steps should be taken to generate the required funds. In accordance with the Vedic dictum of utilizing one-tenth of one's personal income for *janakalyan* (public welfare), he, then and there, offered ten per cent of his yearly net income for the Sadachar Bharati work of the Bhavan. And the cheque is meticulously sent by 31 March every year.

Palkhivala held Paramacharya Jagadguru Sri Chandrasekharendra Saraswathi of Kanchi in the highest esteem. In 1977, before leaving for Washington to take up the post of India's Ambassador to the USA, he went to Kanchi specially to seek the Paramacharya's blessings. Later, at the behest of the Paramacharya, Palkhivala became the Chairman of the Veda Rakshana Nidhi Trust. The main purpose of this foundation planned by the Paramacharya is to extend financial assistance to indigent Vedic scholars who have devoted their lives to learning and fostering Vedic teachings. Preparing a detailed list of eligible Vedic scholars all over India was the first step initiated by the Foundation at the suggestion of Palkhivala.

'Do it today—tomorrow may be too late', Palkhivala tells himself, especially when it comes to doing good. Recently he made a munificent donation of Rs 2,00,00,000 to Sri Sankara Nethralaya at Chennai, and handed over the cheque to the eye surgeon Dr Badrinath without delay, lest fate intervene before he acted. He was deeply impressed by the work of this institute in bringing eye care to the poor, particularly in rural areas.

His books have created history. His magnum opus is *The Law and Practice of Income-tax,* described by reviewers as a 'monumental work' and 'an incredible performance'. It went into several editions, becoming right from the first edition a standard reference book, 'an invaluable vade-mecum' to quote another reviewer, for lawyers, Courts and the Income-tax Department. Chief Justice Chagla, while hearing income-tax references, referred to it as '*the* book'; and often when a ticklish question of law arose on which precedents were silent, he would ask, 'What does the book say?' When the second edition of the book was in the press, a suit was filed in the Madras High Court against Palkhivala, with Sir Jamshedji Kanga as the co-defendant, on the false ground that it was a plagiarized work. He successfully defended himself. During his cross-examination, which went on for days, he cited from memory case after case with the exact page number on which the relevant words in the judgment were to be found to prove that he had gone to the original source for writing his commentary. At the end of Palkhivala's cross-examination, Homi Seervai, counsel for the defendants, wrote from Madras to Sir Jamshedji, 'I have never witnessed a cross-examination so destructive of the case of the cross-examiner'.

He was the co-author of *Taxation in India* published by the Harvard University in the World Tax Series.

The Highest Taxed Nation shook the Finance Ministry and compelled it to take the first step towards simplification of the tax structure and reduction of the tax rates. Five thousand copies were sold within two days and another five thousand within the next three weeks. *Our Constitution Defaced and Defiled* is a scintillating book, with the spirit of liberty—the Eternal Flame—as its theme. It was meant to arouse the people to their duty as the keepers of the Constitution. *We, the People* and *We, the Nation,* which are collected extracts from his speeches and writings, bear testimony to his life-work and his passionate commitment to public causes. *India's Priceless Heritage* and *Essential Unity of All Religions,* published by the Bhavan, show how deeply he has delved into the spiritual treasure of India.

A number of honours came his way. The Honorary Membership of The Academy of Political Science, New York, the first National Amity Award, the prestigious Dadabhai Naoroji Memorial Award and Padma Vibhushan are only some of the many honours. His own profession honoured him with Bar Association receptions during his extensive tours, and, later, on his completing fifty years at the Bar. Recently he was awarded a Certificate of Honour by the Bar Association of India 'in recognition of outstanding contribution to the development of Constitutional Law and for commitment to the Rule of Law and for selfless service to the legal profession'.

During his tenure in the USA as India's Ambassador, Princeton University, New Jersey, and Lawrence University, Wisconsin, conferred on him the honorary degree of Doctor of Laws. Years later, Annamalai University, Tamil Nadu, and the University of Mumbai followed suit. The citations show how the academic community looked upon him:

> 'Defender of constitutional liberties, champion of human rights, he has courageously advanced his conviction that expediency in the name of progress, when at the cost of freedom, is no progress at all, but retrogression. Lawyer, teacher, author, and economic developer, he brings to us as Ambassador of India intelligent good humour, experience, and vision for international understanding . . .'
>
> —*Princeton University,* June 1978

> 'What is human dignity? What rights are fundamental to an open society? What are the limits to political power? . . . You, more than most, have pondered these great questions; and through your achievements have answered them.
>
> 'As India's leading author, scholar, teacher and practitioner of constitutional law, you have defended the individual, be he prince or pauper, against the state; you have championed free speech and an unfettered press; you have protected the autonomy of the religious and educational institutions of the minorities; you have fought for the preservation of independent social organizations and multiple centers of civic power . . . You have battled stifling economic controls and bureaucratic red tape. You have always believed that even in a poor and developing country the need for bread is fully compatible with the existence of liberty . . . You have given unstintingly of your time and wealth to strengthen the roots of Indian democracy.
>
> 'You are also an enlightened patriot and nationalist . . .
>
> 'Never more did you live your principles than during the recent nineteen-month ordeal which India went through in what was called 'The Emergency'. When those who had eaten

of the insane root, swollen with the pride of absolute political power, threw down the gauntlet, you did not bow or flinch. Under the shadow of near tyranny, at great risk and some cost, you raised the torch of freedom.'

—*Lawrence University,* March 1979

[A man] 'in whom one sees the rare combination of a legal practitioner, an academic, a critical thinker, an upholder of human rights, a crusader against authoritarianism and an expounder of India's cultural heritage. His has been the eventful career of a many-sided personality whose mission has been advocacy of the cause of justice, whether political, economic or social. With an analytical mind he approaches any problem and comes up with a solution such as to compel our attention . . .

'. . . In Dr Palkhivala we see a man whose overarching life purpose is to provide a dynamic motivation for the people to be open-minded and open-hearted and pursue a line of valid direction . . .'

—*Annamalai University,* December 1986

'You have, as India's leading jurist, through your scholarly writings, not merely articulated the definitive treatise of our tax system and laws, but through myriad essays, articles and speeches . . . succeeded in educating the people and making them realize and appreciate their unique legacy . . . You have done all this with rare intellectual integrity, simplicity and sincerity, with devotion and dedication, with courage and conviction and above all frankness, so that our democracy remains vibrant and alive . . .

'In a country besieged by materialism where lasting values are steadily being eroded, you have spread the timeless message of the great Indian philosophers, crossing the narrow confines and boundaries of caste and religion, which are but barriers of the mind . . . Towering as your accomplishments are, you have not lost the common touch.

'All through your remarkable achievements and works runs the silver thread of patriotic, dedicated service to the people, their betterment, their spiritual and economic growth and advancement. You have lived and worked by the creed that the highest life is the life of service to one's fellow being . . .'

—University of Mumbai, January 1998

Palkhivala's talents are God's gift to him. The use he makes of them is his gift to God. A 'living legend' as he is frequently described, generations to come will see the footprints he has left on the sands of time through his inestimable contribution towards preserving the basic values of India's democratic Constitution and her noble traditions.

Much can be written about Palkhivala, the intellectual. Much more about Nani, the man. His accomplishments as a jurist and economist have been universally acknowledged and admired. In his public life he has been described as 'the keeper of national conscience' and 'Tribune of the people of India'. But the human being surpasses his intellectual achievements. Dr P.C. Alexander, Governor of Maharashtra, while honouring Nani at a public function, summed up the assessment of the public when he said, 'Above all, Nani Palkhivala is a good human being and we need more people like him in this country.'

Nani is humility on two legs. The junior members of the Bar who were engaged with him in different cases would testify to this. Before fixing a joint conference, he, so hard pressed for time, would ask the junior, who had all the time at his disposal, which day would be convenient to the junior. A man with incredible ability to pick up points in a flash, during the conference he would listen with patience and respect to whatever the junior had to say.

Nani values his dignitv so much that he never stands upon it. Once, when he was deeply engrossed in a conference, a stranger suddenly stepped into the chambers and inquired when his conference was fixed. Obviously there was some misunderstanding on his part, and Nani told him that there was no such conference noted in the diary. The stranger kept saying something unintelligible in his own language. Nani got slightly irritated and asked the stranger not to disturb him in his conference. The stranger went away. A couple of minutes later a disturbed Nani abruptly excused himself and left the chambers. After about five minutes he returned, with relief writ large on his face. He had sought out the stranger at the other end of the High Court and apologized for his impoliteness.

There is at least one subject on which Nani cannot speak—himself. The world will never have his autobiography.

'The greater the genius, the more simple and common the man.' Yes, Nani is the living proof of this. His simplicity is disarming. The principal of Sophia College, presiding over his lecture in the early seventies, said, 'Mr Palkhivala is a great national figure; he is a great international figure; but the man is far greater.' She supported her remark by narrating an incident. While taking a morning walk on Marine Drive with a friend of hers, Mani Patel, she told Mani that she wanted to invite Nani to address the students of the College, but did not know how to approach this man of formidable reputation. Mani, who happened to know Nani, smiled and straightaway took her to Nani who lived nearby. He was in his sleeping suit, having breakfast in his study. Without any reservation he came out, brought them in his study room, and insisted they shared his breakfast. The principal later left with a convenient date for the lecture.

A lady member of the Bar gratefully recalls how she, a raw junior then, happened to meet Nani in Court. She asked him if she could see him later for fixing an appointment for personal advice. She was as delighted as surprised to get the reply, 'No need for a formal appointment. You may see me in my chambers at any time convenient to you.'

Nani is a man of unfailing courtesy. At the end of the parties given at his residence, he would invariably take the lift down with his guests to see them to their cars. He received thousands of letters from members of all strata of society, and despite his perennially heavy daily schedule he would personally reply to them.

In his personal dealings with people, Nani charms everyone not only with his genuine humility, simplicity and courtesy, but also with his deep concern for others, especially the poor. His little, nameless, well remembered acts of kindness and of love can fill a volume. Only a handful of them may be recalled here.

In 1991 Nani had a coronary bypass in London. The avid and lifelong student that he is, in the post-operative period he read up on all aspects of heart ailments and their treatment. When, next year, S. Ramakrishnan, Director-General of the Bhavan, was advised bypass surgery by two eminent cardiologists of Bombay, Nani, with his newly-acquired knowledge, vehemently argued with them against such a step. In deference to his passionate pleas, they reluctantly agreed to closely 'observe and monitor Ramakrishnan's heart condition for six months' and thereafter take the final decision. Nani discussed the matter with C. Subramaniam, President of the Bhavan. They both felt that the six-month observation period might cause Ramakrishnan some mental depression. It was, therefore, decided to have a check-up in London by the renowned cardiologist Dr Walter Somerville. Nani, only recently out of his own operation, insisted that he should be informed as soon as the appointment was fixed, and he would also go to London to join the discussion with Dr Somerville. And he did. Ramakrishnan was saved from the operation. He remembers the remark made by C. Rajagopalachari when the latter visited the Bhavan decades ago: 'Nani is God's gift to India.'

Himself facing some of the most serious physical ailments, Nani would phone to inquire after a relative or friend having a mild disorder. Well or ill, he worked on endlessly, but saw to it that his co-workers and subordinates had the required rest. A member of his ambassadorial staff in Washington wanted leave to see his seriously ailing father in India. Nani was informed that according to the Government rules the employee would have to make an application to the Ministry in India and obtain the Government's approval which would take considerable time. Nani would have none of it. Taking the responsibility on himself, he released the employee.

When the tea tray arrived in his office, a piece of cake or a few biscuits were first put aside for the peon of his chambers. He ensured that his servants, on their retirement, were financially comfortable; and the same consideration was extended to the family of a servant after his death. While in Karnataka on a lecture tour, he found time from his packed programme to meet his retired cook. At the end of a reception given in his honour, his stenographer told him that the latter's wife was eager to be introduced to him but could not attend the function because of the household chores. Hearing this, Nani himself went to see her at her residence, not very close to the venue of the meeting.

His care and concern were not confined to those near him. 'My father taught me compassion and kindness for the less privileged. I remember, I was not more than two years old. I was about to help myself to a bowl of almonds when my father reminded me of the poor orphan who lived next door. I was so moved by his words that I immediately handed over the entire bowl to the boy. That incident has made a deep impression on me ever since . . . I have always treasured that lesson. It has proved far more important than any legacy of land or wealth he may have left me.' That day the seeds of charity were sown. Today the man is virtually a charitable institution. His silent charities have benefited countless recipients—both the donees and the beneficiaries under the various charitable trusts created by him—but are hardly known to outsiders, for he does not let his left hand know the good his right hand does.

Nani's love for his country is proverbial, and so also his pride in her 'fantastically rich' spiritual heritage. He has travelled both in and outside India so frequently that one closely associated attorney remarked, 'Nani has spent more time in the air than on the land.' But he has never liked to be away from India for long. Whichever part of the world he might be in, his motherland was always uppermost in his mind. He clings to his country as a child to his mother. Even when he accepted the ambassadorship in the USA, he had decided not to have it for the full term but only for a couple of years. While leaving, he confided, 'I cannot remain away from India for long. I'll keep coming here oft and on.' And he did, at his own expense. Just to be in India.

The man who so loved his country could not love his family less. From Washington he wrote regular letters to those he held dear, keeping them informed of his day-to-day activities. When he had been at the Bar for hardly a few years, he was offered judgeship of the Supreme Court which he declined because he did not want to be away from his parents with whom he was living in Bombay.

He has deep abiding faith in God, and he has always listened to the inner voice before taking any important decision in his life. It was this inner voice that deterred him from accepting the post of Attorney-General (offered more than once)—and he later fought the historic cases for the citizen against the government. It was this inner voice that made him step down as ambassador—and shortly thereafter the Janata Government which had made his appointment fell. It was, again, this inner voice which helped him withstand the pressure from the public to stand for the next election—the one in which the Janata Party suffered a heavy defeat and Mrs Gandhi came back to power.

Nani has an infinite capacity for bearing physical pain. While playing with his school friends he once dislocated his shoulder but would not speak about it to anyone at home and kept bearing the pain. It was only when a friend came home the next day to inquire after his condition that his parents came to know about the incident. In later life he had to undergo an operation for appendicitis. When the nurse entered the room to give the pre-operation injection, she found the bed empty and some people light-heartedly talking among themselves. The perplexed lady, with syringe in her hand, had to inquire, 'Who is the patient?' Still later, Nani developed kidney trouble, the stone ultimately blocking the urinary tract. Many conferences were fixed in the chambers for the evening. When clients for the first conference arrived, his juniors informed them of his condition and were about to cancel all conferences. Just then, to the amazement of all, Nani walked in and stayed on to finish all his conferences. 'I feel less pain when I work', he explained. Ultimately he had to be taken to the hospital to remove the stone. Knowing his nature and tendency, the R.M.O. gave him strict instructions to remain completely in bed for a few days. The very next day, unknown to the R.M.O. and to the consternation of the pleading nurse, Nani quietly slipped out of the hospital, held some meetings in his office, and as quietly slipped back into his hospital bed.

In a brief profile it is impossible to do justice to a man who in the words of Matthew Arnold is a personification of 'sweetness and light'. No more beautiful words can describe him than those uttered by Justice Kuldip Singh of the Supreme Court while presenting him a citation on behalf of the various Rotary Clubs of Bombay on 3 December 1997:

> 'Nani has tirelessly defended our freedom and Constitution against the evil designs of politicians who would have otherwise succeeded in twisting the Constitution for their personal needs and gains. I have heard Nani, watched him, known him and befriended him for the last five decades. I have seen him working in the field of law, in the field of education, in the field of economy and finance, and in every field he has excelled to the hilt. But what impresses me most is his disposition—how he behaves towards people, how he talks with them, how honest he is and what a good heart he has. One feels that he is not a man of this world but someone from outside. I have many times tried to explain him as a man. But it is very difficult. One can only feel his essence and enjoy, as one enjoys the fragrance of a flower or the smile of a child. He is like cool breeze on a warm sunny day. That is Nani, the gentleman.'

L.M. Singhvi
M.R. Pai
S. Ramakrishnan

I

LIFE, RELIGION AND ENVIRONMENT

PHILOSOPHY OF LIFE

◆

A FRIEND OF Nani Palkhivala, Buji Chinoy, had the following as his philosophy of life. Palkhivala said that this also represented his philosophy of life.

> When I die
> Give my sight to the man who has never seen a sunrise.
> Give my heart to one who has known the agony of the heart.
> Give my blood to a youth pulled from the wreckage of a car
> so that he might live to see his grandchildren play.
> Let my kidneys drain the poison from another's body.
> Let my bones be used to make a crippled child walk.
> Burn what is left of me and scatter the ashes to the wind to
> let the flowers grow.
> If you must bury something, let it be my faults and my
> prejudices against my fellowmen.
> Give my sins to the Devil.
> Give my soul to God.
> If you wish to remember me, do it with a kind deed or word
> to someone who needs you.
> If you do all I've asked, I'll live for ever.

CONCERN FOR THE POOR IN ZOROASTRIANISM

◆

THE TIME WHEN Prophet Zarathushtra flourished cannot be determined with any precision, since he lived in prehistoric times. Mary Boyce, a great authority on the subject, said that Zoroastrianism is the most difficult of living faiths to study, for three reasons—because of its antiquity, because of the vicissitudes which it has undergone, and because of the loss of many holy texts. Zoroastrianism is the oldest of the revealed world religions. According to Mary Boyce, it has probably had more influence on mankind, directly and indirectly, than any other single faith. In its own right, it was the state religion of three great Iranian empires which flourished continually from the sixth century BC to the seventh century AD, and some of its leading doctrines were adopted by Judaism, Christianity and Islam, while in the East it had some influence on the development of Buddhism. Mary Boyce is one of those distinguished scholars who believe that Prophet Zarathushtra must have flourished around 1700 BC i.e., about the same time as the Vedas were composed in India. Other scholars think that he must have flourished in the sixth and fifth centuries BC, while still others think he must have lived between the ninth and sixth centuries BC.

What is infinitely more important than the date when the Prophet flourished, is his teaching. The general belief, till the Prophet appeared on the scene, was that there were tribal gods, i.e., different gods presiding over the destinies of different tribes. The message of Prophet Zarathushtra in Iran, and of the Vedas in India at about the same time, marked a new phase in human evolution. The new teaching was that there is one God for all creation and that the same Divine Spirit is to be found in all human beings.

Zarathushtra preached a religion which may be called a 'reflective religion'. It is a fusion of a view of the world and a way of life. The focus of his teachings is on a world afflicted with suffering, iniquity, and imperfection—the goal being to transform it and bring it to perfection.

Zarathushtra was one of the earliest of the great prophets of civilization. He looked at the world as we look at it today. The poor are left in their distress without a helping hand. The rule is of might, and right is abandoned. Violence, even in the Prophet's time, was rampant, and strife with the threat of destruction brought the pathos of human existence to the minds of those with a conscience.

The essence of Zoroastrianism is based on the three tenets—*Humata, Hukhta, Huvarshta*—Good Thoughts, Good Words, Good Deeds. Besides these three tenets, the religion also imposes a duty on man to take care of the environment around him. To my mind, no prophet laid greater stress on ecology and environment than Prophet Zarathushtra. He emphasized the prime need to preserve the cleanliness of air, earth, water and fire. He preached that fire was the ultimate symbol of purity. He exhorted man to take care of not only his surroundings but also the animals which inhabit the earth, and his fellow human beings.

It is because of these invaluable tenets which have been imbibed by Zoroastrians over the centuries, ever since the time of the Prophet's life on earth, that goodness and charity towards others have become the principles of a Zoroastrian's life.

The earlier generations of Zoroastrians considered it their duty to see that as they prospered in life they also cared for the well-being of fellow Zoroastrians. Their concern for the poor, not only of their own community, but for all others, was so deeply ingrained that, while they prospered, they also bequeathed to generations to come, rich legacies of their work towards the poor and the needy by way of schools, hospitals, housing, libraries, and generous funds in charitable trusts for the benefit of the public at large. It would be interesting to note that the census of Bombay of 1864 does not record one single beggar in this illustrious community. Their life's motto was—life is not worth living without service, and no love is complete if it does not gradually expand into loving service, not only of kith and kin, but of all humanity.

Fortunately, even today, concern for the poor in Zoroastrianism is stressed by Zoroastrians not only in India but all over the world. But the problem looming over the community in the present times is large and frightening. The economic plight of many of the Zoroastrians is pathetic.

Over 3,000 years have passed since the path of Truth and Right, leading to the desired goal, was pointed out by Zarathushtra. Thereafter, we have had similar teachings by successive prophets in different lands. After all these teachings, after all the knowledge and experience which we have received and garnered, the world stands today in a hardly better condition than it did in that distant past—on the force of arms it would still rely, even today.

ARE WE MASTERS OF OUR FATE?

◆

ON THE SUBJECT of destiny, everyone of us forms his own beliefs on the basis of his own experiences. All that I propose to do is to tell you a few incidents in my own life. You are welcome to draw your own conclusions. I request you to keep an open mind and decide, without bias or prejudice, what you think are the right conclusions to be drawn.

Perhaps the key sentence to the whole problem was that of Dr Johnson who is quoted in *The Oxford Book of the Supernatural*—'All argument is against it, but all belief is for it.'

It is erroneous to think that a nation or an individual that believes in fate is necessarily backward. The Germans have begun to believe in growing numbers in the occult and the supernatural. The French radio gives the day's horoscope along with the daily weather forecast, and France is home to 10,000 taxpaying clairvoyants. Astrology has claimed reinstatement at the Sorbonne after having been banished in 1666 under the influence of Descartes.

Some of the greatest men who have ever lived, have believed that certain events in their lives were preordained and that certain individuals had the rare gift of precognition.

An example which comes straight to mind is that of Dr Radhakrishnan who was merely a professor of philosophy, years before be became the Vice-President, and later the President of India. If you read the life of Dr Radhakrishnan by his son Gopal, you will come across the following passage:

'Sometime during these years when Radhakrishnan was

> spending the summers in Europe, he met "Cheiro", the best-known palmist of his day. "Cheiro" studied Radhakrishnan's palms and forecast that he would reach the top, be the head of a state, but would, before his death, lose his mind. Both these prophecies seemed at the time so wildly off the mark that they became a family joke.' (p. 143)

The above passage bears eloquent testimony to two facts—preordination and the gift of precognition by rare individuals.

The voice of destiny has spoken in the past to some of the greatest thinkers and saints who have flourished down the decades. In the *Times* (of London) of 5 July 1993, William Rees-Mogg in a very perceptive article bewails that the inner guide that showed mankind the way forward has fallen strangely silent, and quotes a few examples. Speaking of the 'unknown guest', Maurice Maeterlinck said, 'From the darkest corners of our ego it directs our veritable life, the one that is not to die, and pays no heed to our thought or to anything emanating from our reason.' Plato quotes Socrates as saying, 'In the past the prophetic voice to which I have become accustomed has always been my constant companion, opposing me even in quite trivial things if I was going to take the wrong course.'

One of the most famous incidents of that type in our times is that of Winston Churchill who had a lucky escape from a bomb attack in a car. On that day he happened to choose to sit on the far side from his usual place. Lady Churchill asked him why. 'I do not know. I do not know,' he replied. Then he said, 'Of course I know. Something said to me "Stop" before I reached the car door which was held open for me. It then seemed to me that I was told I should open the door on the other side and get in and sit there.' Needless to add, Churchill escaped unhurt.

Let me quote one more example of the 'unknown guest' whose guidance can change your life. Mother Teresa is eighty-six years old. In 1946, when she was thirty-six, she was no more than a teaching nun in India. On 10 September 1946 when she was on a train ride to Darjeeling, she felt the touch of a divine command—the message that she must quit her cloistered existence and plunge into Calcutta's slums to care for the poorest of the poor. Two years later, with permission from Rome, she left the convent with only five rupees in her pocket.

Then she applied for and got permission from the Pope to start her own order in 1950—The Society of the Missionaries of Charity. She never looked back after the divine guidance was given to her by her 'unknown guest'. She has had no difficulty in collecting funds for the countless homes started by the Missionaries of Charity. In her own words, 'Donation is a big word. I like to call it Sharing. Like the four-year-old Hindu child who gave up sugar for three days and gave it for our work. That is real sharing.'

As Malcolm Muggeridge says in his autobiography, 'In all the larger shaping of a life, there is a plan already, into which one has no choice but to fit.'

On the subject of destiny, let me state what I believe as briefly as possible.

First, I believe that the basic pattern of an individual's or a nation's life is predetermined.

Secondly, very few individuals have the gift of clairvoyance to foresee what is predetermined.

Thirdly, guidance is sometimes vouchsafed to receptive human beings by means for which there is no scientific explanation.

Fourthly, I do believe in the existence of free will but that again is within preordained parameters. To my mind, the simplest analogy to the case we are talking about is that of a dog on a long leash—the dog has the freedom to move about as far as the leash permits, but not beyond.

Pandit Jawaharlal Nehru expressed the same idea in more felicitous language. He was interviewed by Norman Cousins, the doyen of American editors, and a writer of high repute. After dealing with the political questions, Cousins put the last question somewhat as follows:

> 'You have a modern mind as a result of your upbringing in England, while your roots are in this ancient land. How do you reconcile free will and destiny?'

After pausing and pondering over the question, Pandit Nehru replied as follows:

> 'Both have a place in our life. The best analogy one can think of is to compare life with a game of bridge. The cards dealt to you are out of your control, but the way you play your hand is your free will. Given a good hand, you can still mess up the game, and vice versa.'

There have been examples of other men who have been humble enough to admit that they had reached certain positions in life not because they deserved them but because they were destined to attain them.

A typical example of this is the following conversation between our former Prime Minister, Sri Deve Gowda, and the correspondent of *India Today,* which appeared in the issue of 15 February 1997:

> *India Today:* Will your government last its full term?
>
> *Sri Deve Gowda:* I never aspired to be prime minister. Destiny dragged me here. I don't know how long I will continue. But I do know that the design of destiny cannot be altered. Even in the given atmosphere I will run this government for a full term.

I come now to the experiences in my life on which I have based the four beliefs which I have just enumerated.

Upon joining the Bar in 1944, I started reading Briefs, and I kept on reading past Diwalis, past Christmases, past Ramzan Ids, past long vacations—like the Rajdhani Express speeding past railway stations. I believe that the journey will be over at the predestined hour, irrespective of the medical care that money can buy.

I am alive today only because of a virus that infected me more than forty years ago. I was engaged to argue a Special Leave Petition which was to be heard in the Supreme Court on 9 May 1953. Chandrakant Mehta, a partner of Gagrat & Company, was the instructing attorney. We booked our return tickets from Delhi to Bombay by the night flight on the same day. On 6 May, I developed a very bad cold with fever and had to return the Brief. The next day I agreed to change my mind and do the case since it meant a lot to a poor and deserving litigant. But on 8 May my temperature rose higher and I had no option but to return the Brief once again. Mr C.K. Daphtary, the Solicitor-General, who lived in Delhi was gracious enough to agree to step into my place. Since I did not go to Delhi, Chandrakant Mehta, who disliked flying by night, went to the airline office and changed his own return ticket to the morning flight on 10 May. The plane, which left Delhi on the late evening of 9 May with a full passenger load, crashed. The father of Mr Mani Shankar Aiyar, the well-known columnist who writes for the *Indian Express,* was one of those who died in the crash. There were no survivors.

As a child I suffered from a dreadful stammer. It seemed that I had as much chance of becoming an advocate or a public speaker as a victim of multiple sclerosis has of becoming an Olympic athlete. With the recklessness characteristic of a child, I ventured to take part in elocution competitions; but I believe that without providential grace my own will to get over the handicap would have been in vain.

At certain turning points in my life, when I would have made wrong decisions with my limited intelligence, I have felt as if my will was perceptibly bent by some Higher Power which saved me from myself.

'There's a divinity that shapes our ends,
Rough-hew them how we will.'

In 1968, Mr Govinda Menon was the law minister in the Congress government. He pressed me hard to accept the office of the Attorney-General of India. After a great deal of hesitation I agreed. When I was in Delhi I conveyed my acceptance to him, and he told me that the announcement would be made the next day. I was happy that the agonizing hours of indecision were over. Sound sleep is one of the blessings I have always enjoyed. That night I went to bed and looked forward to my usual quota of deep slumber. But suddenly and inexplicably, I became wide awake at three o'clock in the morning with the clear conviction, floating like a hook through my consciousness, that my decision was erroneous and that I should reverse it before it was too late. Early in the morning I profusely apologized to the law minister for changing my mind. In the years immediately following, it was my privilege to argue on behalf of the citizen, under the same Congress government and against the government, the major cases which have shaped and moulded the constitutional law of India—Bank Nationalization (1969), Privy Purse (1970), Fundamental Rights (1972-73) and the *Minerva Mills* case (1980), among others. Thus, the most momentous decision of my life was made by a Force other than myself.

On 26 June 1975 the Emergency was proclaimed. After that I went through a period which was the darkest period of my life.

Nothing happened to me personally but I was deeply distressed about the future of our democracy. There was an employee of ACC whose surname was Thacker. I hope and trust he is still alive. He had a gift for sometimes seeing into the future. I remember my friend, Wadud Khan, who at that time was the chairman of SAIL, telling me that he was thunderstruck by Thacker predicting that Wadud Khan's brother who was in the USA would die in a plane crash. Unfortunately, the brother of Wadud Khan did die in a plane crash. So, naturally, I was keen to speak to Thacker and ask him what he thought the future held in store for me.

One morning in 1976 I invited Thacker for a quiet chat at my residence. Predicting the future, he said to me, 'I see you occupying a beautiful, spacious mansion in Rome.' I told him that I was not interested in being comfortable abroad but I would like to do what I could for my own people. He continued, 'You will stay there for about two years though you will have a number of opportunities to come back to India.' I put the incident out of my mind.

In 1977, when the Janata government came to power, I received a communication from Shri Atal Behari Vajpayee, the then External Affairs Minister, offering me the assignment of ambassador of India at Washington. I was not at all keen to take up this assignment, because the Emergency had just been lifted and I was very keen to stay on in the country instead of taking up an assignment abroad. I sent a courteous reply to Shri Vajpayee requesting him to kindly pardon me for my inability to accept the offer which he had made to me. But afterwards, I changed my mind, and I accepted the offer. When I went to Washington, the words of Thacker came back to my mind. Thacker had made one mistake—he had referred to Rome when actually it was in Washington that I occupied the beautiful, spacious mansion. I did stay there for almost two years during which period I had the opportunity of coming back to India a few times at my own cost. It was one of the most rewarding experiences in my life, and yet I was so foolish as to decline it in the first instance.

The most incredible experience of clairvoyance or precognition in my life was connected with Mrs Indira Gandhi's case which culminated in the declaration of the Emergency.

The Allahabad High Court had, in the month of June 1975, decided that the election of Mrs Indira Gandhi to Parliament should be set aside. That meant that she would cease to be a member of the Lok Sabha with a potential risk to her prime ministership. Mrs Gandhi filed an appeal in the Supreme Court and her application for interim relief was argued by me on 23 June 1975.

Mr Justice Krishna Iyer heard the application and passed the order of interim relief on the next day. The interim order was that pending the hearing and final disposal of the appeal, Mrs Gandhi could continue to sit in the Lok Sabha and participate in the proceedings of that House like any other member, and could also continue to be the prime minister of India. The only restriction on her was that she was not given the right to vote. The judge mentioned that this did not involve any hardship because Parliament was not in session at that time and that I could renew the application for the right to vote when Parliament reassembled. The evening of that very day (24 June 1975) I saw Mrs Gandhi at her residence and told her that I found the interim order very satisfactory and she should not worry about the case since the judgement of the trial court did not seem to be correct on the recorded evidence.

On the plane which I boarded to return to Bombay, next to me was seated an elderly, simple man dressed in khadi, carrying a khadi cloth bag. He asked me what had happened that day in the prime minister's case and I told him briefly what the judge had decided. He related how he was an inmate of a Gandhi ashram in Bangalore and that he had been out of the ashram since May 1975 to conduct one of his periodic tours in different parts of India. He mentioned the name of a clairvoyant in Bangalore who had made some predictions which he thought were rather curious. The conversation between us ran somewhat as follows:

'When I left the ashram in May 1975 the clairvoyant told me that the prime minister would lose the case which she was fighting in the Allahabad High Court and yet, after losing the case, she would become the most powerful woman in the world.'

I asked in surprise. 'How can Mrs Indira Gandhi become any more powerful than she is today? When she is already the head of the largest democracy on earth, what can possibly add to her power?'

'I do not know. I am only repeating to you what he said.'

Unimpressed, I did not bother even to make a mental note of the name of the clairvoyant. But to carry on the conversation, I asked, 'Did the soothsayer say anything else?'

'Yes. He said that the extraordinary power which the prime minister is to acquire will end in March 1977.'

'Did he mention the precise month and year?'

'Yes, he mentioned specifically that the cessation of the extraordinary power would be in March 1977.'

'Did he make any other prediction?'

'Yes, he said that Jayaprakash Narayan who is today the most popular figure in India's public life, would be stricken by a fatal illness which would carry him away in about two years. He also said that Shri Y.B. Chavan who aspires to be the prime minister of India would never attain that position.'

I came home, wondering what the future would bring. In less than thirty-six hours the Emergency was declared, the invaluable fundamental rights of the people were suspended, and the prime minister virtually acquired all the powers of the leader of a totalitarian state. That was the black morning of 26 June 1975.

In the days immediately following the declaration of the Emergency, my mind kept on reverting to the four forecasts. I invited for a quiet dinner at my residence the then editor of the *Times of India* and a few other well-known journalists and related to them my coversation with the Gandhian ashramite in the plane. The next month I repeated the story to Ramnath Goenka of the *Indian Express,* who was literally hounded by the Congress government during the Emergency. Those were the days of gloom and despair, and the only streak of light was the prediction that the totalitarianism would end in March 1977. I need hardly mention that all the predictions were accurately fufilled—the assumption of supremacy which made Mrs Indira Gandhi the most powerful woman in the world, the cessation of that supremacy in March 1977, the death of Jayaprakash Narayan in October 1979, and Shri Y.B. Chavan dying in November 1984 without fulfilling his ambition of becoming the prime minister.

I did not meet Mrs Gandhi again till the evening of 22 March 1977 when the results of the election showed that the Janata Party had won a landslide victory and Mrs Gandhi had to resign as the prime minister. I was in Delhi on that day and called on Mrs Gandhi at her residence. I related to her the incident of my conversation with the total stranger on the plane in June 1975 and said, 'Indiraji, if it be any consolation, may I tell you that what has happened since the election case was filed against you in the Allahabad High Court seems to have been preordained.' She had tears in her eyes—the only time I saw her in such a sad mood.

It would be preposterous to try to give any explanation for the episodes I have related truthfully except on the hypothesis of preordination and precognition.

I am sorry to find that the hubris of modern science has passed into a byword. In his latest book *Black Holes and Baby Universes,* the brilliant physicist, Professor Stephen Hawking writes, 'I do not agree with the view that the universe is a mystery.' This shocks me beyond words. To me it is not only a mystery of the most profound nature, but an infinite cluster of millions and millions of incredible, insoluble mysteries which the human mind (as distinct from the human spirit) will never be able to unravel. Albert Einstein, the greatest scientific intellect of our age, had the right attitude: 'The most beautiful experience we can have is the mysterious . . . the fundamental emotion which stands at the cradle of true art and true science.'

I do not believe that the human brain, which according to Professor Hawking contains 'about hundred million billion billion particles', will ever be able to discover the 'set of laws which completely determine the evolution of the universe from its initial state'—until the human spirit reaches a higher stage of evolution which Sri Aurobindo called the supramental stage.

Some years ago, there was a dinner party in Bombay where among the guests were India's leading scientist, Dr Homi Bhabha, and a humble, simple man from Lucknow who was reputed to have some unusual powers. At the persuasion of some of the guests, Dr Bhabha consented to test the man's powers. Dr Bhabha took out a one-rupee note from his wallet and without looking at it, put it in his side pocket and asked the stranger whether he could tell the number on the note. The man mentioned the number with total accuracy. It could not be a case of mind-reading because Dr Bhabha had deliberately refrained from looking at the note. Later, when I met Dr Bhabha in Delhi, I asked him whether there was any scientific explanation for the unusual faculty of the Lucknow man. He confessed that up to now no explanation known to science was available.

When you read Dr Raynor Johnson's *The Imprisoned Splendour* and Fritjof Capra's *The Tao of Physics,* you understand why Sri Aurobindo and Rabindranath Tagore were convinced that India is destined to be the teacher of all lands. Saints never contradict one another and mystics have never been known to disagree. Eastern culture and Western culture share the same heritage of spiritual experience. More and more men have begun to realize that we are the Peeping Toms at the keyhole of eternity. I should like to echo the wish with which Arthur Koestler ends *The Roots of Coincidence* that we would take the stuffing out of the keyhole, which blocks even our limited view.

THE MESSAGE OF THE PROPHETS

◆

NOTHING COULD BE more explicit than the message of universal brotherhood and mutual respect preached in every great religion.

The Lord says in the *Gita,* 'Whatever may be the form in which each devotee seeks to worship Me with faith, I make their faith steadfast in that form alone.'

The Vedas proclaim, 'That which exists is only One; the sages speak of it variously.'

The Bible preaches, 'No man liveth unto himself. We are all parts of one another. God hath made of one blood all nations that dwell upon the face of the earth.'

The Koran affirms, 'All creatures are members of the one family of God.'

Guru Nanak said, 'Neither Hindu nor Muslim am I/We are God's children all.'

Guru Nanak followed the principle of giving no appointment to anybody who came to see him unless the visitor had first partaken of food in the community kitchen *(langar)* where Muslims and Hindus, Brahmins and Shudras, all sat together: a fine way of inculcating humility, equality and fraternity and driving home the lesson that we are all children of the Eternal Master.

ESSENTIAL UNITY OF ALL RELIGIONS

◆

THE HARMONY OF all religions has been beautifully and comprehensively dealt with by Dr Bhagavan Das in his magnum opus—*Essential Unity of All Religions.* The Bharat Ratna has never been conferred on a more deserving Indian than Dr Bhagavan Das. An abridged edition of his great work ought to be made compulsory reading in every school and college.

A thinker had observed that Christianity has been tried and has failed: the religion of Christ remains to be tried. The same can be said about every other religion—such is the universal propensity to encrust and encumber truth with dogma, religion with ritual, essence with trappings. An enlightened spirit would go straight to the truth behind the dogma, the religion behind the ritual, the essence behind the trappings.

It is amazing that the experience and insight of all mystics, *rishis* and *sufis* is identical. 'All mystics', it has been truly observed, 'speak the same language because they belong to the same country.' That country is the Kingdom of Heaven which, as Christ taught us, is within us and not without. All seers perceive the ultimate reality with the eyes of their soul.

No one knows whether the great poet-saint Kabir was a Hindu or a Muslim. The story goes that when Kabir died, both the Hindus and the Muslims claimed his body: the Hindus wanted to cremate it according to the Hindu rites, and the Muslims were desirous of burying the *pir* in the Muslim way. But when they came to take charge of the earthly remains of the saint, both groups discovered that there was only a heap of flowers under the shroud! If the story is not true, it deserves to be true. In the words of Dr S.R. Sharma, 'How like Kabir again—dead or alive—a divine weaver of the hearts of men, who alchemised old hatreds into the gold of love . . .'*

*Soul of Indian History, *(Bhartiya Vidya Bhavan)*

TEACHINGS OF INDIAN LEADERS

◆

SHIVAJI IN HIS famous epistle to Emperor Aurangzeb wrote:

> 'Islam and Hinduism appear as contrasted terms; but they are diverse pigments used by the Divine Painter to fill in His picture of the whole human race. If it be a mosque, the call is chanted in remembrance of Him; if it be a temple, the bell is rung remembering Him alone. To show bigotry towards any man's creed and practices is tantamount to altering the words of the Holy Book. To draw new lines on a picture is to find fault with the Painter.'

Muslim leaders have been no less emphatic in their teaching that Hindus and Muslims must live in peace and harmony. Sayyid Ahmed Khan (1817-1898) uttered the following memorable words:

> 'Centuries have passed since God desired that Hindus and Musalmans may share the climate and the produce of this land and live and die on it together. So it appears to be the will of God that these two communities may live together in this country as friends, or even like two brothers . . . I have frequently said that India is a beautiful bride and Hindus and Muslims are her two eyes . . . If one of them is lost, this beautiful bride will become ugly.'

Maulana Abul Kalam Azad (1888-1958) told our countrymen in 1921 that Hindu-Muslim partnership was sanctioned by the Prophet's own example:

> 'When the Prophet Muhammad migrated to Medina he

> prepared a covenant between the Muslims and the Jews of Medina. In the covenant it was mentioned that ultimately the Muslims and non-Muslims would become one nation *(ummah vahidah).*
>
> '*Ummah* means a *qaum* or nation; *vahidah* means one.
>
> 'Thus if I say that the Muslims of India cannot perform their duty unless they are united with the Hindus, it is in accordance with the tradition of the Prophet who himself wanted to make a nation of Muslims and non-Muslims.'

Trusted by the divergent groups within the Congress, Maulana Azad was asked to preside when the Congress met in September 1923 to decide its future course. No one younger had been, or would be, given the honour. Maulana Azad was clear as to what was vital to the struggle for *swaraj,* and what was indeed greater than the struggle itself. His stirring words which came from the heart were:

> 'If an angel descends from the heavens today and proclaims from the Qutb Minar that India can attain Swaraj within twenty-four hours provided I relinquish my demand for Hindu-Muslim unity, I shall retort: "No my friend, I will give up Swaraj, but not Hindu-Muslim unity, for if Swaraj is delayed, it will be a loss for India, but if Hindu-Muslim unity is lost, it will be a loss for the whole of mankind." '

THE SPIRIT—SUPREME AND INFINITE

◆

THE MOST FUNDAMENTAL of all fundamental principles is that a Spirit, supreme and unchanging, pervades the entire universe and the material world is merely a manifestation of that Spirit. More than 3,000 years ago, India perceived this principle even more clearly, and understood its implications even more deeply, than the most highly civilized nations do today. You may call it a principle or evolution or consciousness or God. Each will speak in his own tongue.

'A fire mist and a planet,
A crystal and a cell,—
A jelly-fish and a saurian,
And caves where the cavemen dwell;
Then a sense of law and beauty,
And a face turned from the clod,
Some call it Evolution,
And others call it God.'

It is precisely because the Spirit alone is the everlasting reality that the infinite mystery of the material world can never be explained merely in material terms. In the words of Loren Eisley, 'In the forty-five years of my existence every atom, every molecule that composes me has changed its position or danced away and beyond to become part of other things. New molecules have come from the grass and bodies of animals to be part of me a little while, yet . . . my memories hold, and a loved face of twenty years ago is before me still.'

The body of an adult human being has a thousand billion cells. Each cell is blind; senses it has none. It works in the dark and yet all of them cooperate in the interest of the whole. Sir Charles Sherrington, the eminent physiologist, says: 'It is as if an Immanent Principle inspired each cell with knowledge for the carrying out of a design.' Sir Arthur Eddington expressed the same idea: 'Physical science has limited its scope so as to leave a background which we are at liberty to, or even invited to, fill with a reality of spiritual import.' These conclusions of the most learned of modern scientists were the very basics taught at the zenith of Indian civilization:

> 'From the unreal lead me to the Real;
> From darkness lead me to Light;
> From death lead me to Immortality.'
>
> —*Upanishads*

One of the lessons of the *Upanishads* is that you must regard 'the universe as a thought in the mind of its Creator, thereby reducing all discussion of material creation to futility.' The *Upanishads* teach that both space and time are endless or infinite. Modern science completely agrees. If the biggest railway station in India contained only six microscopic specks of dust, it would be more crowded with dust than space is with stars. A naya paisa coin held at arm's length blocks from your field of vision a thousand galaxies 350 million light-years away.

The Vedas emphasize that the internal *suksma-sarira,* the finer or subtle body of man, the equivalent of 'soul' in modern thought, is of transcendental importance; and that *suksma-sarira* is of the nature of infinite existence and infinite consciousness. In this luminous philosophy, material substance is wholly insignificant. Compare the observations of Einstein:

> 'We may therefore regard matter as being constituted by the regions of space in which the field is extremely intense . . . There is no place in this new kind of physics both for the field and matter, for the field is the only reality.'

BRAHMAN—THE ALL-PERVADING REALITY

◆

IN THE ENTIRE history of human knowledge, there has been no concept greater or deeper than the concept of Brahman evolved by ancient India. There is a unity underlying the entire creation. All parts are related to and interdependent on one another. Brahman is the ultimate and all-pervading reality: the inner essence of all things. Einstein worked for decades on the Unified Theory, an aspect of Brahman.

Dr Jagdish Chandra Bose, at the opening of the Institute which bears his name, observed:

> 'I dedicate today this Institute as not merely a laboratory but a temple . . . In the pursuit of my investigation I was unconsciously led into the border regions of physics and physiology. To my amazement, I found boundary lines vanishing, and points of contact emerging, between the realms of the living and the non-living. Inorganic matter was perceived as anything but inert; it was a thrill under the action of multitudinous forces . . . In time the leading scientific societies of the world accepted my theories and results, and recognized the importance of the Indian contribution to science. Can anything small or circumscribed ever satisfy the mind of India? By a continuous living tradition and a vital power of rejuvenescence, this land has readjusted itself through unnumbered transformations. Indians have always arisen who, discarding the immediate and absorbing prize of the hour,

> have sought for the realization of the highest ideals of life—not through passive renunciation but through active struggle.'

Emerson was fascinated by the concept of Brahman:

> 'All science is transcendental or else passes away. Botany is now acquiring the right theory—the avatars of Brahman will presently be the textbooks of natural history.'

The basic oneness of the universe which was a part of the mystical experience of the Indian sages is one of the most important revelations of modern physics. Eminent scientists like John Wheeler point out that in modern science the distinction between the observer and the observed breaks down completely and instead of the 'observer', we have to 'put in its place the new word "participator". In some strange sense the universe is a participatory universe.'

The *Upanishads* had taught the same lesson of the subject and the object fusing into a unified undifferentiated whole:

> 'Where there is duality, as it were, there one sees another; there one smells another; there one tastes another . . . But where everything has become just one's own self, then whereby and whom would one see? Then whereby and whom would one smell? Then whereby and whom would one taste?'

Sri Aurobindo speaks about 'a subtle change which makes the sight see in a sort of fourth dimension'. The intuition of Indian mystics led them to understand the multidimensional reality and the space-time continuum which is the basis of the modern theory of relativity. In the words of D.T. Suzuki, the significance of the Avatamsaka school of Mahayana Buddhism 'is unintelligible unless we once experience . . . a state of complete dissolution where there is no more distinction between mind and body, subject and object . . . We look around and perceive that . . . every object is related to every other object . . . not only spatially, but temporally . . . As a fact of pure experience, there is no space without time, no time without space; they are interpenetrating.'

Vedanta taught the technique of self-development. The ultimate destiny of man is to discover within himself the true Self as the changeless behind the changing, the eternal behind the ephemeral, and the infinite behind the finite. Greater wisdom was never compressed into three words than by the *Chandogya Upanishad* which proclaimed the true Self of man as part of the Infinite *Spirit-tat tvam asi:* 'That Thou Art.' In the beautiful words of Vedanta:

> '*Samvit* or pure consciousness is one and non-dual, ever self-luminous, and does not rise or set in months and years and aeons, past or future.'

ALL MATTER IS NOTHING BUT ENERGY

◆

DYNAMISM IS THE great law of the universe. Change and movement occur eternally, symbolized by Shiva's dance.

The recurring theme in Hindu mythology is the creation of the world by the self-sacrifice of God—'sacrifice' in the original sense of 'making sacred'—whereby God becomes the world. *Lila,* the play of God, is the creative activity of the Divine; and the world is the stage of the Divine play. Brahman is the great magician who transforms Himself into the world and He performs this feat with His 'magic creative power', which is the original meaning of *maya* in the *Rig Veda.* 'As long as we confuse the myriad forms of the Divine *lila* with reality, without perceiving the unity of Brahman underlying all these forms, we are under the spell of *maya* . . . *Maya* is the illusion of taking these concepts for reality, of confusing the map with the territory' (Dr Fritjof Capra).

To the *rishis* the divine play was the evolution of the cosmos through countless aeons. There are an infinite number of creations in an infinite universe. The *rishis* gave the name *kalpa* to the unimaginable span of time between the beginning and the end of one creation. They understood the staggering scale of the divine play. Many centuries later the scientific mind still boggles at the scale of creation which makes infinity intelligible.

The *rishis* clearly perceived that the most fundamental characteristic of this incomprehensible creation was that it was in a perpetual state of movement, flow and change. *Lila* is a rhythmic play which goes on in endless cycles, the One becoming the many and the many returning to the One. In the *Bhagavad Gita,* Lord Krishna describes this rhythmic play of creation in the following words:

> 'At the end of the night of time all things return to my nature; and when the new day of time begins I bring them again into light.
> Thus through my nature I bring forth all creation and this rolls around in the circles of time.
> But I am not bound by this vast work of creation. I am and I watch the drama of works.
> I watch and in its work of creation nature brings forth all that moves and moves not, and thus the revolutions of the world go round.'

How uncanny is the identity of the ancient insights with the latest conclusions of modern science which are well summed up in the fascinating book, *The Tao of Physics* by Fritjof Capra:

> 'In physics, we recognize the dynamic nature of the universe not only when we go to small dimensions—to the world of atoms and nuclei, but also when we turn to large dimensions—to the world of stars and galaxies. Through our powerful telescopes we observe a universe in ceaseless motion. Rotating clouds of hydrogen gas contract to form stars, heating up in the process until they become burning fires in the sky.
> 'When we study the universe as a whole, with its millions of galaxies, we have reached the largest scale of space and time; and again, at that cosmic level, we discover that the universe is not static—it is expanding! This has been one of the most important discoveries in modern astronomy . . . Whichever galaxy you happen to be in, you will observe the other galaxies rushing away from you; nearby galaxies at several thousand miles per second, farther ones at higher speeds, and the farthest at velocities approaching the speed of light. The light from galaxies beyond that distance will never reach us, because they move away from us faster than the speed of light. Their light is—in the words of Sir Arthur Eddington—"like a runner on an expanding track with the winning post receding faster than he can run" . . .'

Modern physics has come to the conclusion that mass is nothing but a form of energy. Einstein's world famous equation is

$$E = mc^2$$

where 'E' stand for energy, 'm' for mass and 'c' for the speed of light. Thus the amount of energy contained in a particle is equal to the particle's mass multiplied by the square of the speed of light. It would not be an exaggeration to say that the principle underlying Einstein's equation, the basis of the theory of relativity, and the space-time character of the universe, were perceived by the old Indian *rishis* in their advanced stage of spiritual consciousness. In their state of higher consciousness they realized that the ultimate constituents of the universe—energy and mass, particle and wave—were but different aspects of the same basic process, the same Oneness which pervaded the entire universe. Today science has relearned that lesson. In the words of A.N. Whitehead:

> 'Matter has been identified with energy, and energy is sheer activity. The modern point of view is expressed in terms of energy, activity and the vibratory differentiations of space-time. Any local agitation shakes the whole universe. The distant effects are minute but they are there. The concept of matter presupposed simple location . . . but in the modern concept the group of agitations which we term matter is fused into its environment. There is no possibility of a detached, self-contained existence.'

Very old are we men. We have always been, and will always be, both spectators and actors in the great drama of Life. Veering away from the Spirit, we try to learn and understand through our puny minds and are startled by the devastating discovery that matter is almost entirely Void. The vastest knowledge of today cannot transcend the *buddhi* of the *rishis;* and science, in its most advanced stage, is closer to Vedanta than ever before.

ANCIENT INSIGHTS AND MODERN MAN

◆

THE VALUES WHICH have been taught in India over the last 5,000 years have great relevance to the times we live in. And yet so few Indians are aware of our priceless heritage.

It has been my long-standing conviction that India is like a donkey carrying a sack of gold—the donkey does not know what it is carrying but is content to go along with the load on its back. The load of gold is the fantastic treasure—in arts, literature, culture, and some sciences like Ayurvedic medicine—which we have inherited from the days of the splendour that was India. Adi Sankaracharya called it 'the accumulated treasure of spiritual truths discovered by the *rishis*.' Rabindranath Tagore said, 'India is destined to be the teacher of all lands.'

The golden voices of ancient India have come to us down the ages in unbroken continuity through countless *rishis* and saints—some of them world famous and some of them nameless. Our culture which is primarily concerned with spiritual development is of special significance in our age which is marked by the obsolescence of the materialistic civilization. Sri Aurobindo said, 'India of the ages is not dead, nor has she spoken her last creative word; she lives and has still something to do for herself and the human race.'

India is eternal, everlasting. Though the beginnings of her numerous civilizations go so far back in time that they are lost in the twilight of history, she has the gift of perpetual youth. Her culture is ageless and is as relevant to our twentieth century as it was twenty centuries before Christ. Dr Arnold Toynbee, after surveying the story of the entire human race, observed:

> 'It is already becoming clear that a chapter which had a Western beginning will have to have an Indian ending if it is not to end in the self-destruction of the human race . . . At this supremely dangerous moment in human history, the only way of salvation for mankind is the Indian way—Emperor Ashoka's and Mahatma Gandhi's principle of non-violence and Sri Ramakrishna's testimony to the harmony of religions. Here we have an attitude and spirit that can make it possible for the human race to grow together into a single family—and, in the Atomic Age, this is the only alternative to destroying ourselves.'

Toynbee echoes the ideal placed before mankind by India's ancient *rishis*—*Vasudhaiva Kutumbakam*—'The World is One Family'.

It would be hard to improve upon the sense of values which made ancient India so great. Our old sages judged the greatness of a state not by the extent of its empire or by the size of its wealth, but by the degree of righteousness and justice which marked the public administration and the private lives of the citizens. Their timeless teaching was that man's true progress is to be judged by moral and spiritual standards, and not by material or physical standards. Sacrifice was far more important than success; and renunciation was regarded as the crowning achievement. The citizen ranked in society, not according to wealth or power, but according to the standard of learning, virtue and character which he had attained. The finest example of that is the well-known story of Emperor Ashoka, a true follower of Buddha, making it an invariable practice to bow in reverence before Buddhist monks. His minister Yasha thought that it was wrong and improper for a great emperor to bow before monks. Ashoka's answer was:

> 'After all, I am doing obeisance to them as a mark of my deep respect for their learning, wisdom and sacrifice. What matters in life, Yasha, is not a person's status or position, but his virtues and wisdom. The finest minds and hearts may be hidden in ugly mortal frames. Only when you have raised

> yourself up from ignorance can you recognize the greatness of a few in a sea of humanity, just as a good jeweller alone can spot a gem among worthless pebbles.'

The Sanskrit word *dharma* cannot be easily translated into English. It has within it elements from the different concepts of law, righteousness, duty, and basic morality.

India has had an unrivalled tradition of religious freedom and tolerance. That tradition was born of the consciousness that truth can never be the monopoly of any one sect or creed. The words of the *Rig Veda* are world-famous:

> 'Let noble thoughts come to us from every side.'

The *rishis* realized that each man has to work out his own salvation and that everyone's own spiritual experience is vital to the attainment of the ultimate state of soul's evolution. A blind obedience to authority is the surest prescription for spiritual paralysis. Mere acquiescence, even in the dictates of the *sruti,* is not enough. There is nothing like salvation on the cheap. There is no spiritual enrichment which money can buy. There are no fixed formulae, no rules of thumb, no prescriptions as in a pharmacopoeia. The path of the Spirit is narrow and there are yawning abysses on either side.

In the words of the *Kathopanishad:*

> 'Sharp as a razor's edge and hard to traverse is that difficult path, so the sages say.'

Realization of the Divine is possible through meditation and contemplation. The inner spirit must dwell serene on the heights of eternity. However, action can be as efficacious as contemplation. The way to salvation may be through prayer or it may be through action or through knowledge. Men like Sri Aurobindo are examples of the mysterious reconciliation of incessant work and uninterrupted rest in one and the same person. That is the ideal which the *Bhagavad Gita* sets before us: 'He who sees rest in activity and activity in rest—he is wise among men, he is a *yogi* and a thorough man of action.'

The doctrine of Brahman, the Ultimate Reality, must necessarily involve tolerance and understanding, peace and goodwill, and recognition of the immense variety of paths by which the soul can fulfil its ultimate destiny.

Ahimsa, peace and non-aggression were the hallmarks of Indian culture. In her crowded history of over 5,000 years during which she had thrown up vast and puissant empires, India never practised military aggression on countries outside her borders. Thanks to our ethos, even today the Indian people patiently suffer miseries and endure injustices which would result in devastating explosions in any other country.

In these days of spiritual illiteracy and poverty of the spirit, when people find that wealth can only multiply itself and attain nothing, when people have to deceive their souls with counterfeits after having killed the poetry of life, it is necessary to remind ourselves that civilization is an act of the spirit. Material progress is not to be mistaken for inner progress. When technology outstrips moral development, the prospect is not that of a millennium but of extinction. Our ancient heritage is a potent antidote to the current tendency to standardize souls and seek salvation in herds.

Centuries have gone by but the lustre of that heritage remains undimmed. Invading forces have descended on this country but its culture has remained indestructible.

> 'The East bow'd low before the blast,
> In patient, deep disdain.
> She let the legions thunder past,
> And plunged in thought again.'

C. Rajagopalachari observed: 'If there is any honesty in India today, any hospitality, any chastity, any philanthropy, any tenderness to the dumb creatures, any aversion to evil, any love to do good, it is due to whatever remains of the old faith and the old culture.'

The old faith and the old culture referred to by Rajaji are not merely for Hindus, not merely for Indians, but for the whole world. Schelling, in his old age, thought the *Upanishads* contain the maturest wisdom of mankind. Today that wisdom is essential not only for the rebirth of the Indian nation but also for the re-education of the human race.

A HOLISTIC VIEW OF THE WORLD

◆

IN THE ENTIRE history of human knowledge, there has been no concept greater or deeper than the concept of Brahman evolved by ancient India. There is a unity underlying the entire creation. All parts are related to, and inter-dependent on, one another. Brahman is the ultimate and all-pervading reality: the inner essence of all things. *[See pp. 24-26]*

This evening I shall not deal with the concept of Brahman which reaches the frontier of human knowledge. But I shall deal with a narrower topic—a holistic view of the world. The narrower view dictates that all *animate* life may be taken as constituting a distinct unified part of the world—all trees and vegetation and all animals. The holistic view looks at the unity underlying all animate creation.

This holistic view, even in the narrow sense, is a distinct advance in human thought. I believe that this theory was evolved by J.C. Smuts, the great South African thinker, statesman, and general in his book entitled *Holism and Evolution* published in 1926.

The holistic or humanitarian viewpoint looks at the world in a broad manner which is compassionate and liberal, without being too rigid or too intolerant. On the other hand, those who take a holistic view of the animate world on solely religious, moral or intellectual grounds are inclined to believe fanatically in the moral equality of all membes of the animal kingdom. They believe that the slug and the saint are of equal value in God's eyes and that an amoeba ranks equal with Kalidas or Leonardo da Vinci, Beethoven or Shakespeare.

A holistic view of the world is always the main topic of total agreement between all delegates at every international vegetarian conference. For instance, at the Thirtieth World Vegetarian Conference which was held in New Delhi three years ago, the names of vegetarians among world renowned celebrities were mentioned—the Greek philosophers Socrates and Aristotle, world- famous geniuses like Pythagoras, Plutarch, Sir Issac Newton, Leonardo da Vinci, Alexander Pope, Percy Bysshe Shelley, Tolstoy, Dr Annie Besant, Mahatma Gandhi, Albert Einstein and George Bernard Shaw. The famous words of Einstein were quoted, 'Vegetarian food leaves a deep impression on our nature. If the whole world adopts vegetarianism, it can change the destiny of humankind'.

Incidentally, India is the only country in the world which preached the religion of reverence for all forms of life—Jainism. No other religion has ever preached reverence for all forms of life as Jainism which was proclaimed more than 2500 years ago.

Even among those who love animals, there can be two purposes for which animals may be killed with some justification, or a semblance of justification. First, animals may be killed for the purpose of human consumption by non-vegetarians. Every day, Americans slaughter 25 million chickens and Europeans consume 340 million eggs. Human ingenuity will always find a justification for pandering to the needs of man who is a carnivorous animal.

Secondly, much can be forgiven to those men who are not inclined to be cruel to animals but who are concerned with genuine scientific research which aims at alleviating human suffering. In 1991, leading medical charities launched a campaign to justify the use of animals in experiments, and attacked the growing use of violence and intimidation by anti-vivisectionists. They said that many of the biggest advances in public health, including the development of vaccines, transplant surgery, antibiotics and other life-saving drugs would have been impossible without laboratory animals. The eight leading medical charities said that the time had come to take a stand against the lies and disinformation issued by extreme animal rights supporters.

Likewise, the winners of the Nobel Prize in Medicine have repeatedly emphasized that there would not be a single person alive today as a result of an organ transplant or bone marrow transplant without animal experimentation. The moral issue that must be faced is whether the achievements of medical research—aimed at saving human life and alleviating human suffering—justify the use of animals.

Sir Walter Bodmer who is the Research Director of the Imperial Cancer Research Fund, said in a recent lecture, 'Our concern as scientists must be to ensure that the facts are presented as dispassionately and as objectively as possible. The case justifying the use of animals in research is overwhelming'.

Those who are inclined to be kind to animals on religious grounds, moral grounds or intellectual grounds tend to go to extremes in their condemnation. Dr Steven L.R. Clark was a Fellow of All Souls College, Oxford, and a Professor of Moral Philosophy at Glasgow University, and he thought that those who do not accept the moral status of animals are 'worthy of the asylum, the prison, or the hangman's rope'. He put meat-eaters in the same category as the Germans who were willing to torture Jewish children to death.

The intellectual grounds on which a holistic view of the world can be founded are clear and cogent.

'All animals are born with an equal claim on life and the same rights to existence'. This is the First Article of the Universal Declaration of the Rights of Animals which was finalized in 1977. It was adopted in 1978 at a ceremonial meeting of UNESCO.

In 1876, the first Prevention of Cruelty to Animals Act had been passed in Britain. At that time there were about 350 experiments on animals per year. Now there are more than five million each year—many unfortunately for commercial purposes.

In our relations with animals, as Colman McCarthy says, human beings think that any treatment they mete out to animals is justified and proper. We humans eat, hunt, trap, ride, brand, wear, cage, own, sell, breed, dissect, exploit, tame, capture, torture, sacrifice and kill animals. This is for starters; and does not count the estimated twenty-seven species which are made extinct every hour of every day. Much of this torture and suffering is legal, with such laws as the Prevention of Cruelty to Animals Act, 1960 providing a comforting balm.

Our knowledge of the animate world is abysmally poor.

If a species of plant or animal vanishes before scientists even detect its presence, did it really become extinct—or did it never exist? To scientists it is not just a philosophical teaser. Rather, it gives us an idea of the world's lack of knowledge of bio-diversity. In simple language, bio-diversity means the total of all life forms on earth. The nations of the world took a pledge at the Earth Summit in Rio de Janeiro four years ago to preserve bio-diversity.

The United Nations Environment Programme commissioned a global bio-diversity assessment by more than 1000 experts around the world. Their report, released a year ago, concludes that the earth has between thirteen and fourteen million species of plants, animals and microbes and of these, science knows only 1.75 million. Many of the rest will die undiscovered.

The central argument of one of the writers is that regulatory laws for animal welfare do little or nothing to establish or protect the interest of animals. 'Animal welfare is the view that it is morally acceptable, at least under some circumstances, to kill animals or subject them to suffering as long as precautions are taken to ensure that the animal is treated as humanely as possible.' The authors discuss the idea that animals have the same life force and the same will to live as humans.

The basic question is this—is it moral to pass laws that treat animals as property?

Some thinkers who have derived their philosophy from Hellenistic sources believe with Aristotle that humans alone have a rational capacity and that animals have no other purpose save that of serving human beings.

Much of it is also out of sight, with the hamburger consumer unaware of the pain inflicted on animals in factory farms and in slaughterhouses: the violence caused by human beings to animals has been normalized, either through habit or culture, so that it is only the odd person who sees life also from the animal's view point who is considered abnormal. As T.S. Eliot wrote, in a world of fugitives those running in the opposite direction are treated as mad.

Luckily, we still have men who write about animals with vivid compassion. Two such books were published last year—*Animals, Property and the Law* and *Animal Theology*. The authors have argued their case with intellectual calmness.

Animal rights groups are trying to educate the people, lifting the veil of ignorance that obscures the realities of farming. Since

1984 the percentage of Britons who are vegetarians has more than doubled to 4.5 per cent.

All farming involves some cruelty. Where would our milk, butter and cheese come from if cows were not separated from their mothers at birth? No one would condone separating babies from their human mothers. Even vegetarians are accepting here a moral distinction between the two species.

Gone are the days when people solemnly argued that animals do not have rights. The argument urged in support of this view was that rights exist only within a social contract as part of an exchange of duties and entitlements; and, therefore, animals cannot have rights. In this view of the matter, any concern for the suffering of animals was seen as a mistake. Torturing a chimpanzee was treated as morally equivalent to chopping wood. Civilization has advanced sufficiently to make such an argument untenable.

In Europe, the trade in live animals has started a moral debate which is not going to go away. In articles published six months ago, *The Economist,* one of the finest newspapers published in any part of the world, showed Britons taking to the streets to fight trade in live animals. It wrote about cows shoved from lorries and thrown from lorries' upper decks; the bull suspended by one broken leg, then dropped from a height to a hard deck below; a man in an apron kicking a pig again and again as the pig shrieks from the blows; pigs and sheep suspended upside down, fully conscious (they are supposed to have been stunned, but have not been), but still blinking and gulping for a few excruciating seconds as blood floods from their throats. Those who witnessed the tragedy of the animals said that no humans in Nazi concentration camps were treated as badly as these animals.

In those articles, *The Economist* pointed out how cruel humans are to animals. The odds are that the hen which laid the egg for your breakfast is a battery hen. She is confined to a tiny cage with four or five others for her entire adult life. The egg-laying hen is squeezed into a space barely enough to move. She may exercise her pecking instinct by pecking out her neighbour's feathers—unless her beak has been cut off with a red hot blade, probably causing pain for life.

Men have never treated animals as our neighbours but only as our subjects. For example, take the largest living species which we have in our midst in India today—the elephant. The World

Wide Fund for Nature called last year for an international effort to save the species which is now believed to number only between 31,000 and 51,000, of which 24,000 are in India. The other species of elephants is the African elephant which is a much bigger animal and is estimated to number about 600,000.

Surveys indicate that an increasing number of Asian elephants are being poisoned or shot, to stop them from trampling or eating crops. The trade in elephants tusks, hide for shoes and handbags, and ingredients for Chinese medicines—is growing, despite being banned under the Convention on International Trade in Endangered Species. Once the lord of the jungle from Iraq to China, the Asian elephant seem to share a depressing destiny with its African counterpart—both are in danger of extinction.

Many people have begun to think that some form of civil disobedience is definitely justified. To the surprise of the country's political elite, the promotion of animal rights has emerged as Britain's closest thing to a mass social movement. The issue is becoming for Britain what abortion is for America: a deeply divisive social conflict in which the morally simple positions are the extreme ones and the middle is morally treacherous. The Royal Society for the Prevention of Cruelty to Animals, founded in 1824, was the first of its kind, preceding the National Society for the Prevention of Cruelty to Children by half a century. Today the Royal Society for the Prevention of Cruelty to Animals has five lakh supporters. In America, there are four hundred animal advocacy groups.

To us it seems incredible that the Greek philosophers should have scanned so deep into right and wrong and yet never noticed the immorality of slavery. Likewise, it seems incredible that the Indian sages and thinkers should have scanned so deep into right and wrong and yet never noticed the inhumanity of the theory of treating human beings as untouchables. Perhaps three thousand years from now it will seem equally incredible that we do not notice the immorality of our oppression to animals. A holistic view of the world would ensure that the human being is blessed with an intelligent heart and a kind brain.

The holistic view of the world has never been more beautifully expressed than by Ralph Hodgson in his poem 'The Bells of Heaven'—

'I would ring the bells of Heaven
The wildest peal for years,
If Parson lost his senses
And people came to theirs,
And he and they together
Knelt down with angry prayers
For tamed and shaggy tigers
And dancing dogs and bears,
And wretched, blind pit ponies,
And little hunted hares.'

THE AILING PLANET: THE GREEN MOVEMENT'S ROLE

◆

ONE CANNOT RECALL any movement in world history which has gripped the imagination of the entire human race so completely and so rapidly as the Green movement which started nearly twenty-five years ago. In 1972 the world's first nationwide Green party was founded in New Zealand. Since then, the movement has not looked back.

We have shifted—one hopes, irrevocably—from the mechanistic view to a holistic and ecological view of the world. It is a shift in human perceptions as revolutionary as that introduced by Copernicus who taught mankind in the sixteenth century that the earth and the other planets revolved round the sun. For the first time in human history, there is a growing worldwide consciousness that the earth itself is a living organism—an enormous being of which we are parts. It has its own metabolic needs and vital processes which need to be respected and preserved.

The earth's vital signs reveal a patient in declining health. We have begun to realize our ethical obligations to be good stewards of the planet and responsible trustees of the legacy to future generations.

The concept of sustainable development was popularized in 1987 by the World Commission on Environment and Development. In its report it defined the idea as 'Development that meets the needs of the present, without compromising the ability of future generations to meet their needs', i.e., without stripping the natural world of resoures future generations would need.

In the zoo at Lusaka, Zambia, there is a cage where the notice reads, 'The world's most dangerous animal'. Inside the cage there is no animal but a mirror where you see yourself. Thanks to the efforts of a number of agencies in different countries, a new awareness has now dawned upon the most dangerous animal in the world. He has realized the wisdom of shifting from a system based on domination to one based on partnership.

Scientists have catalogued about 1.4 million living species with which mankind shares the earth. Estimates vary widely as regards the still-uncatalogued living species—biologists reckon that about three to a hundred million other living species still languish unnamed in ignominious darkness.

One of the early international commissions which dealt, *inter alia,* with the question of ecology and environment was the Brandt Commission which had a distinguished Indian as one of its members—Mr L.K. Jha. The First Brandt Report raised the question—'Are we to leave our successors a scorched planet of advancing deserts, impoverished landscapes and ailing environment?'

Mr Lester R. Brown in his thoughtful book, *The Global Economic Prospect,* points out that the earth's principal biological systems are four—fisheries, forests, grasslands, and croplands—and they form the foundation of the global economic system. In addition to supplying our food, these four systems provide virtually all the raw materials for industry except minerals and petroleum-derived synthetics. In large areas of the world, human claims on these systems are reaching an unsustainable level, a point where their productivity is being impaired. When this happens, fisheries collapse, forests disappear, grasslands are converted into barren wastelands, and croplands deteriorate. In a protein-conscious and protein-hungry world, over-fishing is common every day. In poor countries, local forests are being decimated in order to procure firewood for cooking. In some places, firewood has become so expensive that 'what goes under the pot now costs more than what goes inside it'. Since the tropical forest is, in the words of Dr Myers, 'the powerhouse of evolution', several species of life face extinction as a result of its destruction.

It has been well said that forests precede mankind; deserts follow. The world's ancient patrimony of tropical forests is now eroding at the rate of forty to fifty million acres a year, and the growing use of dung for burning deprives the soil of an important natural fertiliser. The World Bank estimates that a five-fold increase in the rate of forest planting is needed to cope with the expected fuelwood demand in the year 2000.

James Speth, the President of the World Resources Institute, said the other day, 'We were saying that we are losing the forests at an acre a second, but it is much closer to an acre and a half to a second'.

Article 48A of the Constitution of India provides that 'the State shall endeavour to protect and improve the environment and to safeguard the forests and wildlife of the country'. But what causes endless anguish is the fact that laws are never respected nor enforced in India. (For instance, the Constitution says that casteism, untouchability and bonded labour shall be abolished, but they flourish shamelessly even after forty-four years of the operation of the Constitution.) A recent report of our Parliament's Estimates Committee has highlighted the near catastrophic depletion of India's forests over the last four decades. India, according to reliable data, is losing its forests at the rate of 3.7 million acres a year. Large areas, officially designated as forest land, 'are already virtually treeless'. The actual loss of forests is estimated to be about eight times the rate indicated by government statistics.

A three-year study using satellites and aerial photography conducted by the United Nations, warns that the environment has deteriorated so badly that it is 'critical' in many of the eighty-eight countries investigated.

There can be no doubt that the growth of world population is one of the strongest factors distorting the future of human society. It took mankind more than a million years to reach the first billion. That was the world population around the year 1800. By the year 1900, a second billion was added, and the twentieth century has added another 3.7 billion. The present world population is estimated at 5.7 billion. Every four days the world population increases by one million.

Fertility falls as incomes rise, education spreads, and health improves. Thus development is the best contraceptive. But development itself may not be possible if the present increase in numbers continues.

The rich gets richer, and the poor beget children which

condemns them to remain poor. More children does not mean more workers, merely more people without work. It is not suggested that human beings be treated like cattle and compulsorily sterilised. But there is no alternative to voluntary family planning without introducing an element of coercion. The choice is really between control of population and perpetuation of poverty.

The population of India is estimated to be 920 million today—more than the entire populations of Africa and South America put together. No one familiar with the conditions in India would doubt that the hope of the people would die in their hungry hutments unless population control is given topmost priority.

For the first time in human history we see a transcending concern—the survival not just of the people but of the planet. We have begun to take a holistic view of the very basis of our existence. The environmental problem does not necessarily signal our demise, it is our passport for the future. The emerging new world vision has ushered in the Era of Responsibility. It is a holistic view, an ecological view, seeing the world as an integrated whole rather than a dissociated collection of parts.

Industry has a most crucial role to play in this new Era of Responsibility. What a transformation would be effected if more businessmen shared the view of the Chairman of Du Pont, Mr Edgar S. Woolard who, five years ago, declared himself to be the Company's 'Chief Environmental Officer'. He said, 'Our continued existence as a leading manufacturer requires that we excel in environmental performance.'

Of all the statements made by Margaret Thatcher during the years of her Prime Ministership, none has passed so decisively into the current coin of English usage as her felicitous words: 'No generation has a free hold on this earth. All we have is a life tenancy—with a full repairing lease'. In the words of Mr Lester Brown, 'We have not inherited this earth from our forefathers; we have borrowed it from our children.'

II

FREEDOM AND INSTITUTIONS OF DEMOCRACY

OBEDIENCE TO THE UNENFORCEABLE

◆

I AM SPEAKING today in a State where one of the greatest civilizations known to history once flourished. In the age of Emperor Ashoka, Pataliputra blossomed where modern Patna is located today. The civilization was great because it rested on certain enduring principles—compassion of the strong towards the weak and the suppression of immediate gratification for the more rewarding goals of national glory and progress.

It is important that citizens obey the law. It is even more important that citizens obey the high standards of decency which are not enforced by the law but are the hallmark of a truly civilized and mature democracy. Sir Thomas Taylor of Aberdeen University summed up the position in a few memorable sentences. As he put it, beyond the sphere of duty which is legally enforceable, there is a vast range of significant behaviour in which the law does not and ought not to intervene. This feeling of *obedience to the unenforceable* is the very opposite of the attitude that whatever is technically possible is allowable. This power of self-discipline is the very opposite of the fatal arrogance which asserts, whether in government, science, industry or personal behaviour, that whatever is technically possible is licit. All through history, men have needed it to preserve them from the temper which hardens the heart and perverts the understanding.

Such obedience to the unenforceable is, by definition, not easy to practise or inculcate, particularly in an age characterized by escalating violence, intemperate thirst for power, and social and ideological conflicts. It is specially difficult in industrial relations.

It will be a long time before such standards of mature public conduct prevail in India. So, far from having learnt the value of obedience to the unenforceable, we have a growing tendency not to show obedience even to the enforceable laws.

Maintenance of standards of decency dictated by a high moral sense is impossible unless the people have a sense of discipline. A democracy without discipline is a democracy without a future. Undisciplined trade unionism is as dangerous as undisciplined capitalism; and undisciplined demagogy is as dangerous as undisciplined student power.

It is a painful truth that in labour relations what is claimed by certain unions is not freedom but licence. When freedom degenerates into licence, people resort even to means prohibited by law in their endeavour to secure coveted objectives. In the year 1979, forty-three million man-days were lost in India on account of strikes—forty-three million man-days' loss to society's detriment, resulting in a fall in the gross national product and an increase in inflation. The workers themselves have nothing to gain, in the long run, by such irresponsible leadership.

The question whether in a free democracy strikes can be banned is of utmost importance, because it exemplifies the distinction between a democracy which has just attained majority and a mature democracy which is rich in traditions and in standards of public behaviour. There were long periods in our country's hoary history when there were very few laws, but the people practised the ideal of obedience to the unenforceable. In India, for generations people lived without a government. There was no central government, not even an effective regional government but life went on. The nation had a certain moral depth and knew how to behave.

Let us now consider specifically the right to strike and the moral validity of a law banning strikes. The basic question is whether a government which is concerned with the interests of the working classes can pass a law preventing the exercise of the right to strike. The most significant fact is that in countries which represent the dictatorship of the proletariat, where the working classes themselves are supposed to be in power, strikes are totally and absolutely banned. In communist countries people inciting or taking part in strikes are promptly imprisoned or otherwise removed. This should make you pause and ponder. If strikes are banned in states where the workers are supposed to be in the saddle, surely there is some wisdom behind the view that a handful of individuals cannot, for their selfish gain, hold the whole society to ransom.

Physical violence and strong-arm tactics are still practised by irresponsible trade union leaders and their followers. Such tactics are the relic of a bygone, semi-civilized age. William the Conqueror introduced in England the method of trial called 'ordeal by battle'. That mode of trial was perfectly simple. The plaintiff and the defendant in a civil suit, or the prosecutor and the accused in a criminal proceeding, fought each other. Both parties to the litigation were required to be engaged in physical combat. Only women and the Church were permitted to appear by their champions: and the champion was the precursor of the modern advocate. It was assumed that in such physical combat God would help that party which was in the right. The party who was beaten was pronounced to be guilty, and the party who won was declared to be innocent and to have justice on his side. The method of employing an 'advocate' to appear in place of the litigant was extended later from priests and women to other categories of litigants. In the thirteenth century the most famous 'advocate' was a gladiator called William Graham. It is an interesting comment on the eternal spirit of private enterprise that a businessman soon employed William Graham on a good salary and then he let out, for a certain fee per fight, Graham's services to any litigant. Graham was a most successful advocate. When he was engaged by any party, the case usually went uncontested!

This form of trial fell into disuse, but it remained open under the law to litigants in England until the nineteenth century. It was in 1818 that a man convicted of murder went in appeal and his counsel in the appellate court claimed for his client the right to challenge the prosecutor to physical combat. Lord Ellenborough, the chief justice, had no option but to find that such a right existed. It was this case which led to the abolition in 1819 of the antiquated right to trial by battle.

The points I am making for your consideration is this. If all civil matters can be decided by a court of law, if all criminal matters can be decided, equally satisfactorily, by a court of law, why can industrial disputes not be decided in industrial courts or tribunals—instead of being sought to be decided by muscle power, by physical force, by brutal violence? I am all in favour of a fair deal for workers. But a fair deal can undoubtedly be meted out to workers by an impartial industrial tribunal or adjudicator.

The economic situation in India is so disturbing that as a temporary measure, all strikes and lockouts, and all other modes of action savouring of physical force and coercion, either on the part of labour or on the part of management, should be totally banned by law in every industry for a period of at least two years.

India is too poor a country to lose millions of man-days every year on account of strikes. You must remember that in organized industry we are paying unskilled workers in places like Bombay a wage which puts them among the 5 per cent top wage-earners in India. There are companies in big cities where peons get more than qualified physicians and lecturers in universities.

In those countries where people are mature enough to practise obedience to the unenforceable, there is no need for a law to ban strikes or the use of physical force in industrial disputes. For example, in Switzerland there is no militant trade unionism. In Japan the worker, even during the period of strike, keeps on working—only a band round his arm indicates that he is 'on strike' though he puts in a full day's work. But in countries where self-discipline and self-restraint do not prevail and where the economic miseries of the people may one day result in a violent explosion, the law has to step in and make the machinery of tribunals compulsory in all industrial cases, exactly as adjudication by courts is made compulsory in all civil and criminal cases.

There is no hope whatever of improving the lot of the working classes, both in the cities and in the rural areas, and at the same time of checking inflation, unless and until we attain a sustained level of increased production all round. Industrial peace alone can lead to fast economic growth and, as I am never tired of repeating, without economic growth there cannot be social justice in a poor country like India.

THE FUTURE OF DEMOCRACY IN INDIA

◆

WHAT A SAD contrast between Sri Aurobindo's vision ('Mother India is not a piece of earth; she is a Power, a Godhead') and the cesspool of degradation to which professional politicians have reduced this country!

Sri Aurobindo predicted that the sun of India's greatness would rise and its light would overflow India, overflow Asia and spread throughout the world. This was the vision of Sri Aurobindo, a seer in the true sense of the word. So, when we are faced with troubles for the moment and the path seems to be engulfed in darkness, let us not lose faith in ourselves or lose sight of the rare destiny we have to fulfil.

By voting ignorant professional politicians to power, we have kept a singularly gifted and enterprising nation in the ranks of the poorest on earth. 67 per cent of our people are still illiterate; and if the calibre of our politicians does not improve, India will contain 53 per cent of the world's illiterates by the year 2000 AD. Many politicians seem to have a vested interest in illiteracy—their survival as public figures depends upon the continuation of the forces of ignorance. It appears cynical but it is true that for portly politicians, goodly in girth, poverty is good business: they talk continually about *garibi* without having the will, the expertise or the imagination to eradicate it.

The moral crisis is writ large on the entire political scene. In the fifties we had many eminent men in public life who were every inch gentlemen. In the sixties we had many public figures who were every alternate inch gentlemen. Unfortunately, in the seventies we have an unacceptably large number of politicians who are no inch gentlemen.

As we enter the eighties we have to realize the fundamental importance of four things.

First, the time has come when citizens must wrest the initiative from professional politicians and from political parties, and insist upon men of knowledge, vision and character being chosen as candidates for parliamentary and state elections. It is only such men who can give India the type of government it needs—a government which is strong without being authoritarian, and humane without being weak. Poverty can be eradicated only by experts in finance, production and marketing, and specialists in social engineering and deployment of resources. Singapore is a most striking example of how fast a nation can progress when its cabinet is composed of outstanding talent and probity.

The difference between a minister selected for his political cunning and a minister of high mental and moral calibre is the difference between a lightning bug and lightning.

We have hardly an economic problem which would be beyond the capacity of a knowledgeable organizer with an iron will. A technocrat would never try to repeal the laws of economics—the futile exercise to which our Central and state governments have been addicted so long. He would realize that development begins with people and not with goods. Only men of stature can evoke the response from the people, without which governmental plans turn to ashes.

Secondly, there is a deep-felt need for an intelligent and adequate organization of voters. There should be a Citizens' Council in every constituency, consisting of impartial non-party individuals who would appraise the candidates and recommend the right candidates to the voters, and after the elections ensure that the candidate does not defect or otherwise disgrace himself and his constituents. The voters should unmistakably insist upon the right type of candidates, instead of allowing the political parties to palm off ignoramuses on them.

Thirdly, we must shed the divisive tendencies which split the votes on caste and sub-caste lines, and which are so devastating to our unity as a nation. One Indian is an intelligent human being;

two Indians are a political group; three Indians are two political groups.

Fourthly, our people must cast off the shackles of political feudalism. The modern ruling class consists of the 5,000 members of Parliament and the state legislatures. It is pathetic to see the servile behaviour of our people towards ministers and legislators. When Jayaprakash Narayan talked of total revolution, he meant a total transformation of the spirit, which would enable the people to control the government instead of being dominated and dragooned by the government.

The average age of the members in the last Lok Sabha was 52 years and in the current Rajya Sabha it is 53.5 years, while the life expectancy in our country is only 47 years. By contrast, the average age in the US House of Representatives as well as in the US Senate is significantly lower than in our Parliament, although the average span of life in the United States is 74 years. Our republic would have a new lease of life when younger people, with well-equipped minds and with the ability to have a bright career outside politics, take to public life as a matter of national service.

'It is a funny thing about life,' observed Somerset Maugham, 'if you refuse to accept anything but the best, you often get it.' This is equally true of democracy. If people refuse to accept any but the best citizens as candidates, it would usher in the golden age of our republic. Democracy gives, as life gives, what you ask of it. The following lines of Jessie B. Rittenhouse would be wholly apposite if democracy were substituted for Life:

'I bargained with Life for a penny,
And Life would pay no more,
However I begged at evening
When I counted my scanty store;
For Life is a just employer,
He gives you what you ask,
But once you have set the wages,
Why, you must bear the task.
I worked for a menial's hire,
Only to learn, dismayed,
That any wage I had asked of Life,
Life would have paid.'

The great French thinker, Montesquieu, said in the eighteenth century: 'The tyranny of a Prince in an oligarchy is not so dangerous to the public welfare as the apathy of a citizen in a democracy.' A bad government is the inevitable consequence of an indifferent electorate. Politics will never be cleaner, and our economic future will never be brighter, unless and until our citizens are willing to give of themselves to the land which gave them birth.

THE TASKS BEFORE A FREE PEOPLE

◆

The elections to the Lok Sabha in March 1977 resulted in overwhelming defeat of the Congress. India had a rebirth of freedom.

THE IMPOSSIBLE HAPPENED; and the inevitable did not happen. The triumph of the Janata-CFD party must have rung the bells of heaven the wildest peal for years. Reason, that torch of smoky pine, anticipated results which hovered between narrow victory and narrow defeat for the Congress. The difference between the expectation and the reality was the difference between a tremor and an earthquake, between a drizzle and a hurricane.

The last parliamentary election in India was one of the most significant in the entire history of freedom. At one stroke it doubled the number of free people on earth. In the words of Bernard Levin, India voted in a manner which put ancient and sophisticated democracies to shame. Notably, the 'illiterate intelligence' of the masses brought about a result which the 'educated incapacity' of the intelligentsia could not foresee.

A free nation can be stifled by indigenous autocrats only through its own apathy and folly—apart from brute military force.

Jawaharlal Nehru's description of the condition of India under British domination must have come home with the atrocities of the Emergency to countless people:

'We seemed to be helpless in the grip of some all-powerful

> monster; our limbs were paralysed, our minds deadened . . . The dominant impulse in India was that of fear—pervasive, oppressing, strangling fear; fear of the army, the police, the widespread secret service, fear of the official class; fear of laws to suppress and of prison.'

The first act of the liberated people should be to thank, from the depths of their souls, whatever Higher Forces they believe in—for the deliverance.

> 'Above blind fate and the antagonist powers
> Moveless there stands a high unchanging Will;
> To its omnipotence leave thy work's result.
> All things shall change in God's transfiguring hour.'

Human propensity to err is the favourite instrument of Providence for achieving its beneficent designs. Hitler, despite his super-efficient organization, attacks Russia instead of invading Britain—and it is the beginning of the end of the engulfing night. Nixon, notwithstanding his unsurpassed political cunning, tapes his own misdeeds—and the United States enters a brighter phase. The Indian autocracy, although armed with an all-powerful and all-pervasive secret intelligence force, calls for elections at a time of seething discontent simmering under the surface—and India secures a fresh lease of freedom.

Next, since public memory is so alarmingly short, let us reiterate our gratitude to the men who suffered for freedom and whose sacrifices have not been in vain. *[See pp. 62-63]*

William Makepeace Thackeray observed in *Pendennis:* 'Men serve women on their knees. When they rise, they go away.' It is the same with our electorate. They love and worship their leaders. But when the spell is broken, they unfailingly transfer their allegiance elsewhere. In history there are few more telling examples of this truth than the difference between the results of the 1971 and the 1977 elections.

Today the people are in a mood which comes rarely in the life of a country. They are looking forward, starry-eyed, to a new direction, a new era, a new life. It is time not merely for a new budget or a new licensing policy or a new price structure. It is the moment for shaping and moulding a new society, for giving a new and clear orientation to the nation.

Although we developed highly sophisticated technical skills, we basically remained a feudal and caste-ridden society. A deep and sudden realization dawned on the people last month which made their vote cut across the immemorial feudal and caste lines. The election could be made the matrix of a reborn nation.

The mood of the people today clearly marks a transition from the feudal age to the modern age. The outdated values of feudalism—birth, wealth, position and power—have been drastically eroded, and the age of the common man has begun. This is the golden moment to transform our caste-ridden society into a modern society.

Our people take their morals and their mores from their leaders. What can dynamic leadership, imbued with vision and understanding, with knowledge and dedication, not do for this country at this historic juncture? We have in Shri Morarji Desai a prime minister who is a firm believer in moral values and high principles, and a Cabinet with vast talents and high administrative competence. All the auguries are auspicious for tackling the daunting tasks.

The first task is to have leadership at all levels—from the prime minister's to the panchayat's. True leadership is the exact opposite of the concentration of all power and decision-making authority in one individual. To be a true leader is to unleash the full power of the organization and to release the potential and energy in the rank and file by means of personal impact. Given a selfless and dedicated leadership at this juncture, the objective, in the Janata Party manifesto, of removing destitution within ten years can be achieved. We have to motivate the people so that they put the national interest above the sectional interest. It would be a tragedy if, having regained our freedom, we do not use it wisely and well.

The crying need of the hour is self-discipline and self-restraint. During the post-war period, trade unions in Germany voluntarily applied a wage freeze on themselves, on the condition that industry ploughed back its profits to increase the output and create further employment. The consequence of this self-imposed wage freeze was more and more investment, resulting in more and more employment. Real wages per person were steady during this recovery period, but real wages per family increased because of more employment. In a country where all the groups function harmoniously, the results are fantastically gratifying—totally out of proportion to the inputs. Germany and Japan are examples of the synergistic effect of such harmonious cooperation. Great Britain and Italy serve as warnings of the consequences of its absence.

Plato thought poorly of democracy because it always degenerated into mobocracy. On the other hand, Gandhiji had great faith in the masses and believed that given the right leadership they were capable of self-restraint and self-discipline. Let us so conduct ourselves that we prove Gandhiji right and Plato wrong.

At the Centre we must establish Government of India Limited—limited not in responsibility, but limited by the role of law, by the discipline of the Constitution, and limited in its capacity to release an unending torrent of ill-digested laws on the people.

One of the primary duties is obviously to undo the mischief perpetrated by the 42nd Amendment—that monstrous outrage on the Constitution. Our original Constitution provided for stability without stagnation and growth without destruction of human values. The recent amendments have only achieved stagnation without stability and destruction of human values without growth.

The government need not worry about getting a two-thirds majority in both the Houses of Parliament to nullify the features of the 42nd Amendment. The Supreme Court can do the job equally effectively in appropriate proceedings taken by a citizen.*

The members of the last Parliament, after taking the oath of true faith and allegiance to the Constitution, had no compunction in altering or destroying its basic structure. The members of the present Parliament, who took the pledge at Rajghat on 24 March 1977, 'to uphold the inalienable rights to life and liberty of the citizens of our republic', cannot fulfil the pledge unless they are prepared to accept the supremacy of the Fundamental Rights in the Constitution.

It is to be hoped that the present government will pass such laws and take such executive action as are not meant merely to deal with the difficulties of the moment but calculated to ensure

---

**In 1980 the Supreme Court struck down the 42nd Amendment in the* Minerva Mills' *case.*

the good of the country in the long years ahead. Though the present electoral system has brought the Janata Party to power, the party would be rendering a lasting national service by effecting electoral reforms. Despite its shortcomings, proportional representation would, on the whole, be more just and fair than the present system of 'first past the post'.

The Janata Party manifesto is admirably drafted. With the amount of zeal and dedication that we have in the Cabinet today, there is every hope that the manifesto will not remain a historic parchment in a glass case but will be translated into action with all convenient speed.

There can be no two opinions on the point that the topmost priority must be given to amelioration of the lot of the 40 per cent who still live below the minimum subsistence line. Our first concern must be to look after the weakest—the man who is bowed by the weight of centuries, stolid and stunned, 'dead to rapture and despair, a thing that grieves not and that never hopes'.

There are at least forty million unemployed today—in a country which cannot and does not afford any social benefits.

Poverty is cruel, but it is curable. The only known cure is economic pragmatism instead of woolly ideology. In the field of economics the tree of ideology has never borne any fruit. We have countless chances for development. Opportunities multiply when they are seized; they die when neglected.

We have barely tapped our immeasurable potential for growth. Immense man-power, superb skills and enterprise are to India what oil is to the Middle East. The only difference is that the oil will be depleted one day, but our human resources will never be.

At least 250 million of our citizens are contributors to the national product. There is one way, and one way only, in which India can banish poverty, and that is by putting to the maximum productive use the 2,000 million man-hours which fleet over India every day, never to come again. To every economic policy and legislation we must apply the acid test—how far will it bend the talent, energy and time of our people to fruitful ends and how far will it dissipate them in coping with legal inanities and a bumbling bureaucracy.

'Much to cast down, much to build, much to restore;

Let the work not delay, time and the arm not waste;
Let the clay be dug from the pit, let the saw cut the stone;
Let the fire not be quenched in the forge.'

Irrigation has been sadly neglected during the last thirty years. On an average, India receives 3,000 million acre-feet rainfall in a year,—sufficient to submerge the entire country in a 45 feet deep layer of water. The total area under cultivation was about 422 million acres in 1975-76. Of this area, only about 111 million acres (or 26.3 per cent) was provided with irrigational facilities. At the rate of extension of irrigational facilities achieved in the last fifteen years, we shall not be able to bring even half the arable area under irrigation till 2007 AD.

Three-fourths of the total flow of our rivers is wastefully emptied into the seas. Out of our groundwater resources of an estimated potential of 180 million acre-feet, not even half is being utilized. How much greater would be our agricultural output, with a reduction in prices on account of economics of scale, if irrigation plans were vigorously pursued.

In the Fifth Plan only 0.83 per cent of the total public sector outlay is earmarked for roads, and even out of this paltry percentage three-fourths is intended to cover those road projects which have spilled over from the Fourth Plan. Few countries of the world are so poor in market roads. Road construction is one of the best ways to generate employment and to stimulate agricultural output by opening up enormous new markets.

The country can never prosper or be saved through the efforts of only ministers and civil servants. The people must be associated at all stages with the formulation and implementation of policies. We can have a truly participating democracy for the first time in India. Under the last regime, the government and the people virtually became two hostile armed camps. Now we can have an exciting joint venture between the government and the people.

The very enormity and variety of the challenges facing the country are such as to touch the least tender to tears and the most incredulous to prayer. Shall we maintain discipline—or shall we witness revival of the barbarous *bandhs** when government ceased

---

**Attempts by militant workers to paralyze life in a city*

to govern, mobocracy displaced democracy, and cities were paralysed by groups of men who regarded themselves as above the law? Shall we increase production, create national wealth and settle industrial disputes in the forums provided by the law—or shall we abuse our regained freedom by nine *morchas*† a day?

The nation is mature enough, and the prime minister and his colleagues are experienced enough, to ensure the rule of law while providing liberty under law. Those who talked of chaos as the alternative to authoritarianism overestimated their own calibre and underestimated the intelligence of our people.

The government should have the fullest cooperation from all quarters in the epochal demonstration—watched by the whole civilized world—that liberty is not an 'optional extra' in a democracy, that human rights are not a luxury intended merely for the elite and the affluent, and that our people, poor and downtrodden, are as intensely committed to the free way of life as the richest under the sun.

†*Sizeable processions in the streets, to ventilate a grievance*

MEMORIES OF THE EMERGENCY

Can it Happen Again ?

◆

ON THE TWENTIETH anniversary of the Emergency, let me, first of all, reiterate the nation's gratitude to the men who suffered in diverse ways and whose sacrifices made the restoration of freedom possible.

The first name which springs to my mind is that of Jayaprakash Narayan. Not since the time of Gandhiji, has moral force—personified by a frail individual—triumphed so spectacularly over the forces of evil. He changed decisively the course of history. One life transformed the destiny of hundreds of millions.

It was Jayaprakash who talked of 'total revolution'. He wanted to shake the people out of their apathy and lethargy and make them realize that they are the inheritors of a resplendent heritage which holds them together, despite their differences in caste and creed, region and language.

I had the good fortune to have a long chat with him in Delhi before he administered the pledge at Rajghat on 24 March 1977 to the Members of Parliament 'to uphold the inalienable rights to life and liberty of the citizens of our republic'.

Unfortunately, Jayaprakash passed away in October 1979, and India has remained without true leadership since then.

Only next to Jayaprakash, I would place Ramnath Goenka as the most feared opponent of the Emergency.

Most newspapers, like most people, capitulated. The two national English papers which stood up were the *Indian Express* and *The Statesman*.

Every newspaper had a Censor installed in the office who masqueraded as the editor and decided what should or should not be published. I vividly recall the day, early in the Emergency, when Mr V.K. Narasimhan, the Editor of the *Indian Express,* had written an editorial which the Censor did not allow to be published. Mr Narasimhan, with the concurrence and support of Ramnathji, published the paper with the space for the editorial left blank, so that the discerning reader might understand what was happening in the newspaper world.

During the Emergency I used to meet Ramnathji off and on. And I can say quite truthfully that I have never met a proprietor of a newspaper who had the courage and the public spirit of Ramnathji. He was a dedicated citizen who used his enormous power, as the proprietor of a national newspaper, for what he believed to be the good of the country. He acted on his conviction that the press should never be a poodle of the establishment but should act as the watchdog of democracy. He believed that a courageous and independent press is the noblest servant of society, along with a courageous and independent judiciary.

Ramnathji was against any form of tyranny by the state. He always adhered to the unshakable belief, which he shared with Bernard Levin, that barbed wires will rust, stone walls will crumble, and the tyrant's club will shatter in his fist.

During the twenty-one months of the Emergency, when most papers and journals capitulated, Ramnathji asserted his sturdy independence at colossal personal cost. The government launched innumerable criminal prosecutions against him and his companies in different courts of India; but he faced the onslaught unflinchingly and with terrier-like tenacity.

To the best of my memory, about 166,000 persons were detained without a trial in different parts of India for an indefinite period. Even their close relatives were not told about the place where they were detained. The people detained without a trial included prominent figures like Jayaprakash Narayan, Morarji Desai and Kuldip Nayar—and the humble and nameless who will never be known to the roll-call of honour. A hundred thousand petty tyrants mushroomed all over the country.

II

I come to the next question. What has happened before—can it happen again? The answer is—undoubtedly yes.

No period in the history of our republic is of more educative value than 1975 to 1977. George Santayana said, 'Progress far from consisting in change, depends on retentiveness . . . Those who cannot remember the past are condemned to repeat it.' If our basic freedoms are to survive, it is of vital importance that we remember the happenings during the Emergency when the freedoms were suspended.

Countries which were integral parts of India in the days gone by—Pakistan, Bangladesh and Burma (Myanmar)—have gone through periods of authoritarian rule; and so have highly advanced countries like Germany which had a Constitution which guaranteed freedoms of the type we still enjoy today. (Hitler amended the German Constitution just as Mrs Gandhi did in India and deprived the people of their freedoms.)

Self-knowledge would dictate that we recognize three defects in our national character—lack of discipline and public spirit, lack of a sense of justice and fairness, and lack of a sense of moderation and tolerance. It is these three defects in our character which made a cultured Prime Minister like Rajiv Gandhi say publicly, more than once, that he would not hesitate to reimpose the Emergency if the circumstances demanded such a course of action, although it must be said to his credit that during the dark days of the Emergency, he kept himself totally aloof from the tyranny which stalked the land.

The danger of a reimposition of the Emergency is greater for a country like India where the society is feudal and caste-ridden. I do not think casteism was ever more pronounced in the history of our republic than during the recent past.

Today, India presents a picture of a great nation in a state of moral decay. The noble processes of our Constitution have been trivialized by the power-holders, the power-seekers and the power-brokers. Elections have been reduced to a horse race by contesting politicians—the difference being that the horse is highly trained!

When we look around India today, we can hardly recognize it to be the same country in which a dozen different civilizations of incredible nobility flourished over the last fifty centuries. (This is the only country known to history where men of knowledge and learning had precedence over kings.)

I should like to reaffirm my firm conviction that it is not the

Constitution which has failed the people but it is our chosen representatives who have failed the Constitution. Dr B.R. Ambedkar poignantly remarked in the Constituent Assembly that, if the Constitution which was given by the people unto themselves in November 1949 did not work satisfactorily at any future time, we would have to say, not that the Constitution had failed, but that man was vile.

EMERGENCY REMEMBERED

Preserving the Constitution's Integrity

◆

THE EMERGENCY WAS the culmination of the repeated attempts made by Indira Gandhi to deprive the Indian people of their freedom. The Emergency was imposed in the early hours of 26 June 1975, and lifted in the early hours of 21 March 1977. During the twenty-one months that it lasted, the government of India treated the Constitution as its private property and dealt with Indian law as its personal backyard. In the days of the Emergency, there was widespread governmental propaganda extolling the 'true gains' of the Emergency which was virtually depicted as a great national blessing.

History will record that the true gains of the Emergency were the unification of the opposition, the sharp awakening of the political conscience of the nation, and the dawn of the realization among the people that they are the sole keepers of the Constitution. The people paid a heavy price during the Emergency, but at the polls they exacted an equally heavy price from its architects.

The lifting of the Emergency was calculated to ensure that the past beneficiaries of the abrogation of the rule of law would not become its future victims. With the lifting of the Emergency, the rightful position of the Constitution of India was restored. It is not the MPs dressed in brief authority who are supreme. It is the Constitution which is supreme. It is the eternal human freedoms which are supreme. It is the people who are supreme and it is they who had given the Constitution unto themselves.

The electorate's verdict in 1977 once again proved that sacrifice appeals more to the soul of India than success—the returned candidates were mostly those who had suffered for the good of the country. An authoritarian regime is only as puissant as the sycophants, the time-servers, the cringing and the craven, will make it. No human being can be more powerful than his henchmen will allow him to be. History will apportion the blame and the responsibility for the monstrosities of the Emergency to a wide spectrum of elected representatives who betrayed their trust.

Acute Fear

Fear, born of terror, was more acute—particularly among the innocent—during the Emergency than it was during the two centuries of British rule.

Perhaps the greatest contribution of the republic of India to constitutional jurisprudence is the decision in the *Kesavananda Bharati* case. That judgment was by a Bench consisting of thirteen judges, of whom seven decided in favour of the citizen. The majority held that the power of amendment is limited—it does not enable Parliament to alter the basic structure or framework of the Constitution. For instance, Parliament cannot abolish the sovereignty of India or the democratic character of the republic. It cannot impair the integrity and unity of India or dismember the country. It cannot supersede the jurisdiction of the higher judiciary. Thus something priceless was salvaged out of the tempest that raged over the government's claim to have the power to wreck the Constitution.

The ruling vindicated the citizen's stand that Parliament in exercise of its amending power cannot arrogate to itself the role of the official liquidator of the Constitution. Article 368 which confers the power on Parliament to amend the Constitution cannot be read as expressing the death-wish of the Constitution or as a provision for its legal suicide.

Ten Propositions

After the Emergency was declared in 1975, another Bench of thirteen judges was again convened on 10 November 1975, to hear the plea of the government that the decision in *Kesavananda's* case should be overruled. On behalf of the citizen, I filed ten propositions in opposition to that plea. The degree of tyranny which prevailed during the Emergency may be gauged from the fact that the censor would not allow the propositions to be published or referred to in any newspaper. Even the fact that I had returned the brief of Mrs Gandhi in the case in the Supreme Court, within hours of her declaring the Emergency, was not allowed to be published, till I threatened to file a writ petition to compel the publication. No one could write or say anything in public which was not acceptable to the government.

Anybody could be put in jail without a trial and the barbarous law went to the absurd extent of expressly enacting that apart from the total suspension of the fundamental right to liberty under the Constitution, no citizen could plead a right to liberty based on common law, natural law or rules of natural justice. The law further enacted in effect that a government official might not be permitted, leave aside compelled, to disclose even to a court of law the grounds for indefinite detention without a trial. The judgments and reports of judicial proceedings, or of legislative proceedings, could not be published, however truthful and accurate they might be, except in a form which found favour with the censor.

After arguments extending over two days, however, the Bench constituted to overrule *Kesavananda* was dissolved, and the attempt to confer on Parliament an unlimited power of amending the Constitution happily failed.

Lasting Ignominy

How then did the Emergency continue for twenty-one months despite the decision in *Kesavananda's* case which was rendered two years before the Emergency? The reason is to be found in a patently erroneous judgment of the Supreme Court in *A.D.M. Jabalpur v Shukla*. Let it be said to the lasting ignominy of the Supreme Court that in that case, reversing half a dozen judgments of the High Courts, the Supreme Court had held by a docile majority that upon the suspension of fundamental rights, a detainee could not ask for a writ of habeas corpus or any other order from the court even if he was able to show that his detention was illegal or *mala fide* or was not authorized under the very law under which he was sought to be detained.

The only judge who dissented was Justice H.R. Khanna who rejected this view and held that the suspension of fundamental rights put an Indian citizen in no worse position than a citizen of the United Kingdom where there are no guaranteed fundamental rights, or the citizen of British India before independence, and that an illegal or *mala fide* order of detention could always be challenged in a court of law even during times of Emergency. (It was the same judge, Justice Khanna, who had, in *Kesavananda's* case, by virtue of his decisive vote, preserved the identity of the Constitution and prevented Parliament from tinkering with it.)

In deciding *A.D.M., Jabalpur's* case as he did, Justice Khanna played a memorable role at the most critical juncture in our history. Generations unborn will admire his historic judgment as a shining example of judicial integrity and courage and cherish it for the abiding values it embodies. The twentieth anniversary of the Emergency would be a right occasion for the entire nation to pay a fitting tribute to Justice Khanna whose fearlessness has made it possible for India to live as a free democracy.

HINDUTVA AND STATE

◆

EVERYTHING ELSE PALES into insignificance compared with the policy of the state government to promote Hindutva. The one-year rule by the coalition government in the Maharashtra state makes you conscious of the long way we have to go before we can expect our state government to function in accordance with the Constitution. To my mind, the most distressing point is that the state government does not seem to be aware that, irrespective of its predilections and prejudices, it can only work under a Constitution which continues to be a secular Constitution. Fanaticism and fundamentalism are basically alien to Hindu culture and Hindu dharma, and they are equally alien to the Indian Constitution.

The chief minister of Maharashtra has publicly avowed that 'the first Hindu state will be established in Maharashtra'. Whether it is the expression of a hope as was said by the Supreme Court, or whether it is the expression of the policy of the government, it clearly amounts to mingling religion with politics. The chief minister of Maharashtra has gone to the extent of saying that he would try to prevent the cricket match between India and Pakistan which is scheduled to be played this weekend in Bangalore.

What is as stake is the unity and integrity of India and the possible dismemberment of the republic. It is not only the question of one community against another, but one state against another. Can we afford to take such a grave risk to the integrity of the country?

CORRUPTION IN ADMINISTRATION

◆

MR G.R. KHAIRNAR HAS been charged with misconduct under the Municipal Servants Conduct and Discipline Rules, and a suspension order has been served on him. There is no doubt that he is guilty of indiscipline under the rules. He has no cause to take action against the municipality or against Mr Sharad Kale, the municipal commissioner, who has merely done his duty.

The real issue is completely different. When Mahatma Gandhi was charged with violating the law and was tried before a British judge, he pleaded guilty and requested the judge to pass on him the maximum sentence. India has been rightly called a 'soft state' and it is extremely difficult to make the people aware of their rights and conscious of the degradation to which they have been reduced. The greatest service which Mr Khairnar has rendered, at risk to his own life, is to arouse the citizens from their slumber and make them realize that just as good government is no substitute for self-government, it is equally true that self-government is no substitute for good government. Those who won freedom for India are rightly revered by the people. Now the time has come when those who are fighting to preserve freedom for India must also be held in equal admiration. Most people are incapable of thinking for themselves and of realizing that just as freedom was lost in Pakistan, Bangladesh and Myanmar, it may be lost in India unless we are careful enough to realize our duties and responsibilities as citizens.

Some years ago, the then Pope said that the silence with

which the world witnessed the Holocaust was culpable and criminal. Let not our children ask the question, 'Where were you when mafia rule brooded over our benighted country?'

I am convinced that this nation is doomed to degenerate further, unless we have honest men in our public life.

III

CONSTITUTIONAL ISSUES

HAS THE CONSTITUTION FAILED?

◆

THE CONSTITUENT ASSEMBLY began its deliberations on 9 December 1946. On that historic day, envisioning the constitutional structure of the world's newest and largest democracy, Sachchidananda Sinha, provisional chairman of the Constituent Assembly, quoted in his inaugural address the words of Joseph Story:

> 'The structure has been erected by architects of consummate skill and fidelity; its foundations are solid; its compartments are beautiful as well as useful; its arrangements are full of wisdom and order; and its defences are impregnable from without. It has been reared for immortality, if the works of man may justly aspire to such a title. It may, nevertheless, perish in an hour by the folly, or corruption, or negligence of its only keepers, THE PEOPLE. Republics are created—these are the words which I commend to you for your consideration—by the virtue, public spirit and intelligence of the citizens. They fall when the wise are banished from the public councils because they dare to be honest, and the profligate are rewarded because they flatter the people in order to betray them.'

These words were truly prophetic. The foundations of the Constitution have been shaken by the *folly* of the people, the *corruption* of our politicians and the *negligence* of the elite. In just thirty years, we have reduced the noble processes of our

Constitution to the level of a carnival of claptrap, cowardice and chicanery.

Politics has never been a particularly edifying activity. Daniel Webster said that the unvarying tendency of the mad strife of politics 'is to belittle greatness and corrupt goodness. It contracts the mind and hardens the heart'. John Dewey observed that 'while saints are engaged in introspection, burly sinners run the world'.

Nobody expects politics to be synonymous with ethics. But the unusual predicament facing India is that an unacceptably large percentage of the 5,000 members of Parliament and the state legislatures have sunk to such a level that to call their manoeuvres a rat race for winning elections and personal power would be defamatory of rats.

Hilaire Belloc, after spending a term in the House of Commons, wrote: 'The standard of intellect in politics is so low that men of moderate mental capacity have to stoop in order to reach it.' Indian democracy has reached its nadir because in our average politician we have the sordid amalgam of lack of intellect with lack of character and lack of knowledge

At this moment, when the nation is standing on the escalator of anarchy and corruption, right-minded citizens cannot afford to stand frozen in disgust and dismay. We cannot merely look upon the political developments in sorrow and upon our politicians in anger. The problem facing the country has to be solved without delay—we are racing against time. A problem avoided turns into a crisis; and the crisis not mastered can turn into a disaster further down the road.

Honest and knowledgeable members of our society should reverse the decision, which they have adhered to so long, of opting out of the democratic process. They must devote themselves to the task of educating public opinion and the younger among them should stand for election in large numbers.

The ill-informed are often confused about three distinct concepts which have wholly different connotations—equality, equality before the law and equal opportunity. Equality before the law is the very foundation of a republic. Equal opportunity is the very foundation of social justice. But equality is achieved only in the graveyard.

Granted equality before the law and equal opportunity, men

will attain different positions in life, depending on their intelligence, their character, their capacity to work hard and to take risks. Therefore, equality has never been achieved at any time in any progressive country, even where equality before the law and equal opportunity have existed.

Every democracy must needs have an aristocracy of talent, of knowledge and of character. It is this aristocracy which must take to public life, however distasteful it may be, if democracy is to survive in India. We must go all out to grant the highest recognition to ability, knowledge and integrity. Ancient India was great because it was as enamoured of learning as modern India is of petty politics.

Our Constitution was framed on the basis that our citizens, including the best, would be willing to take a continuous and considered part in public life. If, however, the thoughtful and the selfless fail the country at this juncture, the only other option available would be to have a second look at the type of democratic set-up which is embodied in our Constitution. The question is: how does one get a government of experts in place of the ubiquitous government of professional politicians?

There should be a nationwide debate in depth as to how we can meet the crisis facing the country. To shut our eyes to the gravity of the situation would only be to invite the forces of authoritarianism of the type which overran the country not so long ago.

The peacock must not be replaced as the national bird by the ostrich.

DESIRABLE CHANGES IN CONSTITUTIONAL LAW

◆

THE IMPORTANCE OF India in world affairs is now more widely recognized than ever before. The report submitted in August 1978 by the Committee on International Relations to the US Congress mentions that India has 'finally achieved the ascendancy that had long eluded it' and that India has emerged as 'a significant economic and military power as well as the dominant power in the subcontinent'. Professor Rostow of the University of Texas at Austin has expressed his conviction that the most important phenomenon of the post-war era is the survival of the Indian democracy. The English historian, E.P. Thompson, has said, 'India is not *an* important, but perhaps *the* most important, country for the future of the world. All the convergent influences of the world run through this society: Hindu, Moslem, Christian, secular, Stalinist, liberal, Maoist, democratic socialist, Gandhian. There is not a thought that is being thought in the West or the East which is not active in some Indian mind. If that subcontinent should be rolled up into authoritarianism—if that varied intelligence and creativity should disappear into conformist darkness—then it would be one of the greatest defeats in the human record, sealing the defeat of a penumbra of other Asiatic nations.' These quotations give some idea of the momentous destiny which we are called upon to fulfil.

There is a cavernous gap between India's tremendous potential and the depressing reality. Our economic accomplishment has been woefully insufficient to eradicate poverty and to enable the underprivileged of this country to rise above their ageless squalor.

Our nation has paid heavily for its folly in leaving the governance of this country entirely to professional politicians for whom politics is merely bread and butter—a means of livelihood, or worse, a means of personal enrichment. The tremendous problems facing this country can never be solved by professional politicians, few of whom are equipped for the task. If the corrupt and inefficient administration is to be toned up, it can only be done by ministers with integrity, ability and knowledge who are versed in the art of management. If poverty is to be banished, it can only be done by men of vision and practical understanding of the ways in which the wealth of nations is created. Our bureaucracy without purposeful leadership at the ministerial level operates only as a guarantee of societal inertia.

Arnold Toynbee believed that history bore constant witness to the truth of Meredith's dictum, 'We are betrayed by what is false within.' This profound observation affords the key to our present crisis. Do we deserve our sublime Constitution? Has not the apathy of citizens—particularly of the elite who have almost opted out of the democratic process—been responsible for the corruption, incompetence and inefficiency that we see all around us? Our crisis of character is nowhere more evident than in politics. The moral crisis, combined with the economic crisis, has resulted in a political crisis of unparalleled magnitude. At such a juncture, the question naturally arises whether the constitutional law of India needs to be amended with a view to improving the quality of government.

Our Constitution was framed by men of great vision and knowledge. In these days of people's soul-eroding disillusionment with politicians, some are apt to put the blame wrongly on the Constitution.

However, it is high time that, having regard to the lack of character and calibre in the overwhelming majority of our politicians, we should think of making some badly needed changes in our constitutional law.

The expression 'constitutional law' comprises not only the Constitution but also other parliamentary laws which supplement the Constitution and are concerned with subjects that are constitutional in nature.

There are three ways of amending the constitutional law. The first is to change those parliamentary laws which qualify to be treated as constitutional law—without amending the Constitution itself. The second is to amend the Constitution without altering its basic structure, in accordance with Art. 368 of the Constitution. The third way is to amend the Constitution so drastically that its basic structure is altered: and this can be done, according to the Supreme Court's judgement in *Kesavananda Bharati's* case*, only by setting up a new Constituent Assembly or by a referendum. The third way of amending the Constitution may be ruled out as being clearly inadvisable at the present juncture. When the dangerous divisive forces are so pronounced, this is hardly a time to call a Constituent Assembly or to call for a referendum for changing the basic structure of the Constitution. Convening a Constituent Assembly would be a step fraught with the greatest danger to the unity and integrity of India. Even a small country like Belgium took twelve years (1967-1978) to revise the fundamental laws of that state. Our problems are far more complex and more numerous than those of Belgium. We are therefore, left with the first two alternatives.

There are four desirable changes in our fundamental laws which can be implemented *without amending the Constitution.*

First, no political party should be recognized by the election commissioner or by any other authority unless the party is willing to maintain audited accounts of all its receipts and expenditure. The greatest source of corruption in public life is the total immunity of political parties from accountability while the small baker, butcher and grocer are expected to keep accounts. It is but fair and equitable that political parties should be disciplined by the same requirements of the law which apply to citizens at large. Such a change requires no constitutional amendment but can be effected merely by the addition of a section to the Representation of the People Act, 1951.

Secondly, it seems essential to introduce partial proportional representation in the Lok Sabha†. Half of the Lok Sabha members should be elected on the basis of proportional representation, which is the system in force in several countries including Germany.

**A.I.R. 1973 S.C. 1461*

† *The House of the People, the Lower House of the Parliament of India*

In order to prevent the mushrooming of political parties and splinter groups, it should be provided that the benefit of proportional representation would be available only to those political parties which secure a certain percentage, say, 5 per cent of the votes cast in a region. The advantage of proportional representation is that it would enable the voice of minorities, regional parties, and other significant segments of the public, to be heard in Parliament, and thus allay the feelings of frustration and discontent among them. Further, it would prevent a repetition of the 1971 mischief when the Congress party, which received only 43 per cent of the votes, obtained more than a two-thirds majority in Parliament and was thus enabled to deface the Constitution by passing the disgraceful Forty-Second Amendment Act.

Proportional representation in the Lok Sabha is permissible under Art. 81 of the Constitution which only requires 'direct election'. Therefore, the desired change can be accomplished by amending the Representation of the People Act.

Thirdly, some minimum qualifications should be prescribed for those who seek election in Parliament. This, again, can be done without amending the Constitution. Article 84 already provides that the qualifications for a person who seeks to stand for election to the Lok Sabha are—(a) he must be a citizen of India, (b) he must be twenty-five years old, and (c) he must possess such qualifications as Parliament may, by law, prescribe. The first qualification is usually an accident of birth; and the second is inevitably the result of the inexorable passage of time. Up to now Parliament has prescribed only disqualifications. I advocate some positive qualifications for aspirants to a parliamentary career. When at this convocation you see degrees conferred upon engineers, doctors, surgeons, lawyers and other professionals, you cannot fail to be struck by the grim irony of the situation where the one job for which you need no training or qualification whatsoever is the job of legislating for and governing the largest democracy on earth. You need years of training to attend to a boiler or to mind a machine; to supervise a shop floor or to build a bridge, to argue a case in a law court or to operate upon a human body. But to steer the lives and destinies of more than 650 million of your fellow-men, you are not required to have any education or equipment at all!

The long day's task was done for the Constituent Assembly on 26 November 1949, when it formally adopted the Constitution. On that historic day Dr Rajendra Prasad observed in the Constituent Assembly:

> 'I would have liked to have some qualification laid down for members of the legislatures. It is anomalous that we should insist upon high qualifications for those who administer or help in administering the law, but none for those who make it except that they are elected. A law-giver requires intellectual equipment but, even more than that, the capacity to take a balanced view of things, to act independently and above all to be true to the fundamental values in life—in one word, to have character.'

Fourthly, a salutary change can be made in our constitutional law, without amending the Constitution itself, to reduce to a minimum the detestable exhibitions of the toppling game which has been a craze among our frolicsome politicians for some time past. Legislative rules or other laws can be so amended as to provide that a vote of no-confidence against the government would be inoperative unless the legislature passing the vote of no-confidence chooses at the same time the leader who is to take the place of the prime minister or the chief minister. Such a system prevails in Germany where a vote of no-confidence in the Chancellor has to take the form of a resolution choosing another person as the Chancellor.

Let us now come to those changes which would *require an amendment of the Constitution,* but would not affect its basic structure.

First, Art. 75 requires that a minister at the Centre should be, or become within six months, a member of Parliament. An amendment should provide that while the existing provision would apply to the majority of ministers, a minority of ministers may be selected by the prime minister from outside Parliament, who would not be required to get into Parliament at any time. Even the ministers who are not members of Parliament would have the right to address, and would be responsible to, Parliament; and thus the principle of collective responsibility of the Cabinet to the legislature would not be impaired. In Japan, for example, which has a democractic Constitution on the Westminster model as we have, the majority of the ministers are selected from the

Diet, but it is open to the prime minister to select a minority of the ministers from outside. The advantage of such a system is that it enables the prime minister to have in his cabinet some of the best talent available in the country.

There is a second reform which can be adopted in the alternative, or in addition, to the one referred to in the preceding paragraph. When an MP is nominated to the Cabinet, he should be required to resign his seat in Parliament. There are several advantages in having such a law. The minister would then be able to concentrate on the task of governing the country, and his energies would not be dissipated in politicking and in discharging his time-consuming duties as an MP. In France a person has to resign from the legislature upon his appointment to the Cabinet, and this system has worked extremely well in that country. It is true that in France the presidential system prevails; but this particular feature is equally compatible with the Westminster model, because it does not derogate from the principle of the responsibility of the council of ministers to Parliament.

The third suggestion I should like to make is that Art. 75 should be altered to provide that every one of the twenty-two states of India should be entitled to send two representatives to the Lok Sabha who would not be elected on the basis of adult franchise but would be elected by universities and professional bodies, and a similar provision should be made to have one representative so elected from each major Union Territory. This way we would have about fifty MPs who would represent the professionals and the faculties and would be able to improve the tone and standard of debate in Parliament. Conceivably, they may hold the balance of power among the warring political parties which are chronically engaged in contending for the plums of office.

The various amendments in the Constitution and other constitutional laws, which have been suggested above with reference to Parliament and the Government of India, can be introduced at the state level as well, to great public advantage.

At a time when some of the founding fathers of the US Constitution were still alive, Joseph Story made a profound observation which is very apposite to our own situation when we are fortunate enough to have still in our midst some of the architects of our Constitution:

> 'It depends upon the present age, whether the national constitution shall descend to our children in its masculine majesty, to protect and unite the country: or whether shorn of its strength, it shall become an idle mockery and perish before the grave has closed upon the last of its illustrious founders.'

Freedom cannot be inherited in the blood stream. Each generation will have to defend it and fight for it—then alone will it survive to be passed on to the next. The great lesson of the nighmarish Emergency imposed in June 1975 is that a free democracy can be converted overnight into an authoritarian state where the people fail in their duty as the keepers of the Constitution. Only the husk of democracy—the one man, one vote rite—may survive after freedom has perished.

Justice Frankfurter said, 'Democracy is always a beckoning goal, not a safe harbour. For freedom is an unremitting endeavour, never a final achievement.' You, my young friends, who are passing out of the portals of this famous university today, will, I trust, keep these words engraved on your mind.

ELECTION OF THE PRESIDENT OF INDIA— THE FIVE CARDINAL RULES

◆

IN THE WORDS of Woodrow Wilson, the President is the representative of no constituency but of the whole people. The President of India, unlike that of the USA, has no executive power but he represents 'the majesty of the people incarnate'. His office symbolizes the unity and integrity of the state. He is above the chances and changes of party politics and his election is, therefore, of special importance in a country like India with deep political cleavages and numerous political parties. The present President witnessed two elections and three governments in a brief span of less than eighteen months between December 1989 and June 1991.

Constitutional morality dictates that merit should be the sole criterion for the election of the Head of State. But the motivations and machinations in New Delhi (the customary burial place of constitutional morality) suggest that merit has been subordinated by some groups to caste or creed.

Ours is a noble Constitution, worked in an ignoble spirit. It is inherent in the very process of democracy that men of high character and exceptional calibre do not get nominated or chosen. It is not the fault of the Constitution but flows from the innate limitations of adult franchise. Commenting on American polity, Lord Bryce remarked that the one disturbing, but unavoidable, feature of democracy is that it puts mediocrity in power. The election of Abraham Lincoln was an exception that proved the rule. Will Durant observed that we forgot to make ourselves intelligent when we made ourselves sovereign. The most underdeveloped territory in every continent on earth is situated between human ears.

If the President has to be chosen by the democratic process, it is difficult to conceive of a more satisfactory method than that embodied in our fundamental law. There are five cardinal rules laid down in our Constitution to regulate the election of the President:

> First, the voting at the election is by secret ballot. Since the Head of State is expected to be above party politics, every vote for or against him is expected to be a conscience vote. This is meant to avoid trivialization of the election process by plain parochialism of party politics.
>
> Secondly, the election of the President is indirect. As Pandit Nehru and other pointed out in the Constituent Assembly, indirect (and less expensive) election of the President is unquestionably preferable in a country like India which does not have a presidential form of government. Direct election of the President on adult franchise basis has been wisely eschewed. Nothing would be gained by having the President elected by 'the mass man'—the malleable class of people, unthinking and easily exploited. The Electoral College consists of (a) the elected members of both Houses of Parliament, and (b) the elected members of the legislative assemblies of the states. The reason why the members of state assemblies have been included in the Electoral College is clearly to prevent the President being elected merely by the vote of the party which happens to be in power at the Centre.
>
> Article 62 of the Constitution provides that an election to fill a vacancy caused by the expiration of the term of office of President shall be completed before the expiration of the term. In view of this mandatory time-limit, the election of the President would have to be completed even though there may be some vacancies in the Parliament or in some of the state assemblies; or even if the Assembly of any of the states may have been dissolved and there may be no Assembly in existence in that state. The presidential election cannot be postponed beyond the time-limit which is mandatory. Only those persons

can vote who possess, at the date of election, the qualification of being elected members of either House of Parliament or of a state Legislative Assembly.

Thirdly, there has to be uniformity among the states *inter se*, as far as practicable. This is achieved by ensuring that the rule of one voter, one vote, does not apply. Every elected member of the Legislative Assembly of a state has as many votes as there are multiples of one thousand in the quotient obtained by dividing the population of the state by the total number of elected members of the Assembly. Uniformity in the scale of representation is brought about by the members of the legislative assemblies of thickly populated states having a larger number of votes than the members of the assemblies of less populous states.

This is called 'weightage' which is determined by the population of each state. Needless to add, in a democracy such weightage on the ground of population is possible, but there can be no weightage on the ground of wisdom, knowledge or insight. Human ingenuity has not discovered, and never will, how to get over the perennial injustice of 'the lives of wise men at the mercy of fools'. The foolish, the feckless, and the fatuous among the MPs and MLAs have the same voice in the election of the President as the most well-informed.

The fourth rule is that there should be parity between the states taken together and the Union. This is achieved by the provision that the elected membes of the two Houses of Parliament would have the same number of votes as the aggregate of the votes of the elected representatives of the state assemblies taken together.

Fifthly, the election of the President has to be held 'in accordance with the system of proportional representation by means of the single transferable vote'. The object of this rule is to afford the minorities a better voice in the selection of the Head of State. As Dr Ambedkar explained—

> '. . . Obviously no member of the House would like the President to be elected by a bare majority or by a system of election in which the minorities had no part to play.

> That being so, the election of the President by a bare majority has to be eliminated and we have to provide a system whereby the minorities will have some voice in the election of the President. The only method, therefore, that remained was to have a system of election in which the minorities will have some hand and some play and that is undoubtedly the system of proportional representation.'

This method is known as 'the alternative vote' in a single-member constituency. At the time when the votes are cast, every member of the Electoral College has to indicate which candidate he votes for in the order of preference. If a candidate gets an absolute majority of the votes cast, he would be deemed to have been elected and it would be unnecessary to have a recount. But if no candidate has secured an absolute majority of the votes cast, the subsequent preferences would have to be taken into account. This is the effect of the Presidential and Vice-Presidential Election Rules, 1952.

ELECTORAL REFORMS

◆

SOCIAL REFORMS IS a vast subject and so is electoral reforms. But I think electoral reforms are more urgent than social reforms.

The first and most important electoral reform is the reform for cleansing the electoral system. But in this country, the total lack of character which is reflected in the type of people who get elected, comes in the way. For example, it is easy to say, as some people do, that anyone against whom a charge is pending cannot stand for election, unless and until he is cleared of that charge. Today, the law is that a man who is convicted of a certain crime cannot stand for election. But it is being sought to be changed to anyone who is charged with a crime cannot stand for election. But look at the dangerous implications. A scoundrel is contesting the election against an honest man. All that the crook has to do is to ensure that the honest man is charged with a crime. This means that the honest man can never stand a chance of getting elected. There is no way in which a totally innocent man may not be charged with a crime in our country. I remember the case I fought for the late Mr Aditya Birla where he was charged with the crime of attempt to murder. The charge was preposterous; but nothing prevented the magistrate from admitting the prosecution in which such a nonsensical charge was levelled against one of our most respected citizens. We had then to move the High Court to quash the proceedings against Mr Aditya Birla and I remember arguing strenuously to quash the proceedings. If this is the calibre of our judiciary and the character of our people, how do you expect the contemplated electoral reform to succeed?

I am afraid fair and free elections is a wish rather than a

reality. To my mind, the greatest mistake which the Constitution-makers made was to introduce adult franchise. It should never have been introduced in 1950. I am not aware of any significant democracy which ever started its existence as a democracy with adult franchise. Adult franchise is the culmination of years of experience and training. (It should never have been the starting point of our existence as a democracy.) I can well understand that it is now politically impossible to change the system. Let us have enough understanding to admit that of all the democracies of the world we are paying the heaviest price ever paid for adult franchise. People are able to get votes on the ground of their religion or clan, their caste or creed. Hari Nanda had done more good in Faridabad than any other candidate, alive or dead, and yet when he stood for the Lok Sabha, he was not only defeated but he forfeited his deposit. Can you think of a stronger condemnation of our political system than this incident?

STATES ARE NOT VASSALS OF THE UNION

◆

THE LARGEST EXPERIMENT ever undertaken in human history in the art of democratic living has been carried on in India since 1950. Never before, and nowhere else, has more than one-seventh of the human race lived together in freedom as a single political entity. The uniqueness of this phenomenon is rendered even more impressive by the fact that till 1950 India was never a united country.

In such a situation it is not only natural but inevitable that differences and disputes should arise between the Centre and the twenty-two states that constitute the Union, and even between the states *inter se*. The problem must be resolved in a spirit of goodwill and with far-sighted vision.

There is no doubt about the great injustices done by the Centre to the states; but it must be remembered that the injuries done to the states are, in a sense, self-inflicted. The Centre is nothing but the states in their federal garb: the Parliament and the central government consist of none but the elected representatives of the states (barring the handful of nominated members). The real authors of the injustices are the self-centred representatives of the states who, after being elected to Parliament, have betrayed the true interests of the very states which returned them.

The Constitution provides for a cooperative federation of states with a bias in favour of the Centre. Such a bias, within reasonable limits, is necessary, having regard to the conditions prevailing in our country. The essential question is—what are the reasonable limits within which the constitutional bias in favour of the Union should be contained?

The approach to the problem of Centre-state relations must be governed by the following basic considerations which aim at reconciliation of conflicting viewpoints:

(1) A national consensus should clearly remind the Centre that it has not inherited the viceroy's mantle of paramountcy. What is needed at the Centre today is not an authoritarian government but the moral authority to govern. And the Centre would have no moral authority to govern unless it displays a sense of constitutional morality, particularly a sense of justice and fairness towards the states.

(2) We do need a strong Union. But a strong Union is in no way inconsistent with strong states. On the contrary, by definition, a strong Union can only be a Union of strong states.

(3) Where a paramount national interest dictates a line of action, the narrower viewpoint of a state or the parochial attitude of a municipality must not stand in the way.

For instance, the states should be persuaded in the national interest to agree to the substitution of sales tax by additional excise to be levied by the Centre and fairly distributed among the states—thus providing the states with the same growing revenues as they would derive from sales tax after deducting the cost of collection. Similarly, the states should revoke the power granted by them to their municipalities to levy the antiquated octroi, and resource should be raised for the local bodies in more civilized ways. Delays at check-posts range from 30 to 45 per cent of the effective travelling time of commercial vehicles. The 15,000 check-posts where octroi or entry tax is collected in different states result in 15 per cent of fuel consumption being wasted and virtually involve 80,000 trucks being rendered idle.

But these laudable reforms can and should be effected without detriment to the self-respect or the resources position of the state and the municipalities. The Constitution never intended that the chief ministers of the states would have to be on a perpetual round of pilgrimages to New Delhi supplicating the Centre for its discretionary bounties.

(4) As far as possible, the grievances of the states should be redressed by building up salutary conventions and traditions which are in conformity with the true spirit of the Constitution, rather than by amending the Constitution. There are good reasons why constitutional amendment should be treated as the option of the last resort:

(a) The Constitution is intended not merely to provide for the exigencies of the moment but to endure through a long lapse of years. We should get accustomed to a spacious view of the great instrument. The Constitution was meant to impart such a momentum to the living spirit of our national identity that the Union of States may remain indestructible beyond our times and in the days when our place will know us no more. Therefore, in dealing with a constitution, the wisest principle to act upon is that when it is not necessary to change, it is necessary not to change.

(b) If the Constitution is worked in the right spirit, there would be no need to consider any amendment so far as Centre-state relations are concerned. The problem has arisen today in an acute form because over a period of years the Centre has acted in a manner which at best has been contrary to the spirit of the Constitution and at worst has been tantamount to a fraud upon the Constitution. Many people hastily assume that the working of the Constitution has revealed its grave shortcomings, whereas the truth of the matter is that it is a noble Constitution which has been worked in an ignoble spirit.

(c) Today a crisis of national identity broods over the country. We are in the throes of our rebirth as a single nation. Emotions are running high in Assam, the Punjab and some other states. The forces of passion and ignorance are in the ascendant. At such a juncture, to open the door of large-scale constitutional revision may involve a grave danger to the unity and integrity of the country.

Industries and economic development

The states would have made far greater progress if the scheme of the Constitution has been respected in the field of economics. There are three significant entries in the State List: (a) Industries, (b) Trade and commerce, and (c) Production, supply and distribution of goods. The Union List permits Parliament to legislate in respect of 'Industries, the control of which by the Union is declared by Parliament by law to be expedient in the public interest'. Thus, the basic scheme of the Constitution is that industries and commerce should remain state subjects and should be dealt with primarily by the states; and that it is only those industries, the control of which by the Union is expedient in the public interest, that must be regulated by the Centre.

Parliament passed the Industries (Development and Regulation) Act in 1951, specifying those industries which in the public interest would have to be controlled by the Centre. The Act as originally drafted was fair and reasonable and rightly gave control to the Union over those industries which were vital to national development. However, in course of time, more and more industries were added to the Industries (Development and Regulation) Act till the basic constitutional scheme has now been patently subverted.

Without any amendment to the Constitution, 'Industries' has been nefariously transformed into a Union subject and has ceased to be a state subject. Today at least 93 per cent of organized industries, in terms of the value of output, have been brought under the bailiwick of the Union. Even items like razor blades, paper, gum, matchsticks, household electrical appliances, cosmetics, soaps and other toilet requisites, fabrics and footwear, pressure-cookers, cutlery, steel furniture, zip fasteners, hurricane lanterns, bicycles, dry cells, TV sets, agricultural implements—have all been brought under the Centre's control! There can be no doubt that this is an indefensible violation of the Constitution. It is imperative that the states should regain their legitimate powers over industries and commerce.

The true position of the states in commerce and industry, according to the unmistakable mandate of the Constitution, can and should be restored; and for this purpose no amendment of the Constitution is needed. All that is necessary is to delete various items in the First Schedule to the Industries (Development and Regulation) Act. If only industries which are crucial to the national interest were controlled by the Centre and state were given their rightful jurisdiction over the rest of the field of industry and commerce, those states which have a balanced and pragmatic outlook on economic problems would benefit tremendously. In order that the nation may not suffer as a result of any states not permitting industries to come up, the Centre may reserve to itself the power to start, or licence the starting of, industrial units in such states. In other words, the position should be that the Centre may step in where a state will not allow industries to commence or develop, unlike the position today when the Centre has the veto where the states want industries to start or grow.

Over-centralization has been one of the main reasons for our poor rate of economic growth which is one of the lowest in the world.

President's rule

Under Art. 356, President's rule can be imposed in a state 'if the President, on receipt of a report from the governor of a state or otherwise, is satisfied that a situation has arisen in which the government of the state cannot be carried on in accordance with the provisions of this Constitution'.

This power has been grossly abused and President's rule has been imposed on the states more than seventy times. All states, except Sikkim, have been given at one time or another doses of this pretentious curative. Several cases where President's rule has been imposed by the Centre in a partisan spirit for party ends have already passed into history.

The Rajamannar Committee in its report published in 1971 recommended deletion of Art. 356. The other view is that the Article would continue to serve a useful purpose if it is invoked bona fide in appropriate cases only. It may be better to retain the Article while devising some machinery to prevent its misuse.

K. Santhanam, deprecating the imposition of presidential rule whenever a state ministry is defeated, observed, 'Ordinarily, when a ministry is defeated and an alternative ministry cannot be formed, the proper course should be immediate dissolution and re-election so that people of the state would have a chance to decide for themselves. It is only where law and order cannot be maintained and the legislature cannot function in peace that presidential rule can be really justified. In the discussions in the Constituent Assembly on Art. 356, it was emphasized by many speakers that except in cases of civil disorder, presidential rule should not be imposed without first a dissolution and general elections.'

Appointment of governors

There has to be a governor for each state (Art. 153). The governor is appointed by the President (Art. 155) and he holds office during the pleasure of the President (Art. 156).

According to the judgement of the Supreme Court delivered on 4 May 1979, in *Dr Raghukul Tilak's* case*, the relationship of employer and employee does not exist between the Government of India and the governor, and the governor's office 'is not subordinate or subservient to the Government of India'. While this is the true constitutional position, we have systematically devalued various constitutional institutions including the office of

**A.I.R. 1979 S.C. 1109*

the governor. In practice the governor has been reduced to virtually the same position as that of the resident agent in a Native State in the days of the British Raj. Several governors have debased their high office by lending their services to fulfil the partisan objectives of the political party in power at the Centre.

One of the difficult questions is how to restore the governorship to the high status envisaged by the architects of the Constitution. The Rajamannar Committee made the following recommendations:

> 'The governor should be appointed always in consultation with the State Cabinet. The other alternative will be to make the appointment in consultation with a high powered body specially constituted for the purpose.
>
> 'The governor should be rendered ineligible for a second term of office as governor or any other office under government. He should not be liable to removal except for proved misbehaviour or incapacity after inquiry by the Supreme Court.
>
> 'A specific provision should be inserted in the Constitution enabling the President to issue Instruments of Instructions to the governors. The Instruments of Instructions should lay down guidelines indicating the matters in respect of which the governor should consult the Central Government or in relation to which the Central Government could issue directions to him. Those Instructions should also specify the principles with reference to which the Governor should act as the head of the state including the occasion for the exercise of discretionary powers.'

President's assent to state bills

A Bill passed by the state legislature is presented to the governor and the governor has to declare 'that he assents to the Bill or that he withholds assent therefrom or that he reserves the Bill for the consideration of the President' (Art. 200). The President may direct the governor to return the Bill to the state legislature with a message requesting reconsideration of the Bill; and if it is again passed by the state legislature with or without amendment, it is presented once more to the President for his consideration (Art. 201), but in no case is the President bound to give his assent.

The object of the Constitution-makers in enacting these provisions was simple and clear. While the constitutionality of any state legislation can always be challenged in a court of law, its wisdom cannot be; and, further, it is better to prevent a clearly unconstitutional measure from reaching the statute book than to have it struck down later by the court. A governor is expected by the Constitution to reserve only such Bills for the President's assent as are patently unconstitutional or palpably against the national interest. In practice, governors have been known to surrender their judgement and act as the deferential subordinates of the central government in exercising their extraordinary power. Moreover, the Centre's own record in enacting legislation is not such as to justify the belief that it is superior to the states either in wisdom or in knowledge of constitutional limitations.

The Rajamannar Committee recommended repeal of that provision which permits the governor to reserve any Bill for the consideration of the President. However, this power may be usefully retained, if its indiscriminate use can be checked by some machinery, e.g., by providing mandatory guidelines in the Instrument of Instructions to the governor.

Extra-constitutional authorities

Among the extra-constitutional authorities, the Planning Commission takes the palm. 'Economic and social planning' is in the Concurrent List. But no law has been enacted by Parliament in exercise of this power. The Planning Commission is a body without any constitutional or legislative sanction.

The Chairman of the Fourth Finance Commission in his Supplementary Note to the report described it as a 'quasi-political body'. K. Santhanam observed that the Planning Commission had set up a sort of vertical federation, thus displacing the territorial or horizontal federation established by the Constitution. The Study Team appointed by the Administrative Reforms Commission observed that planning at the hands of the Planning Commission had the result that 'the three horizontal layers of administration, represented by the lists of central, concurrent and state subjects, have been vertically partitioned into plan and non-plan sectors: and . . . within the plan world, the compulsions and consequences of planning have tended to unite the three horizontal pieces into a single monolithic chunk from the Centre although operated in respect of concurrent and state subjects in the states'. Dr K. Subba Rao was of the view that the Planning Commission 'functions in violation of the provisions of the Constitution . . . The Centre through the Planning Commission controlled not only the state sector of the plan but also their implementation'. The Rajamannar Committee was of the view that the 'Centre is able to impose its will on the states in the formulation and execution of the plans by virtue of the non-statutory grants under Art. 282, which are dependent on the absolute discretion of the Centre. It will thus be seen that the process of planning and the activities of the Planning Commission have a very deleterious effect on the autonomy of the states particularly in spheres exclusively allotted to the states by the Constitution'.

The above-quoted words of criticism are fully justified. Today there are two types of grants made by the Centre to the states—(i) grants-in-aid of the revenues of the states as recommended by the Finance Commission (Art. 275); and (ii) discretionary grants by the Central Government (Art. 282) which are usually made in accordance with the recommendations of the Planning Commission. Of the total grants disbursed by the Centre to the states, only 30 per cent is as per the recommendations of the Finance Commission, while the remaining 70 per cent represents discretionary grants given to the states on the advice of the Planning Commission.

To remove this distortion of the constitutional scheme, it is necessary that even discretionary grants under Art. 282 should be dealt with by a constitutional authority like the Finance Commission, and not by the Planning Commission.

Financial relations

Any fair-minded and impartial observer can have no doubt that having regard to the growing responsibilities of the states, the distribution of taxes and revenues is very unfair to the states and far too favourable to the Centre.

Taxes on income are levied and collected by the Government of India and distributed between the Union and the states [Art. 270(1)]. But the expression 'taxes on income' does not include corporation tax [Art. 270(4)]. 'Corporation tax' means any tax on income which is payable by companies and for which no credit is given to the shareholders who receive dividends from the companies [Art. 366(6)]. As a result of the changes made by the Finance Act, 1959, all income tax paid by limited companies must now be treated as corporation tax, and consequently the states are not entitled to any share of it.

Union duties of excise may be shared between the Union and the states but only 'if Parliament by law so provides' (Art. 272). The chairman of the Fourth Finance Commission referred to the possibility of making a constitutional amendment placing excise duties on the same footing as income-tax, that is, making excise duties also divisible between the Union and the states.

Even when a tax or duty is compulsorily divisible between the Centre and the states, the Union has the right to levy a surcharge which is excluded from the divisible pool (Art. 271). This extraordinary power is exercised in the most ordinary fashion: every annual budget contains the levy of a surcharge on income-tax exclusively for the purposes of the Union.

The Seventh Finance Commission had recommended that 40 per cent of the central excise duty should be transferred to the states. In the last three years the Centre stopped raising rates of excise on items like petroleum, iron and steel, aluminium and coal, but only raised the prices. The entire benefit of this increase in prices goes to the Centre which is the producer and seller of the goods. According to a recent speech of the West Bengal Finance Minister, by raising prices instead of excise the Centre gathered additional revenues of Rs 6,500 crores in which the states are not entitled to a share, whereas, if the excise had been increased, Rs 2,600 crores would have come to the states as per the recommendation of the Seventh Finance Commission.

The states must be given a legal right to a larger share in the tax revenues collected by the Centre, instead of having to rely upon the discretionary largesse of the Union under Art. 282.

Inter-State Council and Constitutional conventions

The formation of an Inter-State Council as envisaged in Art. 263 of the Constitution is long overdue. The Conference of the Council of Chief Ministers held on 20 March 1983 on the initiative of the Karnataka chief minister, was a significant constitutional development. Active cooperation among the states should be institutionalized and states must solve their inter-state problems by mutual discussion and negotiation. For example, problems regarding electricity, water and rivers should be sorted out by the states themselves without the intervention of the Centre. Imaginative cooperation between the states would be a most fruitful way of counteracting excessive domination by the Centre.

It is a pity that there should be the need for a union of states—as distinct from the Union of States which the Centre is supposed to be—but the states are left with no other alternative under the present set-up.

The ways in which the Centre unduly dominates the states are beyond enumeration and are symptomatic of the Centre's attitude towards its 'vassals'. Exceptional constitutional powers are used in a routine manner, and standards of constitutional decency are unknown. There is no political will to let healthy conventions grow up to serve as guides to the Centre in its manifold dealings with the states.

An unfailing index to the maturity of a democracy is the degree of its respect for unwritten conventions. By this criterion of maturity, the Indian democracy must be regarded as being still in its swaddling clothes. Not only have we failed to build up any conventions, but we have thrown to the winds even those norms of decency and decorum in public life which prevailed in India when we became a republic.

Dr K. Subba Rao wisely observed: 'Unless the party that happens to be in power in the Centre develops conventions to shed its party affiliations in the matter of its relations with the states, the federal government cannot effectively function in our country.'

The only lasting solution

Those who are in favour of major constitutional amendments to re-define relations between the Centre and the states, must come to terms with one profound truth.

The only satisfactory and lasting solution of the vexed problem is to be found not in the statute-book but in the conscience of men in power. The long-suffering states can be given redress not by a change of law but by a change of heart. The ultimate guarantees of a fair deal to the states are the individual conscience of the representatives they return to Parliament and a vigorous and well-informed public opinion.

We must get away from the fallacy of 'the legal solubility of all problems'. In a constitution what is left unsaid is as important as what is said. Our constitutional equilibrium can be preserved only by Obedience to the Unenforceable.

The survival of our democracy and the unity and integrity of the nation depend upon the realization that constitutional morality is no less essential than constitutional legality. *Dharma** lives in the hearts of public men; when it dies there, no constitution, no law, no amendment, can save it.

**Righteousness; sense of public duty or virtue*

IV

JUDICIARY, LAW AND LAWYERS

THE JUDICIARY AND THE LEGAL PROFESSION

Yesterday, Today and Tomorrow

◆

JUSTICE AND THE rule of law are perhaps two of the noblest concepts evolved by the wit of man. The Romans regarded justice as a goddess, impartial, impassive and unshaken. Ancient Indian culture pays a similar tribute to dispensers of justice. But in our own times there has been a precipitate diminution of admiration and a sharp erosion of the values which ought to actuate the administration of justice.

Doubtless, the law is imperfect, and it would be imperfect even if it were made by a committee of archangels. This is understandable. But according to an eminent writer, the court is no longer looked upon as a cathedral but as a casino: if you are dissatisfied with the trial court's judgement, you double the stakes and go to the Division Bench; if you are dissatisfied with the Division Bench judgement, you treble the stakes and go to the Supreme Court.

A number of observations have been made down the centuries about the legal profession, and few of them have been complimentary. G.K. Chesterton, talking of lawyers, said:

'They fight by shuffling papers,
They have dark, dead alien eyes;
And they look at our love and our laughter
As a tired man looks at flies.'

I asked Sir Noshirwan Engineer, the advocate general of India in 1947, how he viewed, in the light of his decades of experience, the legal system of administration of justice. His answer was, 'I am inclined to the view that it is better to have *Kazi* justice, where one wise man decides what he thinks is right and that is the end of it.'

The reasons for these somewhat disparaging remarks are not far to seek. If some people in our country believe that the difficulties we face in our administration of justice are due to British influence, I would emphatically dissent from such a view. I do not think the British should be blamed for the ailments afflicting our legal system today.

It has become the fashion to talk of Oxbridge (Oxford and Cambridge) as if they were responsible for undesirable influences. Let us not forget that some of the eminent judges of the Nagpur and Bombay High Courts, including Justice M.C. Chagla and Justice Hidayatullah to whom well-deserved tributes have been paid, were the products of Oxford or Cambridge. If we did not have the rules of British jurisprudence, it would be impossible to administer justice in this country. Our history goes back 5,000 years. More than a dozen civilizations waxed and waned in different parts of India over these fifty centuries. Which system could we have possibly adopted as the national system? We fight over everything. We fight on the issue whether towns on the boundary of one state should not belong to another state. What would become of the system of administering justice if we left it to be dealt with by historical antecedents without the influence of any foreign system of administering the law? Further, the rule of law, human rights, equality of all citizens, are not traditionally Indian concepts. If untouchability still continues in practice in our country, if *sati* continues to occur, and thousands flock to the spot where *sati* has been performed, we do have something to learn from other parts of the world.

I would like to give an example of Nigeria to illustrate what happens when the Western concept of the rule of law does not prevail. An Air-India plane was recently detained by the Nigerian forces. Air-India went to the High Court of Nigeria and asked for the release of the plane. The High Court decided that the aircraft should be released forthwith. But defying the court's order the Government of Nigeria would not release the plane, even after that government's appeal to the higher court was dismissed. Some days later, the Nigerian Government issued an ordinance under which jurisdiction in the case was transferred to the Military Court which refused to release the plane. This is what happens when the rule of law does not prevail; and let us not pretend that the rule of law is a concept which can be regarded as a part of the Indian psyche.

Please recall the events during the Emergency. Our fundamental right to life and liberty under Article 21 of the Constitution was suspended. Our High Courts, let it be said to their great credit, ordered certain detenee to be set free—those who had been arrested under a mistake of identity, or as a result of private vendetta, or at the whim and fancy of the executive, or without being heard at all. Our Parliament, to supersede the judicial decisions, passed an extraordinary law to the effect that 'no citizen shall be entitled to liberty on the ground of natural law, common law or rules of natural justice'. This is typical of what can happen in India when the Western concept of common law, natural law and rules of natural justice are treated as a pernicious outside influence! Another law passed by Parliament was to the effect that 'no police officer shall be *permitted* (as distinct from *compelled)* to disclose to a court of law the grounds on which an individual is detained', and that if a man was released by a court because the detention was held to be unsustainable, he could be re-arrested on the same grounds after he left the courtroom. Such are the laws passed by the Indian Parliament when it is unrestrained by the Western concepts embodied in our Constitution.

It is interesting to read what has been said about the present position of the judiciary and the legal profession in Britain and the United States of America. If there is anything critical to be said, it is better to say it in respect of other countries, rather than our own. The reason is that we Indians do not mind other countries being censured, but we do strongly object to ourselves being criticized.

In Britain, Lord Benson, chairman of the Royal Commission on Legal Services, told the International Commission of Jurists that the public was showing unwillingness to accept high costs, inefficiency, prolixity, incompetence and delay in the legal system: and that the traditional attitude of the legal profession is that 'all change is bad, specially change for the better.'

Lord Devlin has pointed to the obsolescence of the British

system of meting out justice, mainly on two counts—the adversary system which wastes time and effort, and the system of taking oral evidence.

Lord Gifford, QC, said last year that British judges were ignorant and biased, the bias being the product of their education and social position. In his book, *Where's the Justice?,* Lord Gifford observes that a male-dominated judiciary is unable to understand the problems of women. Personally, I think the remark was justified in view of some of the amazingly lenient sentences handed down in England in cases of rape where the rapist was let off lightly on the ground that his career would otherwise be ruined, while the judge thought nothing of the girl's career being ruined as a result of the cruel and wicked crime.

Lord Hailsham, the former lord chancellor, has expressed himself strongly about the heavy load of work. He even suggested that judges might have to undergo training and part-time job experience, as is necessary in the case of physicians, surgeons and engineers.

Let me come to the United States. In that country the legal profession is perhaps more commercialized than in any other country of the world, though India comes a close second. In America you can work on a contingency fee basis—i.e., a fee depending upon the monetary redress awarded by the court to your client. You will recall how US lawyers rushed to Bhopal to make money out of the miseries of the poor victims of the Union Carbide tragedy. Ambulance-chasing and acting as scavengers is thought to be perfectly in order. Small wonder that citizens of the States of Massachusetts and Pennsylvania demanded in the eighteenth century that the legal profession be abolished.

Judge Learned Hand said, As a litigant, I should dread a lawsuit beyond almost anything else, short of sickness and death.'

Justice Douglas said that 40 per cent of American lawyers were incompetent. Justice Warren Burger, the former chief justice of the US Supreme Court, said that 50 per cent of American lawyers were incompetent (disagreeing with Justice Douglas' estimate of 40 per cent). He believed that America was approaching a disaster area, not just a problem. He further stressed that the American judicial system 'may literally break down before the end of this century'. He told the American Bar Association:

> 'The harsh truth is that we may be on our way to a society overrun by hordes of lawyers, hungry as locusts, and brigades of judges in numbers never before contemplated. The notion—that ordinary people want black-robed judges, well- dressed lawyers and fine-panelled courtrooms as the setting to resolve their disputes, is not correct. People with legal problems, like people with pain, want relief and they want it as quickly and inexpensively as possible.'

A former deputy attorney-general of the United States has warned that the 'legal process, because of its unbridled growth, has become a cancer which threatens the vitality of our forms of capitalism and democracy.' In the United States, $30 billion is spent annually on lawyers, which comes to about 1.5 per cent of its Gross National Product. In India, thanks to our complicated laws, the percentage spent on lawyers may also well be 1.5 per cent of our Gross National Product.

There are three grave shortcomings of the present system of administering justice.

First, the commercialization of the legal profession. I do not think the legal profession was ever so commercialized as it is today. When I started my practice in 1946 on the Original Side of the Bombay High Court, if a counsel made a factual statement to the judge, it was implicitly believed to be true. You seldom heard of an affidavit, filed on behalf of the government or any public authority, which did not contain the whole truth. But now all that has totally changed. Counsel often make statements at the Bar which are factually incorrect, and affidavits are often filed even on behalf of public authorities, which do not state the truth. Look at what was going on before the Lentin Commission, and how witness after witness perjured himself. Yet there was no surge of public disgust and outrage. Unfortunately, we accept perjury as a fact of Indian life. The worst danger is not that even persons in high public office perjure themselves. The worst danger lies in public acceptance of such degradation of national character. As a man who loves India not wisely but too well, I ask the question—why can we not have standards as high as those of mature democracies in the world? After all, our ancient culture is the noblest ever known.

Secondly, administration of justice suffers from the intractable complexity of modern society. Life has become far more complex, and corruption and all-round lowering of standards are far more pronounced than ever before.

Thirdly, while all the time we emphasize our rights, we do not lay a corresponding stress on our responsibilities. Part IVA of the Constitution, which deals with 'Fundamental Duties', has been a dead letter from the moment it was enacted by the Constitution (Forty-second Amendment) Act, 1976.

If I were asked to mention the greatest drawback of the administration of justice in India today, I would say that it is *delay*. There are inordinate delays in the disposal of cases. We, as a nation, have some fine qualities, but a sense of value of time is not one of them. Perhaps there are historical reasons for our relaxed attitude to time. Ancient India had evolved the concepts of eternity and infinity. So what do thirty years, wasted in a litigation, matter against the backdrop of eternity? Further, we believe in reincarnation. What does it matter if you waste this life? You will have many more lives in which to make good.

I am not aware of any country in the world where litigation goes on for as long a period as in India. Our cases drag over a length of time which makes eternity intelligible. The law may or may not be an ass, but in India it is certainly a snail and our cases proceed at a pace which would be regarded as unduly slow in a community of snails. Justice has to be blind but I see no reason why it should also be lame: here it just hobbles along, barely able to walk.

A charitable trust, with which I am connected, filed a suit to recover possession of its building. It took thirty years to get the final decision of the Supreme Court. Even after that, the trust has been unable to recover full possession, because there are obstructionists' notices in the Small Causes Court (in respect of some floors) which would take another decade to dispose of. If litigation were to be included in the next Olympics, India would be certain of winning at least one gold medal!

The fault is mainly of the legal profession. We ask for adjournments on the most flimsy grounds. If the judge does not readily grant adjournments, he becomes highly unpopular. I think it is the duty of the legal profession to make sure that it cooperates with the judiciary in ensuring that justice is administered speedily and expeditiously. It is the one duty of which we are totally oblivious.

Sometimes judges are asked to intervene on humanitarian grounds, e.g., in the case of encroachments on public property. Courts of law are there to enforce the law. But in matters relating to encroachments and similar cases the courts are expected to *prevent* enforcement of the law. Lawyers who would not allow homeless persons to stay with them in their own houses or build a hutment next to the wall of their own building, act as great champions of the downtrodden in such disputes. Double standards have become shamelessly common in the legal profession.

We take cases in mind-boggling numbers to the court of law. Small wonders that we have colossal arrears in courts. Do we not have to blame ourselves as members of the legal profession for this state of affairs? Lawyers are entitled to earn their living, but not at such an unbearable cost to society.

What are the ways in which the problem can be even partially tackled?

First, we must educate our lawyers better. We produce ethical illiterates in our law college, who have no notion of what public good is. In India the number of advocates today is about three lakhs. We have the second highest number of lawyers in the world, the first being the United States which has seven lakh legal practitioners. These large numbers result in a lot of lawyer-stimulated litigation in the two countries. By contrast, the number of practising lawyers in Japan is less than 14,000. About 30,000 students appear for law examinations in Japan and only about 475 succeed, i.e., less than 2 per cent. So stiff is the examination they have to go through! No wonder that in Japan very few cases are filed and disputes are mostly settled out of court.

Secondly, we must improve the quality of public administration which is today at an all-time low. In the last forty-five years India was perhaps never governed so badly as it is governed today. It has been said that in the state of Bihar nothing moves except the river Ganges!

Nothing happens to the tax officer who makes an assessment which no reasonable man would ever dream of making. Few persons know about the administrative scheme announced during the tenure of Mr V.P. Singh as the finance minister. Under the administrative incentive scheme, if a show-cause notice is issued by an officer asking the citizen why a certain amount should not be collected from him in addition to the amount of tax admitted to be due, the officer and his colleagues are entitled to a reward which may go up to 5 per cent of the amount specified in the show-cause notice, irrespective of the final result of the case. To illustrate: a show-cause notice was served on ITC alleging that a sum of Rs 806 crore was due from that company by way of excise during a period of five years in which the company's total profit was Rs 70 crore. On the alleged excise dues of Rs 806 crore, the officers' reward could go up to Rs 40 crore.

Thirdly, the citizenry must be better educated to evolve a higher standard of public character. Ancient Indian culture must be taught in schools and colleges. The synergic effect of the different cultures, the amalgam of which is called Indian culture, is bound to prove of great ethical value. Will Durant said that just as continuity of memory is necessary for the sanity of an individual, continuity of the nation's traditions and culture is necessary for the sanity of the nation.

LAWYERS IN THE DOCK

◆

PERHAPS MORE UNCHARITABLE things have been said about the lawyer than about any other professional of even half the lawyer's utility to society. To begin with, the Bar has been called not so much a profession as an excuse for not having one. Chaucer in his *Canterbury Tales* portrayed the lawyer who took good care to seem 'busier than he was'. Maybe, the average lawyer has not changed much in this respect since the pilgrims set out from the Tabard Inn.

One of the commonest calumnies hurled against the lawyer is that his profession is one where success depends on trickery and chicanery. A doctor said to Sydney Smith's brother who was a lawyer, 'But admittedly your profession does not make angels of men'. 'No', came the quick rejoinder, 'your profession gives them the first chance of that'.

The lawyer's tricks of the trade and juggling with words have become proverbial, mainly through a repetition of the charge. Dean Swift brusquely referred to lawyers as men who prove that white is black or black is white 'according as they are paid'. Tulliver, in *The Mill on the Floss,* expressed the opinion that 'the law's made to take care o' raskills'. Lawyers are supposed to have so little regard for truth even in solemn documents that Charles Reade said caustically, 'The truth will out—even in an affidavit.'

The common charge against the lawyer is that he is a parasite on society. 'A sty for fattening lawyers in on the bones of honest men,' was the comment of Thackeray on the Court of Chancery. Lord Justice Knight Bruce cynically observed in an administration suit that 'the estate will be divided in the usual way among the s olicitors'. A contested case in which eminent counsel are engaged is the luxury of the rich or the refuge of despair. It often spells ruin to the average citizen. Voltaire used to say that he was ruined twice in his life—once when he lost a lawsuit and once when he won a lawsuit.

In the most famous of all soliloquies, 'the law's delay' is placed by Shakespeare among the chief ills of human life. It has also been recorded that Oliver Cromwell 'spoke somewhat against lawyers' and was pained to see 'what a tortuous ungodly jumble English law was'. Nearer our own times, Tennyson deplored the spectacle of advocates toiling for years—

> 'Mastering the lawless science of our law,
> That codeless myriad of precedent,
> That wilderness of single instances,
> Thro' which a few, by wit or fortune led,
> May beat a pathway out to wealth and fame.'

Disraeli was equally harsh on lawyers. 'The chief characteristics of the legal mind', he said, 'are expounding the obvious, illustrating the self-evident, and expatiating on the commonplace'. Jeremy Bentham, a lawyer himself, is no less severe—'Ignorance of the law excuses no man except the lawyer'. Bentham was more right than would seem at the first blush. English magistrates are not expected to know, and sometimes do not know, any law. Indeed, it has been established as clear law in England that it is not defamatory of a magistrate to say that he knows no law, for there is no reason why he should.

When revolution comes in any land and the people take charge of their affairs at last, the first reform is always the execution of all lawyers. It is often the only reform which subsequent ages do not regret!

A balanced view would suggest that the entire legal profession should not be reviled in this fashion. Perhaps it is a natural weakness to revile that which we cannot do without. So supreme is the value of law that Napoleon said, 'I will go down to posterity not by the battles I have fought but by the Codes I have given to France'.

It is not true that law defiles, it is not true that law degrades. The legal profession has produced some of the finest and most independent characters whose names are imprinted on the scroll of history. No one can pretend that any system of law is perfect, but by its very nature it can never be.

The profession of law, said Justice McCardie, has two aspects. It may be regarded as a pursuit which yields, if success be gained, a reward of fees and emoluments. But it may also be looked upon as a vocation which offers the joy of intellectual achievement, which claims the allegiance of unswerving honour, which asks for the guardianship of high tradition, and which affords a wide field for loyal and generous service to the community.

Thackeray described a great lawyer as a man 'who had laboriously brought down a great intellect to the comprehension of a mean subject, and in his fierce grasp of that, resolutely excluded from his mind all higher thoughts, all better things; all the wisdom and philosophy of historians; all the thoughts of poets, all wit, fancy, and reflection; all art, love, truth altogether, so that he might master that enormous legend of law. He could not cultivate a friendship or do a charity or admire a work of genius or kindle at the sight of beauty. Love, nature and art were shut out from him'. This is a gratuitous libel on a great profession to which Thackeray had himself been apprenticed once. It depends entirely upon the individual himself whether he will allow the legal profession to narrow his mind or will regard it as an opportunity to learn comprehensively the story of human life and human nature.

As Lord Buckmaster observed, it would be more true to say of the finest lawyers that, so far from having a narrow outlook on the world, there is no horizon too large for them to gaze at. There is no learning that comes amiss to the lawyer; there is no phase of all the myriad mysteries of the human heart which may not be the subject of the case which he has to consider.

SENTINELS OF DEMOCRACY

◆

AT THE END of the First World War President Wilson said that the world must be made safe for democracy. Up to now we have gone as far as making it safe for committees and conferences.

A conference like this serves the useful purpose of getting many lawyers together from the far corners of the subcontinent. It enables you to have a respite from the law reports—the musty volumes dark with the shadows of the decades, and grim in the solidity of their binding and in the amplitude of their cubical contents. Secondly, it enables you to have a clearing-house of ideas, where the pros and cons of the multifold problems facing the country can be analysed by trained legal minds.

We must remember that democracy, with freedom of opinion and opposition, is not the normal way of organizing society, but it is a rare human achievement. It involves the cooperation of large numbers of citizens in the active work of the government. The state has a claim on your energy, time and thought. The rich Athenians gave free gifts of money for ships or choruses or public monuments; the poor Athenians gave—themselves.

In a vast democracy like India, many citizens are bound to be undimensional. But no lawyer has any excuse for being undimensional. By his training and equipment and by his professional competence he is better qualified than the rest of the citizenry to take an active part in the making of laws and the formulation of public policies. He would be failing his country if he did not do this duty.

The lawyer has to act as a catalyst. The responsibilities which today lie on the shoulders of the lawyers are far greater than at any earlier time in world history.

A topic worthy of your very careful consideration is that of the absurdly low salaries we pay our judges. Chief Justice Hughes said that an honest, high-minded, able and fearless judge is the most valuable servant of democracy. In order that such judges may still continue to adorn the Bench, it is necessary that the legal profession should ensure that their emoluments are reasonable and not kept so low as to make it difficult for good and honest men to accept the office.

Another important subject is legal education. The quantity of demand has affected the quality of supply. Cheap professionals can be produced on an extensive scale like cheap beer, but that can hardly meet the vital needs of a country for intellectual leadership. We produce lawyers who seem lost without case law to support their propositions. The average lawyer who finds himself without precedent to cite, is like a tycoon without a balance sheet, a jazzman without a trumpet, a gossip without a club.

Further, you might well discuss at a subsequent conference the balance sheet of the legal profession since 1950. You will find many liabilities remaining undischarged.

Unfortunately, in the legal profession we have not only lost the way, but also seem to have lost the map, to quote the words of G.K. Chesterton. What we need are lawyers who are prepared to stand as sentinels of democracy, as standard-bearers of the public cause they believe in. I am reminded of the words of Arthur Koestler, 'If the Creator had a purpose in equipping us with a neck, He surely meant us to stick it out.'

The subjects which you are going to discuss for three days bristle with difficulties. But that is as it should be. A world in which iron did not corrode and wood did not decay, in which gardens had no weeds and washing was as easy as the soap makers' advertisements describe it, in which rules had no exceptions and things never went wrong, would be a much easier place to live in. But for the purpose of training and development it would be worth nothing at all. It is the north wind that made the Vikings. It is the resistance that puts us on our mettle. It is the conquest of the reluctant stuff that educates the worker. I wish you will have enough difficulties in your deliberations to keep you alert and resourceful.

V

ECONOMY AND SOCIALISM

SOCIALISM—ITS KERNEL AND ITS SHELL

◆

WE LIVE IN a world of slogans where socialism has taken the place of the *mantras* and the *shastras,* the Ten Commandments and the Golden Mean. But just as a coin gets defaced and its engraving gets erased after it has been a long time in circulation, words like 'socialism' get denuded of their true content after they have been in constant circulation. Socialism means different things to different people, and to some people it means no more and no less than cabinet rank.

There is the type of socialism which has built up the lucky countries of Europe and of the Third World. And there is also the other type of socialism which has brought down the less lucky countries like Indonesia under Sukarno and Ghana under Nkrumah.

The Preamble to our Constitution does not use the empty label 'Socialist'* at all, but uses the meaningful words, 'Justice, social, economic and political' and 'Equality of status and of opportunity.'

The wrong brand of socialism is extremely popular: in fact it is the fastest-selling brand of socialism today in India. The reason for its popularity is that it is so much easier in practice. This cheap

---

**In Palkhivala's opinion, the subsequent amendment of the Preamble, which inserted the word 'Socialist', is unconstitutional.*

and easy style of socialism mistakes *Amiri hatao** for *Garibi hatao*†; it aims at levelling down and not levelling up; it is content to satisfy the pangs of envy when it cannot satisfy the pangs of hunger; and, since it cannot create income or wealth, it plans for poverty and equal distribution of misery.

True socialism provides four significant measures of a country's development—an increase in the Gross National Product, availability of work, fair distribution of income and the quality of life. You must have all the four if you want economic growth with social justice. There would be no availability of work, no income to distribute, and the quality of life cannot be made less shoddy unless and until we have a fast and sustained rise in the Gross National Product. Without it there can be no increase in gross national happiness.

If we followed the school of Old Economics, we would be content with mere increases in the Gross National Product. If we adopted the New Economics, we would insist on growth with social equality. But we have chosen 'non-economics' where ideology reigns supreme, scarcities multiply and savings evaporate in inflation.

The vital point which is normally missed in political histrionics is that while it is possible, in a poor country like India, to have economic growth without social justice, it is impossible to have social justice without economic growth. 'Economic Growth *for* Social Justice' would be a more rewarding slogan than *Garibi hatao.*

The concept of socialism gets distorted when one stubbornly adheres to state ownership as the only means of achieving the goal. You may adopt state ownership in areas where such ownership affords the only sure and safe launching pad; or you may tap the boundless reserves of the people's response and initiative, energy and endeavour, prosaically called 'the private sector'. The vital point to remember is that the public sector does not necessarily spell public good and the private sector does not merely spell private gain.

Our scarce financial resources should not be wasted on ideological preferences which envisage a dichotomy between the

---

**Liquidation of wealth*

†*Removal of poverty*

public sector and the private sector. The government and the people should think of only one sector—the national sector. The line of demarcation should be between honest and efficient business on the one hand and dishonest and inefficient business on the other. Every effort must be made to encourage and expand the first and to condemn and constrict the second, irrespective of the question whether the enterprise is in the public, private or joint sector. If the same standards of economy, efficiency and managerial competence and the same criterion of dedicated public service are applied to the public sector as well as to the private sector, we shall have achieved the greatest economic transformation of our time.

State ownership is to social justice what ritual is to religion and dogma to truth. State ownership and state control are the shells of socialism which were really intended to protect and promote the growth of the kernel; but rigid shells merely stunt its growth.

The fanatical devotion to nationalization as an end in itself and the confluence of all controls in the hands of the government made Galbraith observe that in the old days the principal enemies of public enterprises were those who disapproved of socialism; while now it is the socialists themselves.

Two great men whose birth centenary has been celebrated this year all over the world have expressed strong views against the monolithic state. Bertrand Russell said in a letter in 1964: The danger to liberty involved in almost any form of socialism comes from the power of officials. If socialism is to permit freedom, powerful officials must somehow be curbed, for, if not, they will inherit all the powers of capitalists.'

And Sri Aurobindo said: 'We are now tending towards such an increase of organized state power as will either eliminate free independent effort altogether or leave it dwarfed and cowed into helplessness.'

The elimination of poverty as a social problem is a formidable objective, but it is not an insurmountable one. We have abundant natural resources and all the manpower we need. Perhaps there is no other nation which has in such ample measure all the enterprise and skills needed to create national wealth, and which takes such deliberate and endless pains to restrict and hamper its creation.

Social justice is different from mere equality. Social justice demands that there should be adequate differentials for ability and other laudable qualities. Elimination of such differentials is the very negation of social justice—it is unfair to those who are denied the fruits of their industry, integrity and intellect; and it is equally unfair to the tens of millions whose hope will die within their hungry hutments, since in a democracy there can be no economic growth without such reasonable differentials.

THE HUMANISTIC FACE OF CAPIALISM

◆

I FEEL DEEPLY honoured by your invitation to be the chief guest at your annual general meeting. Since I am conscious of the almost unbroken tradition of business chambers to choose their chief guest from a particular walk of life, your invitation has had a very unhappy effect on me. I woke up this morning in a cold sweat, dreaming that I was a minister!

Over the whole world there seems to have descended the old Chinese curse—'May you live in interesting times.'

I am a champion of private enterprise, but I do believe at the same time that private enterprise is justified only to the extent to which it displays private initiative. By 'private initiative', I mean that initiative which enables a businessman to act on his own in the cause of promoting public good.

We must evolve new standards of measurement for determining the ranking of business. The new standards would have to be qualitative, and not quantitative in terms of mere output and profits. It is true that a business must do well before it can do good; but, at the same time, it is not enough that a business does well only for its owners. Dr Alexis Carrell observed that it is not so important to add years to your life as it is to add life to your years. That sentence expresses beautifully the new standard of measurement I have in mind. Our financial papers give the figures of capital block, turnover and profits of different companies from time to time. But more important are the figures of the fund of skills, disciplines and productive human resources generated by the enterprise. These are the most valuable assets of the company, though they never appear in the accounts.

What is needed is a commitment of time and energy to public causes which transcend the materialistic objectives of business. The businessman must give not only money but of himself to the human values which are so essential to the quality of democratic life. He must get personally involved, and not merely be content to place his resources at the disposal of others for public causes. It is personal involvement which makes all the difference. The main reason why so little good is done by the public sector and by governmental agencies is the lack of personal involvement.

Gone are the days when the best that was expected of business was that it should provide jobs, give fair wages, make contributions to the public exchequer and place quality goods at reasonable prices on the market. Capitalism has now a different face—it is humanistic capitalism.

The best way in which business can assist the masses is not so much by providing money as by providing expertise, managerial and professional skills, for the advancement of causes which would make life more bearable for the masses.

Businessmen would have to adopt the type of outlook indicated above, if they want to survive in the changing world. They would have to adapt themselves to the new environment in which emphasis is rightly put on social and economic justice. One of the basic laws of nature is that adaptability is the price of survival. In the prehistoric ages, the dinosaur and the mastodon—two of the strongest and largest animals that ever lived—perished, while the insignificant cockroach survived. The reason was that those mighty animals could not adapt themselves to the changes brought about by the passage of hundreds of centuries, while the cockroach could. Incidentally, the cockroach has inhabited this planet far longer than man.

There is one more thought I would like to leave with you this evening. I think the time has come when workmen should have a share in the capital of the company they serve. By some reasonable mechanism we should ensure that workmen, either individually or collectively, get a stake in the capital of the company so that they may have a sense of identification with the enterprise they serve and a sense of involvement as owners in its growth and development.

SOME SUGGESTIONS FOR ACCELERATING ECONOMIC GROWTH

◆

I. More liberalization

The prime minister's intention to liberalize the economy has been substantially thwarted by a number of factors. One can understand that liberalization may be by stages and not be drastic, but the situation is worse than that.

Applications for modernization or expansion still face unconscionable delays and bureaucratic obduracy at various levels.

With the total assets limit of Rs 20 crore under the MRTP Act, the number of companies registered under that Act was 1,912 in March 1985. In that month the limit was increased to Rs 100 crore. It was anticipated that the number of companies registered under that Act would come down to about 800 as a result of the increase in the limit. However, in June 1986 no less than 1,625 companies are still compelled to remain registered under the Act. The reason for this is that the MRTP authorities have started a widespread practice of declaring more and more companies to be 'dominant'—by picking out the species, instead of the genus, of the line of production.

The definition of inter-connection is ridiculously wide and makes such companies inter-connected as are not even aware of the existence of one another.

II. Non-utilization of built-in capacity

As Mr L.K. Jha has pointed out, allocating resources for maintenance is even more important than investment in new projects; and it is a mistake to allocate plan expenditure only for new projects.

III. Black list of companies which have not paid the tax assessed

This system of black listing is ultra vires, unconstitutional, and may even amount to contempt of court. See *Annexure A'*.

IV. Advance rulings

The quality of tax administration in India leaves much to be desired. In Britain there are 29 million taxpayers and the number of references made to the High Court is between 30 and 35 per year. In India there are 4½ million taxpayers and the number of references to the High Courts is more than 6,000 per year, plus high prerogative writ petitions. It is not because the Indian public is anymore litigious than the British, but it is because our tax laws are administered in a spirit which justifies the comment that we live not under the rule of law but the rule of men. Decisions on identical facts depend upon the men for the time being in power, and the rulings and circulars change with new incumbents.

Nothing is more detrimental to economic growth than uncertainty in business circles as to their tax liability which is still pretty high in India in the corporate sector. There should be a provision for advance rulings which would be binding on the Department unless there is a change in or mis-statement of material facts.

V. Private units in fields today occupied by the public sector

Privatization may not be politically possible, but new units of the private sector should be encouraged to come up in areas today dominated by the public sector—e.g., in banking, unit trusts, and the generation, transmission and distribution of electricity. The private sector can start even a 500 MW plant for electricity generation by placing orders exclusively with BHEL, and without itself having to place any order abroad.

VI. Legal forms

An enormous amount of time and energy are wasted in drafting and typing legal forms, e.g. different types of mortgages. There should be statutory forms which may just be adopted by the parties who want to enter into a certain type of transaction and who would merely fill in the details or have such modifications as may be necessary in a particular case.

VII. Credit Authorization Scheme

The Credit Authorization Scheme was evolved in 1965, before the banks were nationalized in 1969. With nationalized banks which have directors nominated by the government, the Credit Authorization Scheme which requires the Reserve Bank's approval for any loan in excess of Rs 6 crore has totally outlived its utility. It is not merely a scheme which serves no public purpose but is in reality detrimental to public interest, because it has entailed a separate layer of bureaucratic control and delay.

VIII. Food processing

Food processing is an important industry which needs encouragement and incentives. It would not only improve the nutritional level in the country but can be a major export earner.

IX. Development of indigenous technology

Suggestions for developing indigenous technology are set out in *Annexure 'B'*.

X. Increasing exports

India is lagging far behind foreign governments which give generous incentives for export. Suggestions for increasing exports are set out in *Annexure 'C'*.

XI. Tax laws

Recent amendments in tax laws leave much to be desired. See *Annexure 'D'*.

Annexure 'A'

Black list of companies which have not paid the tax assessed

Companies which are in tax arrears to the extent of Rs 5 crore or more are penalized in different ways, e.g., by being refused public finance, or by not being granted licences, or by not being given permission to issue shares or debentures. This is a blanket decision, irrespective of the merits of the case and irrespective of the question whether the non-payment of tax is due to a desire to evade tax or is due to the assessment being wholly unsustainable in law.

The cases of those who are in tax arrears fall into different categories. The assessee may have a bad case and might deliberately commit a default, and may even have wrongly obtained an injunction from the Court only to buy time. Or, there may be borderline cases where two views are possible. Or the assessee may have a thoroughly good case and may only be the victim of a whimsical assessment. To treat all these cases alike and deny the assessee financial assistance or approval under different statutes merely because the tax has not been paid—would be illegal for three reasons.

First, different statutes deal with different subject matters. What is germane to the Income-tax Act may be wholly extraneous and irrelevant to questions arising before the Controller of Capital Issues. To deny a company permission to raise capital merely because its tax has remained unpaid for any reason whatsoever, is to do something wholly extraneous to the Capital Issues Control Act, 1947. In other words, the decision of the Controller would be ultra vires the statute under which he is acting.

Secondly, to deny a company the right to issue capital only because it has not paid the tax, however unjustifiably assessed, would be a violation of Article 19 of the Constitution which guarantees the fundamental right to carry on any occupation, trade or business.

Thirdly, where the Court has granted a stay of recovery, it would be a clear case of contempt of court to attempt to deprive the citizen of the fruits of the stay order by coercing him in various ways to make the payment regardless of the stay order.

Annexure 'B'

Development of indigenous technology

The government has rightly stressed the need to upgrade technology in engineering and other industries. Towards this end, government has, in the recent past, permitted *import of technology,* frequently coupled with reduction in customs duty on imported components.

Unfortunately, *indigenous* development of technology, which should have got still higher priority, has not received adequate encouragement in the government policies. This is regrettable in the context of a country like ours which has been wedded to the principle of 'self-reliance' and which today needs to conserve, more than ever before, every bit of the foreign exchange that can be saved. Instead of getting the topmost priority, indigenous development of technology today finds itself faced with some definite disincentives. For instance, in most indigenously developed products, while the import of components is negligible, raw material (particularly special quality steel) has to be imported, as it is not available indigenously. On these steels that are needed to make the very components which would otherwise have to be imported at a much higher foreign exchange cost to the country, the indigenous manufacturer is compelled to pay customs duty at a rate as high as 120 per cent to 135 per cent. On the other hand, those who import ready components pay only concessional duty at the rate of 50 per cent. Such anomalies leave the country with a permanent drain on its foreign exchange reserves.

In order to encourage and reward development of truly indigenous products, any manufacturer who has put on the market a product which meets the requisite standards without the help of foreign collaboration must be given the following incentives:

(i) The total cost of development of the product should be given to the manufacturer as a grant. The financial institutions now have a scheme for reimbursing half the cost of imported technology. Surely, indigenous technology deserves no less encouragement.

(ii) Payment of excise duty on the end products should be waived for a period of five years.

(iii) Customs duty on special quality steels and other raw materials that have to be imported for manufacture of components should be reduced to 25 per cent.

Annexure 'C'

Suggestions for Increasing Exports

1. Cash compensatory support

Cash compensatory support should be free of tax. Today it is treated as a trading receipt with the result that part of it is taken back by the government by way of tax.

2. Weighted deduction for capital expenditure on scientific research

Weighted deduction of $1\frac{1}{3}$ times the expenditure should be allowed under Section 35 of the Income-tax Act in respect of capital expenditure incurred on scientific research.

3. Section 80HHC of the Income-tax Act

Deduction under Section 80HHC of the Income-tax Act should be linked to export earnings and should not be linked to profits. It is true that today export profits are computed on the basis of the overall profit made by an assessee in respect of his entire turnover (both foreign and domestic). But in a concern where as a result of keen domestic competition the margin of profit itself is very low, the benefit under Section 80HHC in respect of exports is negligible.

The minister of state for finance stated in the Lok Sabha on 5 May 1986 that Section 80HHC would be amended 'to allow deductions to the extent of 4 per cent of the net foreign exchange realization plus 50 per cent of the remaining net profit'. The amendment of Section 80HHC in 1986 is in breach of this promise. It specifically provides that the deduction under that Section would be equal to the aggregate of 4 per cent of the net foreign exchange realization and 50 per cent of so much of the export profits as exceeds 4 per cent of the net realization, provided that the deduction 'shall not exceed the profits derived by the assessee from the exports'. In other words, if the average profit of the manufacturer on the total turnover is, say 1 per cent, the deduction under Section 80HHC cannot exceed 1 per cent.

The deduction under Section 80HHC should be at least 5 per cent of the FOB value of exports in the previous year plus a percentage of the incremental FOB value of exports.

Even if Section 80VVA is unwisely retained, Section 80HHC should be taken out of the purview of that Section.

4. Acquisition of know-how

A lump sum capital payment made for acquisition of know-how is allowed to be deducted in six equal annual instalments under Section 35AB of the Income-tax Act. Such payment should be allowed in full in the year in which the expenditure is incurred. Alternatively, it should at least be allowed in three equal annual instalments. This is necessary because depreciation on capital assets has not been increased to 33.3 per cent.

5. Single Window Clearance

Our exports are poor because the governmental agencies involved are more concerned with finding out the likely misuse of the benefits, rather than with the positive promotion of exports. Today clearances are needed from the Ministry of Commerce, from Customs, from the Reserve Bank, and the Finance Ministry. What is needed is a Single Window Clearance mechanism, which can give quick decisions without the exporter having to go from one department to another.

6. Materials at international prices

The International Price Reimbursement Scheme ('IPRS'—administered by Engineering Export Promotion Council) does not give due relief to the manufacturers of value-added products, e.g., commercial vehicles. The benefit is available to producers of components from the primary material which is made available to them at international prices, if they export those components.

When they supply the components to another manufacturer for use in aggregates and end-products, no benefit is available even if the end-products are exported. In other words, the IPRS benefit is available only on the components which the manufacturer of the end-product himself produces. For instance, when the manufacturer of commercial vehicles exports complete vehicles, he has to absorb the higher cost of raw materials used by his component suppliers.

7. Cost of money

(a) Working capital: Indian exporters have to hold larger inventories than their foreign competitors because the infrastructure in our country is much weaker. This is necessary specially when they have to guarantee delivery on time to foreign customers. When Indian exporters have to pay a much higher rate of interest than their foreign competitors, they naturally find it difficult to sell in competitive markets. Even after the recent reduction, the interest rate for pre-shipment and post-shipment credit is 9.5 per cent—much higher than the 5 per cent or 6 per cent rate available to competitors in other countries.
(b) Investment: The rate of investment for capital investment is also higher in India. Recently ICICI has offered loans at 9.4 per cent for export-oriented investments. Even this interest rate is substantially higher than abroad.

Annexure 'D'

Sense of honour and tax amendments—abolition of investment allowance—Section 80VVA

No amendment should be made to the tax laws which involves a breach of faith with citizenry. This comment is justified by the abolition of investment allowance in the Finance Act, 1986, without the originally prescribed three years' notice. [*See p. 175*]

In the Middle East and in other parts of the world, investors have been greatly perturbed by the fact that the Indian Government has no sense of honour or respect for its own laws. The tax evader breaks the law. The government which abolishes the investment allowance without three years' notice breaks the law. Does it make a difference that the government has the power to have an amendment passed to cover up the breach of faith?

Even on merit, the discontinuance of investment allowance is a wholly unwise and retrograde step. The big corporations, which expanded and developed when investment allowance was in force and Section 80VVA did not exist, have contributed far more to the national exchequer by way of (a) excise, (b) sales tax and octroi, and (c) foreign exchange earnings, than the amount of tax now sought to be collected from them by the abolition of investment allowance and the enactment of Section 80VVA.

The abolition of investment allowance is a typical example of the short-sighted manner in which revenue is sought to be collected without regard to larger considerations and broader issues of economic growth.

In the Long Term Fiscal Policy it has been said, 'Consequent on the withdrawal of the investment allowance, the minimum tax provisions embodied in Section 80VVA of the Income-tax Act will be abolished'. Contrary to the statement in the Long Term Fiscal Policy, Section 80VVA has not been abolished.

ASIAN VALUES AND ECONOMIC DEVELOPMENT

◆

IN THE LAST forty years the world economy has grown at a pace faster than in the earlier four thousand years. Many business houses have fallen by the wayside. But Rieter is the great survivor which is celebrating two hundred years of its business activities, and has achieved world renown for its textile machinery and automative components. The countries of Asia are among those which have known the *comfort* of using the products of Rieter.

Let me say a word about Asian Values and Economic Development.

The Asian economic miracle has now passed into a by-word. Look at the four newly industrialized Asian tigers—South Korea, Hongkong, Taiwan and Singapore—which have achieved the average annual growth rate of six per cent in the course of a generation. Japan is well-poised to outstrip the United States of America in per capita income by the end of the century. There are other countries in Asia, including China and India, which are, to adopt the words of Lee Kuan Yew, like the sleeping giants who, when awakened, could make a powerful impact on the global economy. It would not be mere chauvinism to say that India is a giant recovering from a bad cold, not a pygmy with cancer.

The economies of the various countries of Asia are distinct and different. But there is a common denominator which underlies all of Asia's success stories. The newly industrialized countries of Asia have achieved rapid growth through an astonishing mobilization of resources, goaded by the need to break the shackles of poverty. As in the case of individuals, so also in the case of countries, adversity is a great spur to achievement.

Affluence has never been a yardstick for measuring the contribution of a nation to the growth and development of human civilization. Besides, in recorded history, nations and civilizations have perished through affluence but no nation, no civilization, has ever died of adversity.

A nation's worth is not measured merely by its gross national product, any more than an individual's worth is measured by his bank account. The poor of India do not count their wealth in money alone.

The heart of the Indian nation is sound and the human raw material is excellent. To a western mind, the Indian's inner strength and capacity for patient endurance are almost unbelievable. Hundreds of millions, who have no standard of living, still have a standard of life. The nation is able to take in its stride situations which would spark a revolution in other countries. The ancient Indian civilization has survived and will survive when the raucous and fractious voices of today are lost in the silence of the centuries.

Old values—harmony, flexibility and companionship, stable family life, and intermingling of diverse cults and cultures—are even more important than the notion of freedom which takes the pride of place in the West.

It is true that eternal vigilance is the price of liberty. But it is equally true, in an even deeper sense, that eternal responsibility is also part of the price of liberty. Excessive authority, without liberty, is intolerable; but excessive liberty, without authority and without responsibility, very soon becomes equally intolerable. De Tocqueville made the profound observation that liberty cannot stand alone but must be paired with a companion virtue: liberty and morality; liberty and law; liberty and justice; liberty and the common good; liberty and civic responsibility.

Most of East Asia's extraordinary growth is due to the superior accumulation of material and human capital, in the words of Louis Preston, who was the President of the World Bank and who died yesterday. Two years ago, the World Bank published 'The East Asian Miracle'—a carefully researched report. Many Asian economies have had more planning by their respective governments than in the West and have developed even a social framework with fewer civil liberties. 'If there is a secret to Asian growth,' writes Paul Krugman, a Professor of Economics at Standford University, 'it is simply deferred gratification, the willingness to sacrifice current satisfaction for future economic gain'. For instance, the highest savings ratio (gross domestic savings as a percentage of gross domestic product) was achieved by the Indian economy in the year 1990-91. It was 23.7 per cent. It has now declined, but it is still 20.2 per cent.

In 1993, the regional leaders of Asia issued the Bangkok Declaration of Human Rights, in which they characterized the Asian way—harmonious, disciplined and collectivist—as against its western counterpart—chaotic, licentious and anarchic. Lee Kuan Yew, the greatest statesman of Asia, says that Asians will valiantly defend order against the corrosive advance of the western notion of freedom.

Scotland is not an inappropriate country to talk of the values which are common to Wesleyanism and Calvinism and to Eastern culture.

On behalf of all of you, and on my own behalf, I wish Rieter many more decades, so saturated and dripping with success, that its last two hundred years would pale in comparison. After all, in the life of a business enterprise it is only the first two hundred years which are difficult.

THE CURRENT ECONOMIC SITUATION IN INDIA

◆

I AM GRATEFUL to the Indian Institute of Public Administration and the Yeshwantrao Chavan Pratishthan for inviting me to deliver the Yeshwantrao Chavan Memorial Lecture this year.

I knew Yeshwantrao intimately, and shared the thought of Welles Hangen who said in 1963 that Shri Chavan was the fittest person to succeed Nehru. Unfortunately, destiny willed otherwise. Although he became the Deputy Prime Minister in 1979-80, he never reached the top. He died in November 1984 without fulfilling his ambition of becoming the Prime Minister. He had too much of the horse sense of an Indian peasant to become a practising socialist. My only regret is that during the first forty years of India's history as a republic, Yeshwantrao did not dissociate himself from the so-called leaders who suffocated and strangulated our people by state ownership and state control, nor did he oppose their policies. During those lost decades, the pace of our economic growth was sedate, if not glacial.

Then came the economic transformation with a big bang. The period of collective insanity of the Indian nation was over. In July 1991 came the biggest metamorphosis in the economic climate with the enunciation of the New Industrial Policy. The world's largest democracy reached a turning point in its history.

Liberalization and globalization are today dictated by the *zeitgeist*—the spirit of the times. Globalization is a buzzword that has launched a thousand strategies. The borderless corporation is the new phenomenon of our times. The world today boasts of some 40,000 transnational corporations.

The New Industrial Policy fortunately has been continued by the new government. Recently, Lord Rees-Mogg came to India as a guest of the K.K. Birla Foundation, and delivered a lecture on the world outlook for the next century. In the article which he wrote in *The Times* (of London) on the 11th of March 1996, he says, 'Anyone who wants to understand the modern world must make a personal passage to India, which has the deepest and most resilient culture of the four likely economic superpowers of the next century, more stable and politically advanced than China, not yet denatured by the modernism of the United States and Europe. Indian civilization is a great lake into which the rivers of different cultures have flowed . . . each depositing a new layer . . . whatever government is elected in May, this liberalization will not be reversed, because it is working . . . In India one can see the inevitability of Asian economic expansion despite the serious problem of population growth.'

In *The Times* of the 16th of March 1996, a British correspondent, agreeing with Lord Rees-Mogg, said the following about the technological advance of India—

> [Lord Rees-Mogg] 'should know that when he books a seat on British Airways, the computer that handles his booking is in Delhi; that when he pays his British Telecom bill, their computer is in Bombay; that many of the operating systems for IBM's computers are written by roomsful of well-dressed, polite, efficient, English-speaking young ladies, with mathematics degrees, working in well-lit modern offices in Bangalore.'

The rest of the world takes the same view as Lord Rees-Mogg. US foreign direct investment in South Asia has touched a record $2 billion in 1995, with over $1.2 billion of this coming to India, which means that more than half has come to India.

To be globally competitive, a country must be blessed with two favourable factors—an unlimited reservoir of talented and skilled labour and an abundance of capital available for new projects. A World Bank report, published a few years ago, indicated that India had both these factors in abundance.

We have had 5000 years of civilization behind us—a civilization which reached the 'summit of human thought'. During those

5000 years of India's priceless civilization, the Vedas were composed. In the nineteenth century, the Vedas were translated into European languages; and Schopenhauer (1788-1860), the great German philosopher, observed: 'Access to the Vedas is the greatest privilege this century can claim over all previous centuries'. 'In the whole world,' Schopenhauer added, 'there is no study so beneficial and so elevating as the *Upanishads*. It has been the solace of my life. It will be the solace of my death'. Another German philosopher, Schelling (1775-1854), in his old age looked upon the *Upanishads,* which came after the earlier Vedas, as representing the maturest wisdom of mankind. Emerson, talking of the *Upanishads* and the Vedas, said that having read them, he could not put them away. 'They haunt me. In them I have found eternal compensation, unfathomable power, unbroken peace.'

Speaking quite dispassionately, the people of India inherited great skills and many-splendoured intelligence, since the genes had evolved over five luminous millenia. The trader's instinct is innate in our ethos. I am never tired of repeating that an Indian can buy from a Jew and sell to a Scot and yet make a profit!

Giant multinational corporations are engaged in worldwide competition for the most scarce resource of all—talent. India has never been charged with an inadequate supply of this resource. Sir William Ryrie said, as the Executive Vice-President of the International Finance Corporation, that India has some of 'the most creative entrepreneurs . . . the most dynamic business leaders . . . and the sharpest financial brains in the world'. Incidentally, IFC has invested nearly 650 million dollars in India's private sector in the fiscal year 1994, raising this country to the status of Number One in its worldwide portfolio.

Some decades ago, the weekly *Punch,* now defunct, came out with one word of advice to those about to get married—*Don't.* Sir Thomas Bingham, the Master of the Rolls, gave the same advice the other day to those about to embark on a litigation. Today, the opposite would be the advice to those about to invest in India—*Do.* Lord Keynes said that investment is not just a matter of cold calculation, but an act of faith on the part of risk-taking entrepreneurs.

A recent issue of *Forbes,* the American business magazine, says in its lead story, 'India may be the best emerging market of all'. *Forbes* marshals facts in support of its view. There is twice as much

American direct investment now going into India as into China. Unlike China, India operates within the rule of law. When you invest in India, you invest in democracy. India also has a much larger and far more capable infrastructure of local companies which serve as good partners and tough competitors. *Forbes* further added that unlike China, India had much more than cheap labour to offer. English is widely understood and extensively used in international contacts. Some years ago, when the Queen of England visited India, she was agreeably surprised to learn that our laws are passed in English, the arguments in the Supreme Court and in the High Courts are in English, and the judgments of those Courts are delivered in English. The nations of the European Union and the Middle East would find themselves quite at home in dealing with India.

On an objective appraisal of all the circumstances, Motorola is planning to make India what it calls a 'brain centre' for engineering and design work; and the Japanese subsidiary of Digital Equipment Corporation chose Indian software engineers, over its own Japanese employees, to write the tricky computer programmes that translate English code into Japanese characters.

The celebrated investment bank, Merrill Lynch, has opined that liberalization in India had reached a point where it would be impossible to turn the clock back. In a recent report, Baring Securities mentions India as among the best emerging markets.

In the art of living together, India, the world's largest democracy, may have a lesson or two to teach the rest of the world. We have a population of about 940 million—give or take the entire population of Canada! Compare this mass of humanity with the European Union which has a population of 380 million. India comprises twenty-five States under a Constitution which welds them into a quasi-federal entity, as against the European Union which today has fifteen sovereign members. We have in India a larger variety of religions and a larger number of languages and dialects, than in the European Union. The Eighth Schedule to our Constitution lists eighteen major languages and the number of dialects is estimated to be more than 300. In these circumstances, it is natural and inevitable that we would be faced with even more problems than Europe has to contend with.

Credit should go to Dr Manmohan Singh (Finance Minister in the Congress government led by Shri P.V. Narasimha Rao) and

Shri P. Chidambaram (Finance Minister in the Janata Dal government led by Shri Deve Gowda) for their endeavour to introduce fruitful egalitarianism in place of sterile socialism. But in that direction we still have a long way to go. India still waits for the type of revolutionary turnaround effected by the Labour Party of Britain under John Smith, its great leader and one of the finest gentlemen of our times, who passed away recently. A short while before his death, John Smith said that he was relaunching the Labour Party as the party of the citizens and that he intended to chart a future in which the traditional associations of the party with state ownership, high taxation and trade union power would be buried for ever. In a reference to the Labour Party's old attachment to public ownership of the commanding heights of the economy, John Smith said that the new commanding heights were education and training. He categorically said that there would be no commitment to re-nationalization in the next manifesto of the Labour Party and that the most important priority would be to invest in people, to provide opportunities and skills that were the building blocks for individuals and national prosperity.

India purported to become a Socialist Republic by a constitutional amendment in 1976. The nation anxiously waits for the dawn of a new era when our politicians will, like John Smith and the present British Labour leader, Tony Blair, openly dissociate themselves from ideological socialism and espouse social justice which is ethical socialism.

INDIAN ECONOMY—THE SHAPE OF THINGS TO COME

◆

IN THE LAST fortnight, three events have happened which make us feel happy and optimistic about the economic situation in India.

First, the Union Budget of the Indian government introduced on 28 February 1997. By and large, it is the best Budget ever presented in our Parliament. It is almost unbelievable that the same country where our so-called leaders suffocated the people by state ownership and state control for more than forty years, and where enterprising Indians in those years were allowed to enrich a hundred foreign countries but were not allowed to enrich their own, should now be presented with a Budget which does justice to India which was never poor by nature but was only poor by policy. The country always had enough enterprise and enough entrepreneurship to raise our people from the subhuman squalor in which they had been enmeshed for so many years. Entrepreneurship comes naturally to Indians.

It was only at the end of February this year that the world famous journal, *The Economist,* published a special in-depth fifteen-page report on India, in which it critically examined the country's economic climate in global terms. In that report, India's markets are considered as among the most protected, regulated and over-administered in the world.

Now, as all of you know, in this Budget, the rates of direct taxes on individuals, residents and non-residents, companies and associations, have been slashed and the rates of duties on imports and exports have been drastically curtailed. At the same time, the ceiling on foreign investment has been substantially raised.

The *second* event which has served to restore India's confidence in its economic future is the visit of Bill Gates and his generous words of praise for India and Indians. In the words of Gates, 'India is well-positioned for the information age. Given the right investments in education, technology, infrastructure and the Internet, India can become a software superpower. The country's advantages are many. It has an excellent university system. Its computer scientists are among the leaders of companies worldwide. Its technolgy centres in Bangalore, Pune and other places are well-respected. Its corporations are at the cutting edge of technology development and deployment'. He futher adds, 'The world is moving at lightning speed towards Internet-based computing. Software developers in India are already adept at using the Internet, electronic mail, telephone and video conferencing to do business with technological partners of its customers around the world'.

Gates, who was recently described by TIME magazine as one of the most important minds and personalities of our era, added what should have been obvious to every thinking person that 'education is going to be the engine of growth for the Indian information technology'. He was generous enough to say that Indian software engineers are 'among the best in the world'. India can now start in a new era—an era where the government and the people realize the necessity for making Indian industry globally competitive.

The *third* event which is of very far-reaching significance is the proposed meeting of the Foreign Secretaries of Pakistan and India after a lapse of three years—to be more exact, thirty-eight months. No one who is a friend of Pakistan and India would ever want the present tension to continue between the two countries. Both the countries are almost ruined by having to spend on defence and armaments.

When India was on the verge of becoming an independent country, the great mystic and clairvoyant, Sri Aurobindo, said, 'The old communal division into Hindus and Muslims seems now to have hardened into a permanent political division of the country. It is to be hoped that this settled fact will not be accepted as settled for ever . . . The partition must go. Let us hope that that may come about naturally, by an increasing recognition of the necessity not only of peace and concord but . . . by the practice of common action and the creation of means for that purpose'. The Mahayogi hoped that divided India would once again be united 'under whatever form—the exact form may have a pragmatic but not a fundamental importance'. He declared that 'by whatever means, in whatever way, the division must go; unity must and will be achieved, for it is necessary for the greatness of India's future.'

Sardar Vallabhbhai Patel assured our people that India would never subscribe to the idea of a Hindu raj. He described it as a 'mad idea'. In his memorable words, 'It would kill the soul of India'.

Sardar Patel felt that Partition would destroy the reality that we were one and indivisible. 'You cannot divide the sea or the waters of the river. As for Muslims, they have their roots, their sacred places and their centres here. I do not know what they can possibly do in Pakistan.'

He said, 'We wish Pakistan well and hope that under settled conditions, when they realize that we are really brothers and not two nations of different faiths and ideologies, they would come back to us'.

Sri Aurobindo believed that fundamentally the separate parts would return to the motherland to form a united India that all cherish.

Bill Gates could have referred to the fact that at an international conference in the United States held some years ago to decide which language is most suitable for the computer, Sanskrit was chosen as the one language which seemed to be the most suitable. It is lucid, unambiguous and a language in which the most intricate steps can be expressed easily and precisely. No country can wish for a higher tribute to its ancient, basic language which is the foundation of its heritage.

There is a debit side to the balance sheet, which has been there for years, and which needs to be highlighted in fairness to foreign investors.

First and foremost, in the words of Bill Gates, the *first* necessity is to spread education more widely among our people. Today, India is competing, with only half its manpower, with the rest of the world—since half of the Indian population is literally illiterate. We must make education the 'priority of priorities'. *[See pp. 199-200]* The real resource of any country today is knowledge. Instead of capitalists and the working class, we are today having knowledge workers and service workers. Even in America, the Morgans, the Rockefellers and the Carnegies have been replaced by professional managers. Today, the well-established pension funds increasingly control the supply and allocation of money in developed countries. These funds own half of the capital of the country's largest businesses in the United States. The pension funds are run by a new breed of 'capitalists'—the faceless and anonymous employees who run the pension funds, investment analysts and portfolio managers. As Peter Drucker observed, we are living in a new era which is both non-socialist and post-capitalist.

Investing in education is to the 1990s what nationalization was to the 1940s and privatization was to the 1980s—the universal panacea of the day. All thinkers are agreed that in our times human capital is the most precious form of capital there is. The skill and calibre of corporate manpower can never appear in any balance sheet; but it is widely acknowledged throughout the world that the greatest resource of a company is trained manpower. In a book published recently by the famous economist, Julian Simon, the human resource is rightly defined in the title of the book as *The Ultimate Resource.*

Among the nations of the world, India ranks very high in innate intelligence, but abysmally low in wisdom—what the ancient *rishis* called *buddhi.* This is both the cause and the effect of our total indifference towards education. The criminalization of politics and the deplorably low moral tone of our public life are the direct consequences of the failure to impart value-based education. When Indians are better educated, they will know how to behave better as workers and to discharge with greater responsibility their duties as citizens.

Liberty without accountability is the freedom of the fool. Our concept of freedom will remain an impoverished one, until it is rounded and deepened by liberal education.

Education is the rock on which India must build her political salvation. Our country will be built not with bricks but with brains; not with cement but with enlightenment. If we cannot afford education, we cannot afford to remain a civilized society.

Secondly, we must privatize the public sector units. Privatization means that the majority of shares should be allowed to go into public hands, while the government may only retain a minority interest. In India, there is no political will to privatize any of the industries which are today in the public sector—the utmost the government is willing to do is to offer a minority shareholding in public sector enterprises to private parties.

However, the present government has appointed in August 1996 a Disinvestment Commission with Mr G.V. Ramakrishna as the Chairman. Though the programme has not yet started, the target has been set around 5,000 crore rupees. (This year's Budget mentions that the disinvestment programme will be selectively done through the Commission).

Take, for example, the subject of life insurance and general insurance. The then Finance Minister, Dr Manmohan Singh, did nothing for the deregulation of the Insurance sector. In his Budget Speech of 1993, Dr Manmohan Singh had rightly referred to it as one of the urgent tasks of liberalization. The Malhotra Committee was appointed and it made a very balanced, well-thought-out report as one would expect from a man of the calibre of Mr R.N. Malhotra. After that report, Dr Manmohan Singh in his Budget Speech in 1994 again reiterated his proposal to deregulate the insurance sector and to create a competitive and financially strong insurance industry functioning under an independent authority. But in the Budgets of 1995 and 1996, nothing was done. Kingsley Amis was not wrong when he said, 'There is always a gap between an idea and its execution, but in India it is the widest'.

In this year's Budget (1997-98), the Finance Minister, Mr P. Chidambaram, has made a modest opening of one segment of the insurance sector, viz, the health insurance business. Only a few Indian companies, which are Indian-controlled and with majority Indian ownership, will be permitted to enter the health insurance business.

Thirdly, India has vast infrastructural gaps. It has to add one lakh megawatts of power capacity in the next ten years. It has to upgrade, both quantitatively and qualitatively, telecommunications network. The state-run telephone monopoly took one hundred and ten years to instal eight million telephones, but it has taken private cable operators just three years to instal twenty million satellite television hook-ups. About two-thirds of the country's five hundred thousand villages still do not have a telephone.

Fourthly, we should change our labour laws instead of aiming at populism all the time. Five years ago, the government promised an exit policy, but no action whatever has been taken in that direction. India will find it impossible to compete with the rest of the world so long as our law forbids even a humane exit policy and prohibits closure of sick units without the government's permission.

Fifthly, if there is any one political factor which is bound to impede the forward march of India, it is the resurgence of the age-old curse of casteism. In no other country in the contemporary world is there anything comparable to our casteism except perhaps tribalism in Africa. Reservations for the backward classes in different states of India have resulted in the substandard replacing the standard, and the reins of power passing from meritocracy to mediocrity.

Casteism and religion are the two powerful divisive forces in India. Some critics have gone to the length of saying that the Indian people is not a nation but a collection of communities. Winston Churchill said in 1931, 'India is a geographical term. It is no more a united nation than the equator'. Reservations on caste considerations in the Maharashtra State have climbed to 73 per cent.

Under a democratic set-up like ours, there is no short-term solution whatever to the problem we are facing. The only solution is a long-term one. We have to educate our people on the essential unity of all religions, instead of letting them remain cultural illiterates.

In the fifty years of independence, India has never had to

face a crisis of the magnitude and far-reaching effect comparable to what it is facing today. We are a low-arousal people, but we must awake from our apathy and realize that there is a grave threat to the unity and integrity of the country—even to the very survival of our democratic system. All recorded history has one clear lesson to teach—freedom cannot last unless it is coupled with order. Order can exist without freedom, but freedom can never exist without order. That freedom and order may co-exist, it is essential that freedom should be exercised under authority and order should be enforced by authority. India is passing through a phase of disorder which makes you recall the pregnant words of Lord Wavell—'India can be governed firmly, or not at all'.

Democracy is of three types. Democracy, as India knew it in the first fourteen years of its independence. Guided democracy, as Singapore has known it since its inception under Lee Kuan Yew. And misguided democracy, of which India is the prime example today. We suffer acutely from four plagues—regionalism, communalism, casteism, and total absence of moral leadership. These four plagues devour amity and national solidarity. It is these four plagues which have made it possible for self-seeking politicians to convert our democracy into a misguided democracy. India produced Mahatma Gandhi, the greatest moral force of this century. But today the country is pathetically lacking even in mediocre leadership.

The Hindus, the Sikhs, and the Muslims have lost sight of the essentials of their respective religions, and are misled by bigots and fundamentalists whose activities represent the very antithesis of the true teaching of their religion.

Different segments of the Indian nation live in different centuries. It is the same nation but it lives in different eras. For instance, some five thousand people watched Roop Kanwar, a nineteen-year-old widow, perform *sati* or self-immolation in 1987, in the village of Daurala in Rajasthan. The villagers said that she sat calmly, holding her dead husband's head in her lap and chanting prayers, as flames consumed her. The police had charged Roop Kanwar's brother-in-law, Pushpendra Singh, with lighting the pyre, and her father-in-law, Sumer Singh, with forcing her to commit *sati.* The third defendant was another family member. But all the three accused were acquitted because the thirty-seven witnesses who gave evidence turned hostile and did not say that Roop Kanwar had been compelled to commit *sati.* In Rajasthan, among many Rajputs, the warrior Hindu caste to which Roop Kanwar belonged, *sati* is still regarded as a holy rite.

Sixthly, corruption is gnawing at the very vitals of our democracy. The tone of the public life has reached an all-time low. We have democracy without meritocracy. Ignorance, incompetence and dishonesty are no disqualifications for high public office, either in the ministerial ranks or elsewhere.

Lastly, the government must make sure that the fruits of liberalization reach the masses, and the rate of inflation must be brought down from seven per cent which is the prevailing rate today, especially in the prices of food articles of daily use which hit the masses the most. Those who live in India are extremely sceptical whether the rate of inflation is really as low as seven per cent or whether the figure merely shows Indian skill in jugglery.

One bizarre thought, unconnected with the Constitution of India and with our prevailing institutions—and I shall have done.

I wonder whether the majority of the people would approve of this year's Budget if it were put to vote on the basis of adult franchise.

The happiest time India has ever known was under rulers who were not elected by the people but were wise men who deserved to rule the country.

Edward Gibbon, the author of *The Decline and Fall of the Roman Empire,* after surveying the history of human civilization, came to the conclusion that the happiest time the world had ever known was the Age of the Antonines which lasted a little less than two centuries. That was the time when the Roman world was governed by a wise ruler who had been chosen by the last leader to rule the country. Unfortunately, the last emperor, Marcus Aurelius, died without naming his successor, and the regime came to an end.

H.L. Mencken described American democracy as a 'boobocracy' of, by and for the 'vast herd of human blanks' who have neither the interest nor the capacity for intelligent self-government. But as you see how government after government in India succumbed to populism when what the country needed was strong leadership, you are tempted to tell yourself that even what is impolitic and impolite has to be said in a country whose national motto is 'Truth Shall Prevail'.

VI

TAXATION

THE PHILOSOPHY OF TAXATION IN INDIA

◆

THE PREFACES TO Nani Palkhivala's monumental work, *The Law and Practice of Income-tax,* are considered brilliant commentaries on taxation in India. Some extracts are given in this section.

From the Preface to the Fourth Edition (8 February 1958)

The regimentation of the nation's life by means of taxing statutes is only one phase of the stifling governmental control with which modern Indian legislation is saturated and dripping. The State is too much with us. Mr Justice Brandeis observed that the most comprehensive of rights and the right most valued by civilized men which the citizen has, as against the government, is 'the right to be let alone'. Taxation laws have joined multitudinous other laws in corroding that right. Since this corrosion is effected in the name of social justice, it may not be out of place to quote from the same judge whose whole life and work were dedicated to the cause of social justice: 'Experience should teach us to be most on our guard to protect liberty when the government's purposes are beneficent. Men born to freedom are naturally alert to repel invasion of their liberty by evil-minded rulers. The greatest dangers to liberty lurk in insidious encroachment by men of zeal, well-meaning but without understanding.'

From the Preface to the Eighth Edition (21 February 1990)

The Indian income-tax law had its hour of glory in 1985. The finest Budget of the Indian republic was that of 1985-86. That epoch-making Budget was a refreshing contrast to the series of historically retrograde, economically unprogressive and socially stagnant Budgets that had preceded it in a supreme ironic procession for many years. It was presented by Mr V.P. Singh, the then finance minister. Unfortunately, the basic ideals and values underlying it—stability, simplicity, and reasonably low rates which encouraged tax compliance—were quietly swept aside in the years that followed. We gave up the search for genes of ideas which deserve to be called 'a high-yielding variety of economics' and are smugly reconciled to 'low yields from high ideals' to quote the words of the late Dr Sudhir Sen.

Today the Income-tax Act, 1961, is a national disgrace. There is no other instance in Indian jurisprudence of an Act mutilated by more than 3,300 amendments in less than thirty years. Simple provisions like Sections 11 to 13 (which deal with exemption of the income of charitable trusts) have suffered no less than fifty amendments.

The tragedy of India is the tragedy of waste—waste of national time, energy and manpower. Tens of millions of man-hours, crammed with intelligence and knowledge—of tax-gatherers, taxpayers and tax advisers—are squandered every year in grappling with the torrential spate of mindless amendments. The feverish activity achieves no more good than a fever.

Our law reports bear witness to the fact that generally a case reaches hearing in the High Court in twenty years, and in the Supreme Court in thirty years, after the relevant assessment year. The situation is continuously aggravated by the deluge of new amendments—the indigestible verbiage; and the flood of litigation is heavier today than ever before.

Two things strike the student of Indian income-tax law with trepidation and amazement—the precipitate and chronic tinkering with the law by bureaucrats who are the unacknowledged legislators of India, and the anaesthetized patience of the Indian public. Truly, we Indians are a 'low arousal' people. We endure injustice and unfairness with feudalistic servility and fatalistic resignation. The poor of India endure inhuman conditions which would lead to a bloody revolution in any other country. The rich endure foolish laws and maddening amendments which benefit none except the legal and accountancy professions, and instinctively prefer to circumvent the law than to fight for its repeal.

Taxes are the lifeblood of any government, but it cannot be over-emphasized that the blood is taken from the arteries of the taxpayers and, therefore, the transfusion has to be accomplished in accordance with the principles of justice and fair play.

Every government has a right to levy taxes. But no government has the right, in the process of extracting tax, to cause misery and harassment to the taxpayer and the gnawing feeling that he is made the victim of palpable injustice.

THE BUDGET OF MY DREAMS

◆

FROM THE MIDDLE of January of each year the people willy-nilly get caught in a vortex of anxiety about the contents of the impending Budget which, according to our antediluvian practice, can only be revealed at the end of February. A flurry of guesses (both educated and uneducated) are made; a chance remark of the finance minister is dissected and analysed threadbare by the pundits and finally blown up out of all proportion. A torrent of advice flows in and the volatile barometer of the Stock Exchange adds a measure of nervousness to the already fevered atmosphere.

I. Tax rates fixed for three years

The rates of direct and indirect taxes which I am proposing are not only for one year but for the next three years—that is, for the remaining term of this Parliament. The rates will not be changed except for the most compelling reasons arising from unexpected developments. Since the rates of income-tax are not proposed to be changed every year, I have discontinued the practice of prescribing them by the Finance Act and have included them in the Income-tax Act itself. I know that I am depriving myself (or my successor) of the profound psychological satisfaction of being able to keep one-seventh of the human race on tenterhooks on the traditional Budget Day; but I am convinced that, without stability in our fiscal laws, all planned growth is impossible.

I propose to bring a comprehensive Bill before Parliament to reduce the Income-tax Act to about one-fourth of its present size by excising what is useless and simplifying what is useful; and I

Nani Palkhivala's parents, Ardeshir and Shcherbanoo

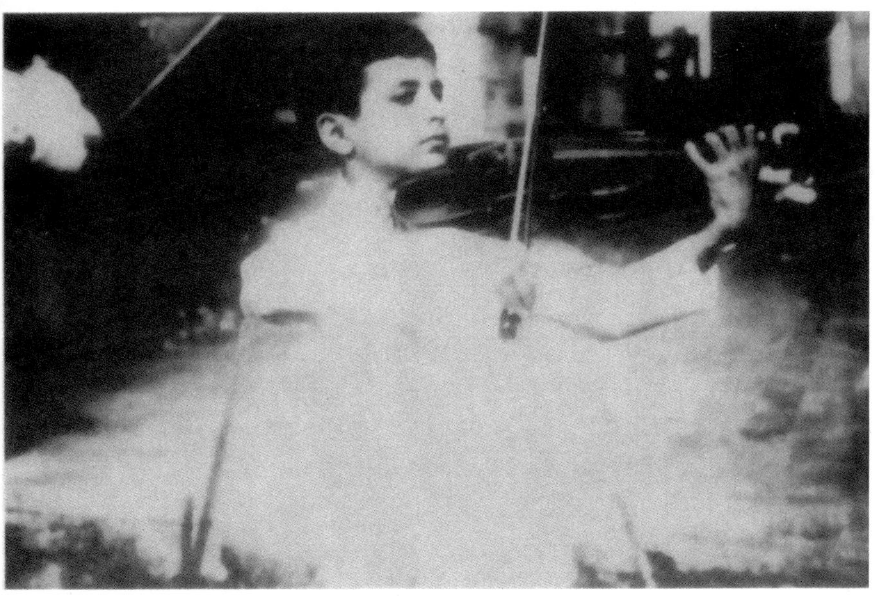

With his violin

With his mother, sister Amy and brother Behram

In his late teens

On his graduation in 1940

Balding with age, shining with knowledge

At the wedding of Nani's brother Behram and sister-in-law Dhan, 1952. Standing: Nani and Nargesh (second and third from left) with his niece Bapsy and nephew Homi Ranina. Sitting: Nani's parents Ardeshir and Sheherbanoo (second and third from left) and brother-in-law Phiroze Ranina and sister Amy Ranina (last two from right)

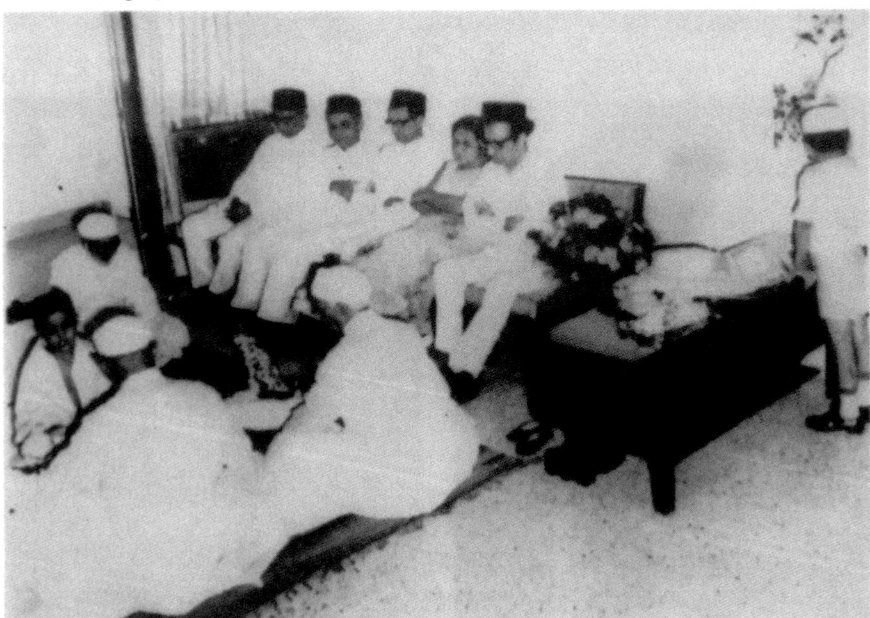

At the navjote ceremony of Nani's nephew Jehangir (Behram's son), 1973. On his right is Nargesh.

At the navjote ceremony of his nephew Phiroze (Behranr s son), 1975. On his right are Nargesh and his Tata colleague the late Adi Billimoria. His sister is in the rear row.

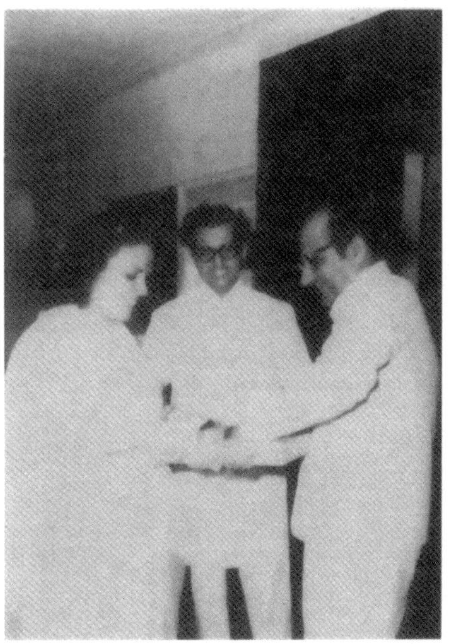

Giving a present to his sister-in-law Dhan and brother Behram after the navjote (1975)

Nani is seen clapping as his nephew Phiroze cuts the navjote cake. Nani's sister Amy is on his right.

In his study at his residence

In his office at Bombay House.

As Indian envoy to USA, presenting his credentials to President Jimmy Carter. Nargesh looks on. (1978)

Being greeted by William Bowen, President of Princeton University, New Jersey, after receiving an honorary doctorate, 1978

Nani, who was honoured with the Lifetime Literacy Achievement Award by the Rotary Club of Mumbai North, with his wife Nargesh.
Courtesy: The Times of India, *1 July 1999*

Sir Jamshedji Behramji Kanga KT

At the centenary celebration of Sri Aurobindo's return to India from England, Apollo Bunder, Mumbai 1993. Others in front are (left to right) his sister-in-law Dhan, Moreshwar Temburde, Deputy Speaker of the Maharashtra Legislative Assembly and Sudhakar Naik, Chief Minister of Maharashtra.

Addressing a large gathering at one of his budget lectures at the Brabourne Stadium, Cricket Club of India, Bombay

Nani seen with Justice M.C. Chagla, former Chief Justice of the Bombay High Court (left), at the 9th A.D. Shroff Memorial Lecture delivered by the latter on 28 October 1974 in Bombay. M.R. Pai is on the right.

Nani with General S.F. Rodrigues who presided over his budget speech at the Brabourne Stadium, 1994

Bharat Ratna and Padma awardees of the Bhavan's family (left to right) S. Ramakrishnan, K.R. Atmanathan, (deputizing Bharat Ratna Smt. M.S. Subbulakshmi), H.K. Dua, Dr. PC. Alexander (Governor of Maharashtra), C. Subramaniam, Nani Palkhivala and Usha Mehta (1998)

Presenting a set of the Bhavan's publications to Her Royal Highness Princess Iren of Greece (1998). Dr. P.C. Alexander and Smt. Ackama Alexander look on.

At the Bhavan with S. Ramakrishnan and Usha Mehta Chairperson, Mumbai Gandhi Smark Nidhi (1999)

With Air Chief Marshal I.H. Latif (Retd.) (1996)

With I.K. Gujral at Bharatiya Vidya Bhavan, New Delhi (1997)

Nani and S. Ramakrishnan with Sri Satya Sai Baba at Dharmakshetra, Mumbai (1999)

With the late Minoo R. Masani (1972)

Observing Mahatma Gandhi 47th Martyrdom Day at Bharatiya Vidya Bhavan, Bombay (30-1-1995). (Left to right) Pravinchandra Gandhi, Morari Bapu, C. Subramaniam, Maulana Wahiduddin Khan and Nani Palkhivala.

Nani seen with Justice H.R. Khanna former Judge of the Supreme Court of India, (left), at the 15th A.D. Shroff Memorial Lecture delivered by the latter on 13 October 1980 in Bombay. On the right is M.R. Pai.

Presenting copies of his books Essential Unity of *All Religions* and *India's Priceless Heritage* to Nobel Laureate Dr Henry Kissinger, former US Secretary of State, on his visit to the Bhavan's head office on 8 June 1999

Cutting the cake on his 75th birthday (16 January 1995) at a function arranged by his admirers. Others seen are: Minoo R. Masani (seated); standing (left to right) Rajsingh Dungarpur, President, The Cricket Club of India, J.R. Gagrat, Solicitor, M.R. Pai and M.A. Rane, Senior Advocate

On his 75th birthday (16 January 1995) with wife Nargesh

propose to have the same type of radical surgery performed on the other statutes dealing with direct and indirect taxes. These changes, which will be made expeditiously in the course of the current year, are calculated to put the fiscal laws on a stable basis, obviating any further amendments till 1985. The same discipline will be observed by the rule-making authorities. The nation will hereafter be spared the maddening consequences of the rule-making exercises which up to now have been undertaken by the Central Boards of Direct and Indirect Taxes once every four or six weeks.

II. Government must live within its means

The past Budget used to estimate first the expenditure and then decide upon the ways of raising the resources. This is the first Budget which has started by charting the available resources and then planned for reduced expenditure within the estimated means.

Over the years the Government of India adopted a Micawber style of living, with little control over expenditure and with the touching faith that something will 'turn up'. Budgets of independent India have vindicated with a vengeance the validity of 'the law of growing public expenditure' enunciated by the economist Adolph Wagner as far back as 1863.

In my Budget proposals there is no deficit either on the capital or revenue account. My fundamental thesis is that the government has no right to live beyond its means—and beyond yours and mine. I have pruned governmental expenditure ruthlessly. One of the small steps in that direction will be reduction of the bloated bureaucracy. There are no fewer than 8.8 million employees of the Central and state governments who are merely concerned with administration, as against 7.2 million employees in organized industry in the private sector. Economic stagnation is the inevitable consequence of such disproportion between productive and unproductive jobs. There will be a total ban for five years on fresh recruitment in the administration section of the government, except in the top cadres. This would mean that, if 2 per cent of the government employees retire in a year, in five years' time the government staff would be reduced by about 10 per cent—a factor which would be conducive not only to economy but, more importantly, to efficiency of administration.

III. Massive tax cuts

Taking human beings as I find them, I recognize that a man will work for himself and his family as he will work for no one else. In its bravest contests with the primordial forces of human nature, the law fights a losing battle. Excessive taxation has sapped the nation's strength, blighted confidence, strangled enterprise and ensured evasion.

I propose to apply the fiscal stimulus and secure fast economic growth through tax cuts. 'Incentives are the prizes in the game of life—the goals individuals seek—the carrots.' Many countries have found that, with every tax cut, the economy boomed and the exchequer garnered golden grain. While reducing the tax rates, I shall get the revenues to grow by making incomes grow and the Gross National Product grow. In other words, our tax revenues hereafter will be self-generating. I have taken credit for substantial increase in excise, customs, income-tax and corporate tax.

I have reduced the rates of taxes both for individuals and for corporations all along the line. The Sixth Five Year Plan says: 'In a large number of areas, our capabilities are almost twenty years behind those in the advanced nations and also behind those established recently in some developing countries. Reduced taxation will enable companies to generate the resources needed to modernise their plants and make technological improvements to increase production.' While making the massive reduction in tax rates, I have also abolished the piddling deductions and rebates which cluttered up the statute-book.

Industry contributes 79 per cent of the central government's revenue, excluding the direct taxes paid by individuals employed in industry. Thus the resources of the central government are crucially dependent upon the health of industry which needs to be promoted by a nutritive budget.

IV. Stealing from the future

Living on excessive borrowings is really nothing but stealing from the future. In eleven years from 1970-71 to 1981-82, the outstanding public debt (external and internal) of the Government of India expanded from Rs 14,043 crores to Rs 46,776 crores. If to this are added the unfunded debts—that is, small savings, provident fund balances, etc—the net liabilities of the Central government now aggregate to Rs 67,489 crores. This means a burden of almost Rs 1,000 on the head of every man, woman and child—in a country in which 40 per cent of the population are never able to save Rs 500 in all their lives.

I view with the most serious concern the alarming growth in internal public debt at ridiculously low rates of interest for the following reasons:

(a) The Government of India borrows at rates of interest far below the long-term market rates. In other words, the government procures funds at a rate of interest which is subsidised by the common man. Hence the government's outlay on commercial and manufacturing projects does not give a realistic measure of the true cost-benefit ratio of the projects.

(b) The commercial banks are compelled to subscribe to a sizeable portion of the government securities, which reduces the banking system's profitability and results in a low rate of interest to the depositors and savings account-holders.

(c) The Life Insurance Corporation, provident funds and public charities are also obliged to invest in government paper, which means that the policy-holders, salaried employees and charities are deprived of a fair legitimate return on their investments.

(d) The Reserve Bank of India has to subscribe to a huge chunk of government securities. This is nothing but disguised deficit financing and is the principal factor in the endemic inflation from which we have suffered so long.

(e) The rising burden of internal public debt also means a sharply enhanced burden of interest payments. The aggregate amount of interest paid on the government's internal debt rose from Rs 443 crores in 1970-71 to Rs 2,875 crores in 1981-82. The assets created out of the borrowed monies do not generate sufficient surpluses in the form of dividends and profits for the government to pay the interest charges.

I have decided to contain within the severest limits any increase in the level of borrowings, internal or external. Surely, there must be a limit to the extent to which we are prepared to mortgage the future of this country; and I am not sure that we have not already exceeded the outside limit. Further, I have provided for a 2 per cent increase in the existing rates of interest on all government securities, which will enure for the benefit of all salaried employees, bank depositors, policyholders and others.

V. The ultimate resource

The human resource is the ultimate resource of a nation. I make no apology for my determination to promote and encourage private initiative which is pejoratively called 'capitalism' with a view to damning it. In formulating my Budget proposals, I have tried to ensure that far more savings will be left in the private sector and with individuals than before. For every rupee earned by a shareholder in organized private sector industry, eight rupees of tax revenues are generated for our Central and state governments.

I cannot shut my eyes to the elementary fact that the performance of the public sector suffers grievously by comparison with the private sector, though not due to any fault of the men in charge of the public sector units. 65 per cent of our industrial fixed assets are in the public sector, but they give only 22 per cent of the total industrial output. If the public sector were to yield what the non-government companies do, the central government revenues would increase by at least Rs 1,000 crores per year.

VI. Abolition of sales tax and octroi

The elementary truth, most often forgotten, is that a nation's progress depends mainly on the extent to which the people's time and energy are released for productive purposes, instead of being frittered away in coping with legal inanities. The full potential of the people must be unleashed to create national wealth. Few levies have been so much responsible for a criminal waste of human time and energy as sales tax and octroi.

The more numerous the points at which taxes are collected, the greater the scope for corruption and evasion, resulting in diminution of public revenues.

The lucky circumstance that the same party is in power at the Centre and in the overwhelming majority of the states has enabled us to coordinate with the state governments in evolving a scheme under which sales tax and octroi will be abolished altogether and, instead, an additional excise duty to be levied by the Centre will serve to raise the resources which will be distributed among the state governments and the local authorities.

VII. Human development

Investment in human development is more productive than investment in physical assets and, moreover, it leads to a faster rate of national growth. We have paid too little attention to human development in the past, particularly in the fields of education, medicine and public health, nutrition and family planning. In these areas, I have provided for very substantial outlays. We shall have a monitoring system to make sure that the amounts are not merely allocated and spent, but that they are fruitfully and productively disbursed. The task of administering these funds will not be in the hands of politicians or ill-paid civil servants, but will be entrusted to private organizations with a proven unblemished record of public service. No more will a 100 million man-days be lost every year in merely fetching drinking water.

Roads are the arteries of the nation—they constitute the road to economic growth. Today as many as 4,07,297 out of 5,75,936 villages—that is, about seven out of ten villages—remain unconnected by all-weather roads, while 3,14,470 (55 per cent) of all our villages do not have any road link at all.

I am unable to see how any state which has any pretensions to practise true socialism can possibly refute the claim of industry that its social responsibilities require it to look after the education, health and general welfare of the people of the locality in which the industry flourishes. I propose to amend Section 37 of the Income-tax Act to provide that any expenditure incurred by an assessee on construction or repair of roads or on other items of public welfare would be fully deductible for tax purposes. I believe that human development would be impossible unless private citizens are associated with this great cause and are given fiscal incentives to promote it.

VIII. Incentives for exports

The trade deficit in 1981-82 exceeded Rs 5,000 crores (it was Rs

5,728 crores in 1980-81) principally because of our export performance which is so poor. Our exports in 1980 totalled \$7.9 billion, as compared to \$17.5 billion exports of South Korea (which has $^1/_{33}$ of our area and $^1/_{17}$ of our population), \$19.4 billion exports of the tiny city of Singapore (which has about one-quarter of Bombay's population) and \$19 billion exports of the city of Hong Kong. India had 1.05 per cent of the world export market in 1960-61, which share has been reduced in the current year to 0.4 per cent. At the end of March 1980, our reserves (excluding gold and special drawing rights) were Rs 5,164 crores. They have now declined to Rs 3,400 crores—an amount barely enough to cover three months' imports.

No solution is afforded by merely taking foreign exchange loans to tide over the crisis and passing on the burden of repayment with interest to the future. The real choice before us is either to push up our exports vigorously or be a defaulter in a few years in respect of our foreign exchange obligations. By various changes in the law, I have provided for streamlined procedures which will remove altogether the element of fiscal levies which makes our goods uncompetitive in the world market. This, coupled with very liberal new incentives and a stable export-import policy, should enable us to have a favourable balance of trade in two years.

IX. Partnership between the government and the people

I believe that the Union Budget should not be an annual scourge but should partake more of the nature of the presentation of annual accounts of a partnership between the government and the people. It is impossible to expect from the people good faith and acceptance of their moral duty to pay taxes, unless the government first proves itself to be fair, considerate and reasonable. I have tried to take the first step towards transforming our apathetic democracy into an anticipatory and participatory democracy.

I am aware of the legal possibility of Parliament retracing its steps in the future and undoing what this Budget attempts to do. The people must make sure that the forces of ignorance and obscurantism are never allowed to put the clock back again. It is necessary to undertake now and in right earnest the task of teaching our lawmakers economic rationalism in place of economic theology, and of educating them in the techniques of the creation of wealth. To this end, I have proposed an amendment to the Income-tax Act to provide that any expenditure incurred by an assessee in undertaking the aforesaid urgent and imperative task of educating the lawmakers will be fully deductible in computing income under any head.

Gone are the years of the locusts. I am happy to stake any entire political future on this Budget which blazes a new trail. Of its immensely beneficial effects on the nation's economy by the end of the three years—that is, 1985—I am as confident as I am of the fact that Halley's comet will reappear in that year.

THE UNION BUDGET 1993-94

◆

IT IS A creative and nutritive Budget. Dr Manmohan Singh has introduced a Budget which a mere politician would have thought possible only through witchcraft or fraud, to use the words of *The Economist.*

The goals of the Budget are unexceptionable. Agriculture and agro-processing industries are sought to be promoted. Another avowed objective is to promote exports. When you realize that Holland, with a population of only fifteen million, has six times the exports of India, and the city of Hong Kong has almost three times the international trade of India, you appreciate that we have a long way to go.

The third objective of the Budget is to curb inflation and to reduce deficit financing. The unborn generations are a group wholly unrepresented in Parliament, and to protect their vital interests it is essential that we bear the burden of our own debts. In the words of Thomas Jefferson, one of the outstanding Presidents of the USA, 'The question whether one generation has the right to bind another by the deficit it imposes is a question of such consequence as to place it among the fundamental principles of government. We should consider ourselves unauthorized to saddle posterity with our debts, and morally bound to pay them ourselves.'

The fourth goal is to increase expenditure on development—health, education, and family planning. It is development which determines the quality of life. The riots and disturbances which recently took place at Ayodhya, Bombay and Surat were the handiwork of hoodlums who made Hitler look like a juvenile delinquent. A long-term plan of value-based educatioin alone can prevent the recurrence of such disasters. It is for the first time that an Indian Budget has emphasized the need for education.

Revival of the economy is another important goal. The Gross Domestic Product of our country is smaller than that of Greater Los Angeles. Even the countries whose currency was weaker than India's for decades have marched ahead.

The sixth and last goal—of tax reforms, remains a distant dream so far as direct taxation is concerned. It is only in the field of indirect taxes that positive measures have been taken.

The Budget is in conformity with recent trends the world over. Fashions in ideas change, as do fashions in clothes. India is much less quick to follow new fashions in ideas than in dress.

It has been observed that nationalization was the fashion in the 1940s, as was privatization in the 1980s. Luckily, education has become all the rage in the 1990s. World opinion is veering round to the view that education is the universal panacea of the day. Dr Warren Bennis, the guru of business management, said that what is needed for our competitive advantage, long-range growth and full deployment of our people are three things: education, education, and education.

On the whole, the Budget is a harbinger of good times to come. It will not take India to heaven but it will check India's precipitate slide to hell.

THE UNION BUDGET 1994-95

◆

THOSE WHO WATCHED the presentation of the Budget on television must have been distressed to see some MPs behave like unruly, irresponsible school children. You are reminded of Rudyard Kipling's dictum 'Politics is a dog's life, without a dog's decencies'.

The biggest curse of the party system in any democracy is that it breeds a tendency to look at every measure on purely party lines. An almost universal tendency of all politicians is to view the Budget not as a national budget but as a party budget. This causes either wholesale approval or total condemnation by those politicians whose critical perception is no higher than forty watts.

The detailed proposals in this year's Budget are, as usual, less important than the overall thrust of the package. The Budget is historically important because it marks a turning point in the way Indians think about their economy—less like a tortoise and more like a tiger. The arthritic economy is increasingly performing like an athletic economy.

Contrary to some expectations, the Budget has not proved to be the biggest bonfire of controls. The expectations of the public were unlimited, while the options available to the Finance Minister were limited. On the whole it is a stimulating Budget, subject to some important reservations.

Lack of Fiscal Discipline

Discipline in incurring non-Plan expenditure is the collective responsibility of the entire government. The Finance Minister by himself can do precious little by way of imposing such discipline. The non-Plan expenditure has been burgeoning at the rate of 15 per cent year after year. The cavalier manner in which the government has sanctioned the expenditure of Rs 1 crore by every member of the Lok Sabha and of the Rajya Sabha at a time when the deficit has reached alarming proportions is an index to the recklessness so characteristic of the Union government.

Service Tax

The Budget has introduced 'service tax' for the first time. No doubt service tax is constitutionally valid, but it is unwise. The proposal today is to levy service tax on three services—brokerage, general insurance and telephones. But nothing is more dangerous in India than the introduction of a new tax. Tax revenues are to Indian politicians what drugs are to junkies—they can never have enough.

The proposed items chargeable to service tax will multiply as quickly as rabbits. Services are rendered by countless professionals—including physicians, surgeons, architects, accountants, business consultants and lawyers. Where will the categories of service tax end?

The least defensible item of service tax is that on telephones. The Indian telephone system is a national disgrace compared to the efficiency of the service in other lands. This obese public sector enterprise represents the low-water mark of efficiency. Our telephones render no service but a blatant disservice. To levy tax on such a disastrous disservice is to betray a degree of audacity which calls for nationwide opposition.

Entry of Foreign Institutional Investors (FIIs)

Globalization in all its forms is the order of the day. Production, investments, communications and information are today globalized as never before.

Throwing open the Indian economy to FIIs is a move in the right direction. We should welcome FIIs who are willing to bring in foreign exchange and to boost the Indian stock exchanges. Their advent into India is in the long-term interest of our country.

Two basic points may be noted about the FIIs. First, they have not come here out of motives of philanthropy or charity, or out of a desire to assist and to be loyal to the Third World. It is true that investment by FIIs can ebb out as fast as it has flooded in. 'The slightest whiff of danger and they will be gone. There is no doubting the depths of their pockets; but you cannot count on their loyalty.' I do not think this veiled criticism is justified. After all, the FIIs are in fact and in law accountable to their own participants and they must sell off their investments at the time which is most beneficial to those who own the fund or the company. If they perform their legitimate and rational duty towards those who own them, they cannot be branded as fickle investors.

The second point, even more important, is regarding the desirability of a cap on investments by FIIs. In an ideal world, the nationality of capital would be irrelevant. But we are not living in such a world.

Instead of wasting our time and energy on non-issues, like the renaming of a university, a well-informed public debate should take place on the question—how long will Indian industries remain Indian?

During the first forty years of our republic, our national industries were suffocated and strangulated, and our entrepreneurial culture was asphyxiated—all in the name of socialism. Would not the national psyche be hurt if today a sizable chunk of Indian industry were to be taken over by FIIs (or the foreign parties to whom they sell) only because they are able to pay an attractive price?

Level Playing Field

Indians can hold their own against their counterparts abroad. But they expect, in fairness, a level playing field. The level playing field should not be merely in relation to the product manufactured by an Indian enterprise but also, equally importantly, in the field of investment. It is here that the Indian investor faces a great handicap. First, because of higher taxation, the Indian resident is left with substantially lower capital (accumulated income) than the foreigner. Secondly, when it comes to capital borrowed for the purpose of investment, the Indian is at even a greater disadvantage. On his borrowed funds, he is obliged to pay, under legal compulsion, a rate of interest which is 200 to 300 per cent higher than the rate which the foreigner has to pay on the loans he raises abroad. In its desire to acquire large reserves of foreign exchange, the Indian government is putting its own nationals at a tremendous disadvantage.

The Budget affords an excellent example of the fact that in India we are accustomed to a comfortable time-lag of thirty years intervening between the consciousness that a particular reform is required in the public interest and a serious attempt to undertake it.

Excessive Secrecy

Excessive secrecy continues to stifle pre-Budget economic debate. Patrick Lenkin, Sir Richard Clarke, and Peter Jay among others have repeatedly pointed out that there is no reason whatever for secrecy about direct taxes. But the fossilized minds in the North Block are totally unresponsive to any new idea unless, per chance, it originates in their own heads.

The legitimate complaint of the NRIs that they have been discriminated against, as compared to FIIs, might not have arisen if there had been an open public discussion regarding the two categories before the Budget.

Instability in Laws

I believe that no civil servant should be allowed to work in the Finance Ministry unless he has taken a Foundational Course which emphasizes one truth. The truth is that stability in tax laws is to a nation what stability in family life is to an individiual; and, therefore, where it is not necessary to change, it is necessary not to change. But stability is anathema to the North Block. Our Finance Ministry is filled with bureaucrats who eternally mistake amendment for improvement and change for progress. In the first decade of our republic, several budgets hardly made any change in the direct tax laws—they merely prescribed the rates of tax. On the top of the 150-odd changes made in the direct tax laws last year, this year's Budget has amended more than sixty sections of the direct tax Acts. Between April 1993 and February 1994, the Import Trade Control was altered by 195 Notifications, and the Export Trade Control by 34 Notifications.

Two-year Budget

There would be tremendous saving in time and energy, cost and public inconvenience, if we adopt the system of a Union Budget for a period of two years at a time. It would make for greater stability in place of the insensate annual changes to which we are accustomed. As many as twenty-one States of the USA have adopted the practice of two-year budgets. President Clinton has publicly said that he intends to introduce the practice of two-year budgets from October 1996. Though we may not be enamoured of the attitude of Americans towards India in some areas, we should learn from them the way of saving the nation's time, effort and energy.

The 5 p.m. ritual

The time of day when the general budget is introduced in Parliament needs to be reconsidered. I am firmly of the view that the general budget should be presented in the morning, just as the railway budget is presented in the morning, year after year. During the British days, the general budget used to be introduced at 5 p.m. for a reason which suited British rulers. Since the British time was 5½ hours behind the Indian Standard Time, the Chancellor of the Exchequer could inform the House of Commons on the same day about the fiscal changes proposed in the Indian budget. No Indian Finance Minister has had the wisdom to change this practice, even though the justification for it has long ago vanished. Dr Manmohan Singh has been an innovator in many areas and I wish he would have the courage to make a change in the timing of presenting the general budget. Once the change is effected, no Finance Minister would ever go back to the 5 p.m. ritual. (Before Mr Morarji Desai became the Finance Minister, the new rates of taxation applied to income earned during the very year in which the Budget was introduced. Mr Desai saw the injustice of it and made the new rates applicable to the accounting year following the Budget. This equitable change has invariably been adhered to. This is how a rational practice, once innovated by a strong man, continues to be followed in subsequent years.)

THE UNION BUDGET 1995-96

◆

THE LAST FOUR Budgets were framed by Dr Manmohan Singh, the technocrat. The fifth Budget introduced this year is by Dr Manmohan Singh, the politician.

The best thing one can say about the Budget presented this month is that it continues the trend which Dr Manmohan Singh started in his first four Budgets—lower taxes, liberalization and globalization. There is no retracing of the steps, no going back on any of the ideals which made those budgets so epoch-making. The justified criticism is that the Finance Minsiter has not taken any step forward in any of the new directions.

It is total misconception to think that in the state elections the people rejected the new policy of liberalization and globalization. The clear message is that the people were disgusted with the prevailing corruption and the inefficiency of the men in power. They voted for change, and that is why in the states where the Congress party was in power they returned non-Congress candidates, and in the states where a non-Congress party was in power they returned the Congress party.

In the Finance Minister's speech are mentioned the new authorities, schemes and programmes which would have to be paid for out of the public exchequer. As Mr Rajiv Gandhi discovered for himself, when he was the Prime Minister, hardly 18 per cent of the expenditure incurred for the welfare of the poor trickled down to the targeted section of the population.

When I was speaking to an audience of non-resident Indians in Muscat and Dubai two years ago, I found them bluntly asking the question—can we trust the Government of India? If we start an undertaking on the strength of tax holiday proposed in a particular Budget, can we be sure that the basis on which we decide to embark on the venture will continue to be the law of India at the time when the tax holiday begins, say, three years later? The majority of the chartered accountants practising in the Arab countries are non-resident Indians themselves and they have full knowledge of what has been happening in India in the recent past.

Prior to the Finance Act, 1986, the then-existing Section 32A(8) of the Income-tax Act provided that the Central Government might notify the discontinuance of investment allowance in respect of any ship or aircraft acquired or any machinery or plant installed after a specified date 'not being earlier than three years from the date of such notification'. The Finance Act, 1986 shamelessly discontinued investment allowance without the three years' notice which was mandatory under the law, by the simple expedient of omitting the statutory words which required three years' notice. Indians have no option but to submit to such strident injustice. But non-resident Indians and other foreigners who can venture in any part of the world are understandably averse to investing in a country where a sense of honour has become totally anachronistic.

A similar breach of faith was involved in the abolition of relief by the Finance Act, 1990 which dealt with certain provisions of the Income-tax Act. It abolished, without notice, reliefs under Section 33A (development allowance for tea bushes planted in new fields); Section 80HH (establishment of new industrial undertakings or hotels in, or shifting of existing units from cities to, backward areas); and Section 80HHA (establishment of small-scale industrial undertakings in rural areas). Those sections had been in operation for a long time—ranging from thirteen to twenty-five years. The government refused to consider the palpable injustice entailed as regards schemes which had been in the process of implementation and which had been undertaken by trusting taxpayers on the basis of existing law.

The question may be asked—how can any finance minister ensure that such breaches of faith are not committed by his successors? In Mauritius they amended the Constitution and provided that changes in certain policies could not be made without a special majority needed to amend the Constitution.

India need not go to that length. There is a simple expedient to deal with the situation. The government should declare its economic and fiscal policy for the remaining term of its office. It should apologize for the breaches of faith committed in the past and publicly avow that its policy hereafter would be to ensure that those who act on the faith of the existing law would be protected. Such a solemn assurance would give rise to the doctrine of 'promissory estoppel' which, in jurisprudence, means that the government is estopped from going back on its promises. The equity of promissory estoppel can be enforced in the High Courts and in the Supreme Court by any aggrieved citizen or foreigner.

I cannot help thinking that Dr Manmohan Singh is the right person who can start the healthy tradition of giving the type of assurance which would amount to promissory estoppel and which would safeguard those Indians and foreigners who act on the basis of our existing enactments.

THE UNION BUDGET 1996-97

◆

THE ONE PROVISION of the Finance Bill, 1996, which is bound to prove the greatest obstacle in the way of attracting foreign capital, is the proposed Section 115JA (tax on companies which have no taxable income). This article is confined to the Minimum Alternative Tax (MAT) embodied in Section 115JA proposed to be inserted in the Income-tax Act.

An acutely perceptive foreigner remarked the other day that he was amazed at the 'compartmentalized' attitude of the Indian government. He said that he could understand a civil servant in charge of income tax being oblivious of the benefits arising to the state from customs or excise revenues. But surely the finance minister is supposed to take an overall national view and is not to be concerned with only one tax, viz., income tax.

Mr P. Chidambaram is one of the foremost lawyers in India today, and it is surprising that he should be the author of the proposed Section 115JA which is an amended version of the old Section 115J which was patently an intruder in the Income-tax Act. The old Section 115J was wisely abolished by the Union budget, 1990, and it is now sought to be whimsically resuscitated. Has the finance ministry collected the statistics regarding the pending matters under the old Section 115J where the decision has yet to be given by the High Court regarding the validity of that section?

Taxable Company

A company which has no taxable income becomes taxable under the proposed Section 115JA in respect of its book profits. Any scheme of taxing a company which has no taxable income must necessarily involve tax at a rate which wanders in the realm of the infinite. Take two individuals, each with an income of Rs 1 lakh. One of them pays income-tax and spends the balance of his income. The other invests his earnings in tax-free bonds, national savings, public provident fund, etc., and has no taxable income. Do you admire the second or do you denigrate him as a zero-tax individual?

In point of complexity and poor quality of administration, our direct tax laws—with the myriad rules and notifications which are beyond count or care—must surely rank as the very worst fiscal system in the Third World. If tax-payers were dogs, the officials of the finance ministry would undoubtedly be convicted under the Prevention of Cruelty to Animals Act.

G.K. Chesterton, in his brilliant essay, 'The Mad Official', analyses how a society goes mad. The rot begins, he says, when wild actions are received calmly by society. 'These are people that have lost the power of astonishment at their own actions. When they give birth to a fantastic passion or foolish law, they do not start or stare at the monster they have brought forth . . . These nations are really in danger of going off their heads en masse, of becoming one vast vision of imbecility'. India is one such country in respect of budgeting and fiscal laws. After the 1996 budget the monster of our tax structure will become even more monstrous.

Companies Hit

The proposed Section 115JA is, in my opinion, constitutionally illegal, economically unsound and morally repugnant. It violates Article 14 of the Constitution inasmuch as (a) it hits only limited companies and thus discriminates against them as compared to other categories of taxpayers, and (b) it discriminates between companies which have adopted the straight-line method of depreciation in their books and others which have adopted the written-down value basis. It further violates Article 19 of the Constitution because it imposes a burdensome restriction on the company's right to carry on business and account for its profits to its shareholders in its own way—which restriction is neither resonable nor in the public interest.

A company may have carried forward losses for tax purposes, but if in the relevant accounting year it shows a profit in the profit and loss account, it would become liable to tax regardless of past losses which may be large enough to reduce the real taxable income to nil. A company may have adopted the regular method of straight-line depreciation (as it is entitled to do under the Companies Act, 1956) and this method may enable the company to show a profit in the profit and loss account, when in fact there is no taxable income on the written-down value method of depreciation which is obligatory in every case under the Income-tax Act; but without deducting even such normal income-tax depreciation the company would be caught by the proposed Section 115JA.

A company may merely revalue its old land and buildings on the market-value basis and take credit for the excess over cost in its profit and loss account; it would find itself liable to tax on such unrealised excess which is not its income at all. A company may not debit to its profit and loss account the capital expenditure on scientific research and development which is fully deductible for tax purposes under Section 35; it would become assessable to tax and would be virtually deprived of the right to such legitimate deduction. The force of tyranny can go no further.

If we are interested in growth, let us remember that among the companies to be hit by the proposed Section 115JA would be some of the most dynamic enterprises in our corporate sector. They undertake plans of development and expansion which result in capital formation, productive investment, increased employment and larger revenues for the Union and the states by way of customs, excise, sales tax, etc. Economists seldom agree with one another but there is a three-word maxim on which all economists are totally agreed, namely, investment produces employment. Now it is proposed to penalise with a vengeance the so-called 'zero-tax companies'—those very companies which make the maximum investment and contribute most to employment and capital formation, and generate the largest revenues for the government by way of indirect taxes.

As an example, I shall take the actual facts of a well-known manufacturing company. That company did not pay any income-tax for six years. But at the end of that period it was employing 10,000 more persons (the number increased from 30,000 to 40,000) and the aggregate amount of tax paid by it annually by way of excise, customs, sales tax and octroi was Rs 295 crore, against Rs 89 crore at the beginning of the six-year period. Could it possibly be said that the company was not making its fair contribution to the national exchequer?

Tax Burden

The mistake lies in shutting one's eyes to the total tax burden discharged by a company and focussing attention only on income tax. In other countries, such vigorous and high-powered companies are put on the roll of honour as national benefactors. But, in India, our fiscal administrators look with great disfavour upon these fast-growing companies.

There is one other point which is of overriding importance. How can a foreigner have faith in the government of India and proceed to invest in this country when he knows that the entire scheme of computation of income for income tax purposes can be set at nought, without any prior notice, by just one new section, as is sought to be done by the proposed Section 115JA?

As I have said before, the Union Budget should not be a scourge but should take on more of the nature of the presentation of annual accounts of a partnership between the government and the people. In the presentation of such annual accounts, good faith and a sense of honour are essential if the partners are to have confidence in each other.

VII

EDUCATION

EDUCATION FOR INDIA'S MORAL AND SPIRITUAL REGENERATION

◆

REVERED CHANCELLOR SRI Sathya Sai Baba, Vice-Chancellor Prof. Gokak, learned members of the faculty, ladies and gentlemen, and my young friends—

I feel truly happy and honoured to have been accorded the privilege of delivering the convocation address this afternoon. Looking around this sea of humanity, I doubt whether in the history of education in any part of the world any convocation has ever been attended by a gathering so large in number, so diverse in character and so disciplined in behaviour.

This Institute is a tribute to the great organizing genius of its founder, Sri Sathya Sai Baba. Without his initiative and inspiration, it would have been impossible to found an institution of this character. We are witnesses to a great event in the history of our country. This 'deemed' University is a memorable experiment in the moral and spiritual regeneration of India. It stands for nothing less. It is a great experiment and I am sure under providence it will not fail. We propose to maintain here standards of discipline and decorum, of decency and dignity, which unfortunately have left the other universities which are far, far older. The standards of discipline and character-building that are proposed to be maintained here, as the vice-chancellor has indicated in his opening address, are equalled by few and surpassed by none in contemporary educational systems. Many of you must have had a look at the Handbook which has been published by the Institute. I would recommend it for your perusal. It has one basic theme. The purpose of this Institute is not merely to churn out BAs and BComs, MAs and MScs. Many universities churn out graduates and double graduates every year—often twice a year. But the objective of this Institute is to turn out men and women who will play a significant role in the future of this country. And in order to do that, the Institute has been dedicated to the five great ideals which Swamiji has been preaching indefatigably and memorably for so many years—*Satya, Dharma, Shanti, Prem* and *Ahimsa*. These five ideals are the very foundation of this Institute; they are the source of its inspiration; they are the criterion of its success; they are the hope for its future growth and development. It would not be out of place to say a word about each of these five values at the first convocation of this Institute. None of these five words has an exact equivalent word in the English language or in any other European language.

First, *Satya*. You will not find a word in English or French or German which will give you the full equivalent of the concept of *Satya*. *Satya* means the truth, as in the maxim 'There is no religion higher than truth.' But *Satya* also means being true to yourself. It connotes intellectual integrity and acting according to your conscience. These various nuances of the word *Satya* have not been encapsulated in a single English word. In our world today, truth seems to be in the background and it is falsehood which is in the ascendant, and yet you need never despair of truth.

'Truth forever on the scaffold,
Wrong forever on the throne;
Yet that scaffold sways the future,
And behind the dim unknown
Standeth God, beneath the shadow,
Keeping watch above His own.'

Take the next concept to which this Institute is dedicated—the concept of *Dharma*. No single word in any European language covers all the elements of *Dharma*. *Dharma* connotes righteousness, nobility, right conduct, a philosophy of life which makes you a worthy citizen of the world. When students of this Institute have understood the ideal of *Dharma*, they will practise what I would call 'obedience to the unenforceable'. We all keep on the right side of the Indian Penal Code because it is enforceable. You will not commit theft because otherwise you can be convicted and imprisoned. But there are norms of nobility and righteousness which are wholly unenforceable by law but which *Dharma* alone enjoins you to observe—this is what I call 'obedience to the unenforceable'. It is *Dharma* which makes a man go into private business and shun the unacceptable face of capitalism which the whole world condemns today. But there is also the acceptable face of capitalism which is illumined by *Dharma*. The man who practises *Dharma* will not be cynical, because he knows that cynicism corrupts and absolute cynicism corrupts absolutely. He will not engage in single-minded pursuit of money because he knows that such pursuit impoverishes the mind, shrivels the imagination and dessicates the heart. He will engage in a commercial activity but without a commercialized outlook. I am confident that the alumni of this Institute will cultivate their minds not merely with a view to offering them as a commodity for sale in the marketplace, but with a view to fulfilling their high destiny as men. If, after passing the portals of this Institute, they go into business or take employment with a commercial enterprise, they will contribute not only to the Gross National Product but also to the gross national happiness. They will go into business to do well, but stay in business to do good. This is the great ideal of a truly liberal education. Historians have been amazed at the fact that India for centuries survived without a central government or any strong authority engaged in enforcing laws. What held the nation together was the ideal of *Dharma*. It is perhaps the greatest, noblest ideal to which human conduct can aspire.

Take next the concept of *Shanti*. *Shanti* is not merely peace. It is something which transcends peace. It is the calm of the mind, serenity of the mind, which makes you find inner peace and total stability within yourself. *Shanti* plays a great role in any integrated personality's life and conduct.

> 'We see all sights from Pole to Pole
> And glance and nod and bustle by,
> And never once possess our soul
> Before we die.'

Those who practise *Shanti* have learnt how to possess their soul before the last hour arrives.

A word about *Prem* of which Sri Sathya Sai Baba has spoken so eloquently in so many places. *Prem* connotes not merely love;

the word has within it also the elements of compassion and understanding. Love is the greatest force in the world—there has never been and never will be a substitute for it. You will find it among the poor, even more than among the rich. The poor need love—it is the strongest nourishing factor in their life.

'In palaces are hearts that ask
In discontent and pride,
Why life is such a dreary task
And all good things denied.
And hearts in humblest huts admire
How love has in their aid,
Love that not ever seems to tire,
Such rich provision made.'

It is love which holds the entire human race together. If the ancient Indian ideal of the entire human race being a single family is ever implemented, it will be only when love becomes universally accepted as the inviolable principle of human behaviour.

Take the last ideal—*Ahimsa.* Again there is no single English word which can be used as its equivalent. In 1979, the world celebrated the centenary of Dr Einstein's birth and volumes were published dealing with the life and achievements of Dr Einstein—perhaps the greatest intellect of this century. One of the writers, Dr Oppenheimer, a great scientist in his own right, said that Dr Einstein was a total believer in *Ahimsa,* and he said he was using the word *Ahimsa* because there is no English equivalent. *Ahimsa* is not merely non-violence; there is far more to *Ahimsa* than that. When you practise *Ahimsa,* you identify yourself with the entire created universe. It is a feeling of kinship, of oneness, with all animate creatures. *Ahimsa* enjoins you to love your fellowmen, as well as animals and birds.

When the students of this Institute—which I feel confident, will be great and glorious as the years go by—have learnt these five great ideals which form the quintessence of Swamiji's teachings, they would be qualified to acquire what the ancients called *buddhi.* Again, there is no equivalent for the word *buddhi* in the European languages. Dr Raynor Johnson, the very eminent Australian scientist, has written a fascinating book called *The Imprisoned Splendour.* He uses there the word *buddhi* and says there is no equivalent in the English language for it. *Buddhi* is that state of mind which makes you not merely wise but gives you an insight into the created universe. A man of *buddhi* is in harmony with his environment and in tune with the infinite. The five ideals can lead a man to attain the state of *buddhi.* I think Swamiji was very far-sighted in concentrating on education for the regeneration of this country. There is no alternative to profound education of the type which this Institute has been founded to impart. This is not merely a university—there are scores of universities but they do not build the nation. This Institute aims at becoming a nation-builder. To build a nation you have to start with youth. The child is father of the man. It is what you learn when you are young that colours your entire life. Whether you will grow up to be a noble citizen or a traitor depends on what you learn when you are young.

> 'In ancient shadows and twilights
> Where childhood had strayed,
> The world's great sorrows were born
> And its heroes were made.
> In the lost boyhood of Judas
> Christ was betrayed.'

Christ was betrayed in the lost boyhood of Judas—what a profound thought!

The quality of the education of the children of today will determine the quality of life in India tomorrow.

An Institute like this is not an academic cafeteria offering junk food for the mind. It aims at shaping and moulding your character. It not only wants to sharpen your skills—it wants to heighten your awareness, to clarify your vision, to purify your heart. This is education in its deepest sense.

Today, the economic recession all over the world is, no doubt, disquieting, but infinitely worse is the moral and spiritual recession. The roots of disarray are in our minds and not in the price of fruits and onions. More than ever you need an elitist Institute like this. I would call it elitist, because it aims at generating excellence. The boys and girls who are privileged to be educated in this Institute cannot do everything. But they must excel in everything they do. This Institute aims at turning out men and women who would leave their mark on public life.

The eighteenth-century French writer, Montesquieu, said that when a new society comes to birth, it is the leaders who produce the institutions; later, it is the institutions which produce the leaders. Today the moral and spiritual leader, Sri Sathya Sai Baba, has produced this Institution. His objective is that one day this Institution will produce leaders who will be able to lead this great nation to the fulfilment of its glorious destiny.

Swamiji has rightly emphasized that nothing is more important than the shaping and moulding of the character of youth. A memorial to George Eliot was unveiled in Westminster Abbey in June 1980, and her own words have been inscribed on the memorial—'The first condition of human goodness is something to love; the second something to reverence.' The objective of this Institute is not merely to teach you Arts and Science and Commerce, but to teach you how to have something to love and something to reverence.

H.G. Wells once said, in a moment of almost despair, that human history is becoming more and more a race between education and catastrophe. That is a pregnant thought. You cannot avoid a catastrophe without education. The same thought was voiced by Thomas Jefferson, one of the founders of the United States of America, who remarked, 'If a nation expects to be ignorant and free, it expects what never was and never will be.' You cannot retain your freedom as a republic unless you are educated and you know how to cast your vote on the right lines.

The concept of education to which this Institute is dedicated is wholly different from training. This is not a training institute. Animals can be trained; only human beings can be educated. In order to acquire education what is needed on the part of students is personal participation and transformation. Education cannot be given to anyone; it must be inwardly appropriated. When Pandit Jawaharlal Nehru became the prime minister of India, he wrote a letter of gratitude to his old professor, Prof. Harold Laski of the London School of Economics, saying that he had now come to occupy the high position because of what the professor had taught him. Harold Laski wrote back to say, 'I did not teach you anything, you learnt.' This Institute gives you a golden opportunity to learn. It aims at turning out not mere graduates but integrated personalities. I have no doubt that in the years to come when the worth of this Institute comes to be widely known and accepted, there would be a great demand for the boys and girls who come out of the portals of this University after an intensive, broad-based programme of five years' study; and they are bound to be offered employment by people who are less qualified than themselves. Andrew Carnegie, the famous multi-millionaire of the United States, wrote his own epitaph which is inscribed on his tombstone—'Here lies a man who knew how to enlist in his service better men than himself.' My hope is that the young graduates who have taken their degrees today will prove to be better men and women than their future employers.

I should like to congratulate the promoters of this Institute upon two things. First, they have insisted upon the medium of English for all courses of study. English is our window to the outside world. If you know English, you have every field of knowledge available to you. The whole world is learning English today. The Russians, the Chinese, the Japanese are feverishly learning that language. A generation ago, in India the English language was spoken and written by the well-educated as ably as anywhere else on earth. In India today knowledge of the greatest modern language is unfortunately on the decline. This Institute will reverse the trend and will assure its alumni of the capability to converse with their countrymen from any state of India and with foreigners from other parts of the world.

Secondly, the promoters have been very wise in selecting this beautiful rural setting for housing this Institute. It was Swamiji's great vision which led him to get away from the impure cities and found this Institute in the unspoilt countryside. Cities are all right if you can accept the impossible, do without the indispensable and tolerate the unbearable. But here you have surroundings where you are close to nature.

'One impulse from a vernal wood
May teach you more of man,
Of moral evil and of good
Than all the sages can.'

All the impulses from the vernal wood are available to you here, if only you are receptive.

In closing, I would say to my young friends—may you uphold the ideal of public good, a great ideal to which every citizen's life ought to be dedicated. There are a number of disciplines taught here, and the interaction between the different disciplines is all important. You will never be a first-rate Commerce graduate unless you know literature also. You will never be a first-rate Law graduate unless you know history and literature. A vast horizon, a wide range of knowledge, is very necessary to make you a good specialist in your own line.

If we are asked what the three-and-a-half decades of self-government have taught us, we must admit ruefully in the words of T.S. Eliot, 'We had the experience, but missed the meaning.'

The man who did not miss the meaning and implications of freedom was C. Rajagopalachari who clearly foresaw what freedom without education would bring in its wake. While in jail for civil disobedience he made the following entry in his prison diary on 24 January 1922:

> 'Elections and their corruptions, injustice and the power and tyranny of wealth, and inefficiency of administration, will make a hell of life as soon as freedom is given to us. Men will look regretfully back to the old regime of comparative justice, and efficient, peaceful, more or less honest administration.
>
> 'The only thing gained will be that as a race we will be saved from dishonour and subordination.
>
> 'Hope lies only in universal education by which right conduct, fear of God and love will be developed among the citizens from childhood.
>
> 'It is only if we succeed in this that *Swaraj* will mean happiness. Otherwise it will mean the grinding injustices and tyranny of wealth. What a beautiful world it would be, if everybody were just and God-fearing and realized the happiness of loving others. Yet there is more practical hope for the ultimate consummation of this ideal in India than elsewhere.'

Sri Sathya Sai Baba's vision aims at doing precisely what Rajaji contemplated—education by which right conduct, fear of God, and love would be developed among the citizens from childhood. Rajaji's faith in India is conveyed by his belief that there is more practical hope for the ultimate consummation of the ideal of Dharma in India than elsewhere. And Swamiji shares that faith.

I shall end with one prayer. May this Institute, by the grace of God and the blessings of Swamiji, replenish our faith in the future of this great country. And may it educate and elevate, motivate and stimulate, generations of youth in the unfolding future.

THE TREASON OF THE INTELLECTUAL

◆

MY TRIBUTE TO your university which has honoured itself by conferring the degree of Doctor of Laws on Mr K. Subba Rao, the former Chief Justice of India, and one of the great judges of our time. Dr Subba Rao combines an amazing grasp of the basic principles of law with outstanding judicial independence. In the years ahead, as the erosion of our basic rights proceeds apace, there will be an ever-widening understanding and appreciation of Dr Subba Rao's vision of our magnificent Constitution as originally drafted. His decisions form a memorable chapter in the history of not only our constitutional law but also of our tax laws and various other branches of jurisprudence.

I extend my hearty congratulations and good wishes to those who have carried away the prizes. My sincere wish is—may God grant them the fulfilment, in their maturer years, of the promise of their college days. I know how much industry, patience and stern discipline, and how many hours of self-denying toil, are represented by the young men and women who have distinguished themselves at the examinations.

To the others who have also taken their degrees at this convocation, I wish a bright future and fulfilling life-work.

As regards those who have not been as successful in their examinations as they thought they deserved to be, I can only recall the words of Professor Walter Raleigh that the College Final and the Day of Judgement are two different examinations. They may also take some consolation from the fact that A.E. Housman, the great scholar of Greek and Latin, and better known as a poet, once failed in the papers on those very languages at the Oxford University. His biographer Richards comments, 'The nightingale got no prize at the poultry show.'

Before I start speaking to my fellow students—I call you fellow students because, I hope, I have not stopped learning—I would like to pay my tribute to the teachers and professors here and at the other universities of our country who trim the silver lamp of knowledge and keep its sacred flame bright from generation to generation. They expend their lives on significant but unadvertised work. Quite a few of them plough the lonely furrow of scholarship. Their dedication bears witness to the selflessness of the human spirit.

In ancient India, kings and emperors thought it a privilege to sit at the feet of a man of learning. Intellectuals and men of knowledge were given the highest honour in society. King Janaka, himself a philosopher, journeyed on foot into the jungle to discourse with Yajnavalkya on high matters of state. In the eighth century Sankaracharya travelled on foot from Kerala to Kashmir and from Dwarka in the west to Puri in the east. He could not have changed men's minds and established centres of learning in the far-flung corners of India but for the great esteem and reverence which intellectuals enjoyed.

Unfortunately, in our own times we have downgraded the intellectual and have devalued the very word. Today an intellectual' means a man who is intelligent enough to know on which side his bread is buttered.

I would like to say a few words to the graduates who are about to face the struggle of life. It has been said that there are two kinds of fools in the world—those who give advice and those who do not take it. I propose to belong to the first category, in the hope that you will not belong to the second.

Education has been called the technique of transmitting civilization. In order that it may transmit civilization, it has to perform two major functions: it must enlighten the understanding, and it must enrich the character.

The two marks of a truly educated man, whose understanding has been enlightened, are the capacity to think clearly and intellectual curiosity.

In the eighteenth century, Dean Swift said that the majority of men were as fit for flying as for thinking. Technology has made it possible for men to fly, or at least to sit in a contraption that flies, but it has not made it possible for men to think. If your education has made it possible for you to think for yourself on the problems which face you and which face the country, your college has done very well by you. If this habit of thinking for yourself has not yet been inculcated in you, you would be well-advised to acquire it after you leave college. As the cynic remarked, a formal education at a university cannot do you much harm provided you start learning thereafter. The capacity to think clearly should enable the student to sift, and reject when necessary, the ideas and ideologies which are perpetually inflicted on him by the mass media of communication. It should enable him to realize that these mass media are in chains—in chains to the foolish and narrowing purposes of selling consumer goods, and to the narrowing and stifling purposes of politics. A liberal education is a prophylactic against unthinking acceptance of the modern 'mantras' which are kept in current circulation by the mass media.

If you have imbibed the ability to think clearly, you will adopt an attitude of reserve towards ideologies that are popular and be critical of nostrums that are fashionable. It is true that in a democracy the majority view should prevail. But never make the mistake of thinking that the validity of a proposition or the correctness of a doctrine depends on the number of people who believe in it. As you grow older, the truth will come home to you that in the fields of politics and economics, the soundness of an ideology is often in inverse proportion to the popular support it commands.

As Alfred Marshall said, 'Students of social science must fear popular approval; evil is with them, when all men speak well of them. It is almost impossible for a student to be a true patriot and have the reputation of being one at the same time.'

Intellectual curiosity would enable the student to continue, nay, to intensify, the process of learning after he has come out of the comfortable cocoon of the university and is thrown into the maelstrom of life. Over the centuries, mankind has built up a treasure-house of art and knowledge—of thoughts that wander through eternity, and of art which is the wide world's memory of things. The pursuit of knowledge and the exploration of the priceless cultural heritage of India and other countries, are too vast for the longest life. After all, any human life, long or short, is just a brief candle—

'Life is but a wintry day;
Some come to breakfast and away;
Others to dinner stay
And are full fed;
The oldest man but sups
And goes to bed.'

A well-furnished mind is as rare as a well-lived life. I hope you will not commit the error, as you go through life, of merely doing your chores day after day. Feel the inner joy of the mind questing for knowledge. Reserve a few minutes for great literature. I would recommend to you the habit of reading at least a few pages of an immortal classic every morning before going down into the battle and the choking dust of the day. It is amazing how great books of yore replenish life and make it fuller and richer. In the beautiful words of T.S. Eliot, which are inscribed on his tomb in Westminster Abbey, 'The communication of the dead is tongued with a fire beyond the language of the living.'

Inevitably, the young men and women who are about to face the world will find disappointment and disillusionment in store for them. They will be inclined to agree with the witty sceptic who suggested that the vast astronomical distances may be God's quarantine precautions: they prevent the infection of a fallen species from spreading.

Let me now come to the second function of education—enriching the character. What we need today more than anything else is moral leadership—founded on courage, intellectual integrity and a sense of values.

As Sir James Barrie said in his address to a famous Scottish university, 'Courage goes all the way.' We are surrounded by too many persons who are willing to compromise and temporize. We have in our midst far too many 'boneless wonders'. With such men, expediency is all. A man who has the courage never to submit or yield is like a rock in the wilderness of shifting sands.

In India today there are shortages of many commodities, but nothing is so scarce as intellectual integrity. Closer contact with the world will convince you that intellectual integrity is a much rarer quality than financial integrity. The treason of the intellectual consists in his not speaking out loud and clear for the values that he, by his vision and the very nature of his personality, holds sacred. What is needed is the resolute courage to stand up and be counted in support of a view which is not popular. Everyone finds it easy to swim with the tide. The great scientist G.H. Hardy said, 'It is never worth a first-class man's time to express a majority opinion. By definition, there are plenty of others to do that.'

There is no replacement for a sense of values. As Einstein observed, 'It is essential that the student acquire an understanding of and a lively feeling for values. He must acquire a vivid sense of the beautiful and of the morally good. Otherwise he—with his specialized knowledge—more closely resembles a well-trained dog than a harmoniously developed person.' These are pregnant words. They do not exaggerate the importance of a sense of values in your future life.

A nation cannot live by the Gross National Product alone. The quantity of life is far more important. In a free democracy like ours the quality of life is to a large extent determined by the availability of the basic human rights and civil liberties, which are placed in the chapter on Fundamental Rights in our Constitution. I have no doubt that as the years go by, you will become more and more conscious of how far-sighted our Constitution-makers were in guaranteeing these fundamental rights to our people, because without them the quality of life would be gravely impaired. We are quite right in making constant endeavours to raise the standard of living of our people. But the standard of life is even more significant than the standard of living. If we lose our sensitivity towards the quality of life, it can only mean that while our knowledge increases, our ignorance does not diminish.

A sense of values will enable you to find happiness within yourself and joy in the most ordinary of things which we often pass by unseeing. As Robert Louis Stevenson said in 'The Celestial Surgeon'—

'If beams from happy human eyes
Have moved me not; if morning skies,
Books, and my food, and summer rain
Knocked on my sullen heart in vain—
Lord, Thy most pointed pleasure take
And stab my spirit broad awake.'

To those of you who are familiar with the immortal heritage of India, the importance of a sense of values will need no elaboration. R.W. Emerson, who knew the literature of a dozen countries, observed that the writings of ancient India, including the *Upanishads* from which some extracts have been read out to you by the vice-chancellor, represent the summit of human thought. The knowledge of our old sages was intuitive. The other type of knowledge which is acquired from teachers and from books is repetitive, imitative, derivative.

After decades of intensive research, science has come to certain conclusions which the intuitive seers of India had already perceived 4,000 years ago. For example, the ancient *rishis* had taught the basic truth that a Spirit or Immanent Principle, supreme and unchanging, pervades the entire universe, and the material world—being merely a manifestation of that Spirit—can never be explained merely in material terms; that all matter is nothing but energy; that inorganic matter is anything but inert and there are inexplicable points of contact between the living and the non-living; and that there is a unity underlying the entire creation. Recent scientific advances illuminate this verity. Likewise, what our old sages said about Brahman or the Ultimate Reality seems to coincide with what our greatest scientists of today think regarding the baffling nature of matter. In the words of Sir James Jeans, the stream of modern knowledge is heading towards a non-mechanical reality. If you have in parallel columns some quotations from our ancient classics and from the findings of modern science, you will be amazed at their correspondence. The farther science advances, the closer it comes to *Vedanta*. Such is our marvellous heritage, and yet we turn so seldom to it, being absorbed in passing trivialities. *[See pp. 22-29]*

Galbraith has remarked upon the contrast between the character and outlook of the poor in India and the poor in other countries. Talking of the inner strength of the Indian masses, he observed that there is a 'richness in their poverty'. The inner strength of our people which enables them to be dignified and to hold their heads high despite their adversity is the result of our age-old tradition of spiritual values. Today, there is a definite risk of our losing that richness, while failing, at the same time, to shed poverty.

There are periods in world history which are characterized by a loss of the sense of values, and the times we live in are pre-eminently such an age. All our troubles may be summed up in three lines (if I may quote T.S. Eliot again)—

> 'Where is the Life we have lost in living?
> Where is the wisdom we have lost in knowledge?
> Where is the knowledge we have lost in information?'

At various recent convocations, students have been known to say bluntly that they want jobs and not degrees. I understand your problem and sympathize with your predicament. But do not forget that problems of poverty and unemployment cannot be solved either by aspirations or by slogans. They are never solved by purblind ideology or by opaque ignorance masquerading as progressive politics. They can be solved—and other nations have solved them—by realistic and pragmatic economic policies which can harness the immeasurable reservoir of the people's faith and response, energy and enterprise.

My gratitude to your university for having enabled me to be with you this afternoon and to dream once more that I am young.

FEMALE EDUCATION—THE PRIORITY OF PRIORITIES

◆

BARBARA WOOTTON, ONE of the great champions of higher education for women, died four years ago at the age of ninety-one. She has written a fascinating autobiography entitled, *In A World I Never Made.* She observed, 'The laughable idealism of one generation evolves into the accepted commonplace of the next.' She lived to see the truth of her dictum proved right time and again, particularly in the field of female education.

Today, some of our most distinguished High Court judges are women like Mrs Sujata Manohar; but no lady was appointed a judge of the High Court before the middle of this century. Till the last century it was assumed that women were unfit to get degrees. London was the first British University to overcome the prejudice against the fair sex. It threw its degrees open to women in 1878. The Bombay University conferred the Bachelor of Arts Degree (First Class) on the first woman student, Miss Cornelia Sorabji, in 1888. The first woman member to be nominated to the Bombay University Senate was in 1891. Oxford and Cambridge took a much longer time to get over their male chauvinism. These facts will give you an idea of the magnitude of Maharshi Karve's achievement, who founded this Women's University in 1916.

Education has been happily defined as the technique of transmitting civilization. It is shocking that the country with the oldest and greatest civilization should be so lackadaisical about the technique of transmitting it.

The Indian psyche remains today wholly untouched by any

thought of the need for wider and more value-based education. Education has never been a high-priority item in any Indian political party's manifesto. The subject which should have galvanized the nation into action forty years ago is still kept in cold storage. Without the guidance which can be derived only from liberal education, a whole generation has grown up which is content to see crime and violence, casteism and communal frenzy, become the order of the day. More criminals have openly entered public life than ever before. No democracy can last long in such circumstances.

It is now acknowledged all over the world that value-based education is the only instrument for transmuting national talent into national progress. Amongst the important countries of the East, India is the least adequately educated. Article 45 of our Constitution enacts:

> 'The State shall endeavour to provide, within a period of ten years from the commencement of this Constitution, for free and compulsory education for all children until they complete the age of fourteen years.'

Elementary education is 'free' in theory; but many one-room schools in rural areas are today without even a blackboard and chalk. 'Compulsory' it is not, even in theory. Men in public life have always looked upon Article 45 as a pious platitude which is not calculated to give any mileage either to the politician or to his political party.

It is only through female education at all levels and the private initiative of well-educated women, that this country will ever be transformed into what our Constitution intended it to be. We have only to look around to see the difference between our apathy and the zeal and dedication of other nations in the field of nation-building.

The rate of literacy in South Korea is 98 per cent. Its economic development is the predictable result of its uncompromising emphasis on education.

When Lee Kuan Yew was recently asked on the BBC as to what he attributed the phenomenal success of Singapore, his answer was in one word—'Education'. He added that no subject had a higher priority in his city-state.

President Mitterrand started his second term of office in 1988 with the promise to make education the 'priority of priorities'. His election manifesto proclaimed, 'In future the nation's power will depend less on its financial wealth than on its grey matter.' He was as good as his word. In France, after the prime minister ranks not the foreign minister, not the finance minister, not the home or the defence minister, but the minister of education.

In February 1991, the British Prime Minister, Mr John Major, in a major speech put education at the top of his personal agenda for the 1990s, and said that education is the key to a 'mobile, dynamic and diverse society'.

In 1983, the National Commission for Excellence in Education, appointed by the United States government, published a report called 'A Nation At Risk'. The report exhorted the government to take prompt and firm measures to raise the level of education, if the future of that country was not to be imperilled. If the United States can be called 'A nation at risk', would it be any exaggeration to call India 'A nation in dire peril'? [*See p. 287*]

A survey was conducted in January 1988 by the American Council on Education. Students were asked about their objective in pursuing higher education. An overwhelming majority of the students said that their objective was to make more money in later years. The motive 'To develop a meaningful philosophy of life' ranked the lowest. The same malaise affects Indian students. No wonder that ancient Indian culture is the subject least often chosen by our youth.

In April 1991, President Bush called for 'a revolution in American education'. He announced a plan for national achievement tests. The President said that he would like to see the creation of non-traditional schools, some of which might be operated by private organizations or businesses.

Right-wingers value education partly because it promises to make labour markets more efficient; left-wingers partly because it gives a respectable role for state activism. Economists on both side of the political divide are agreed that human capital is the most precious form of capital there is.

I hope and trust your university does not have reservations on communal or caste considerations and that, unlike some other colleges, it does not give grace marks in order to enable students to pass where the mark scored on merit is zero. 'Firsts' should not be allowed to multiply; otherwise it would be like inflation—you start destroying the value of the currency.

At the last official count, the number of Indian universities was 181—twice the number that existed twenty years ago. While the number of our universities and the number of our students proliferate, the level of edification does not keep pace. Our education continues to be 'value-agnostic' and 'value-neutral'. Dr Mortimer Adler, the chairman of the Board of Directors of the *Encyclopaedia Britannica,* said that true education can begin only after you have left school or college. All that a school or college can do is to arouse intellectual curiosity and prepare you for lifelong education later.

Education is an end in itself; and not merely a means to an end like financial well-being. There should be no profit motive in liberal education, any more than in friendship. Then alone can knowledge ripen into wisdom.

The timeless lesson of ancient Indian culture is that man is more than man, and there is more to the world than the world. Every age must take a step forward in evolution; but unfortunately India has been taking several steps backwards.

May I end with my best wishes to those who are passing out of the portals of this very fine university. They have been privileged to have been educated well, and they, in their turn, should resolve to return to the people a part of the benefits they have derived.

EDUCATION AND THE ART OF READING

◆

THIS IS THE year of the birth centenary of Ganesh Ramrao Bhatkal. I am personally delighted that celebrations in honour of his Birth Centenary have been undertaken by the G.R. Bhatkal Foundation.

It is a matter of deep personal satisfaction to me that I have the opportunity of making a public acknowledgment of my indebtedness to Bhatkal, to whom I owe a debt of gratitude which I could never repay.

Bhatkal was the proprietor of the Popular Book Depot which he founded in 1924. It soon became the leading book-stall in Bombay. In those days, the Popular Book Depot was situated at Lamington Road which was very close to my residence at Sleater Road.

Bhatkal helped me in three inestimable ways.

He allowed me to treat the Popular Book Depot as if it was a public library. During my career as an Arts student—1936-1942—I remember going to his bookshop almost every evening. I read whatever I wanted and as long as I wanted, browsing among the thousands of books which lined the shelves.

Bhatkal was kind enough to let me take books on approval which I read at home and carefully returned.

I remember many days when I kept on reading in the bookshop even after the front door was closed, and coming out some time later by the back door which was kept unlocked for a while after the main door had been closed.

Not once did Bhatkal tell me that I was taking undue advantage of his generosity and his desire to help. If he were alive today, I would have an irresistible impulse to touch his feet.

It was in those years that I read the lines of Wordsworth which have always been etched in my memory:

'. . . that best portion of a good man's life,
His little, nameless, unremembered acts
Of kindness and of love'.

Bhatkal was a man to whom those lines applied with singular appropriateness. Whatever I am today is, in a large measure, due to Bhatkal's infinite kindness, goodness, and desire to help a struggling young student.

I thought it would be appropriate if I spoke to you today on—Education and the Art of Reading.

I am using the word 'Education' in its profound sense. As I have said before, animals can be trained; but only human beings can be educated. Education requires personal participation and transformation. It cannot be given to anyone; it must be inwardly appropriated.

Some decades ago, in the State of Genoa, the currency in circulation had the following inscription:

'Time is precious; work and save;
Idleness is robbery'.

Today, when I see young boys and girls talking aimlessly in restaurants, I ask myself whether they ever read those beautiful lines which, to the best of my recollection, ran as follows:

'Lost yesterday, somewhere between sunrise and sunset,
Two golden hours, each set with sixty diamond minutes.
No reward is offered; because they are gone forever'.

Today, the students are claiming the liberty to do things which did not happen even once during my entire eight years at different colleges. I remember the morning when I went to deliver a lecture at my own *alma mater,* St. Xavier's College, Bombay. The lecture was to be held in the spacious College Hall. I was told by the then Principal of the College that it would be better if I could close at 11.30 a.m., because at that hour the students would like to have the Hall for their jam session. The jam session was the function which the boys and girls held in the College Hall with all the windows closed. Since that day, I have not acceded to any invitation to speak at that college again.

Culture is what remains after you have forgotten all that you set out to learn. The aim of character-based higher education must be to leave you with a residuum called culture which would teach you a meaningful philosophy of life and enrich your character.

As Dr S. Radhakrishnan, the greatest President India has ever known, said, civilization is an act of the spirit. No one who is familiar with India's priceless heritage would have any doubt on this score.

Mechanical progress is not to be confused with civilization. Ancient India was far more civilized than modern India with its satellites in space.

Our obsession with freedom, openness and equality has produced a generation of Indians bereft of their own civilization and ignorant of their own culture. Today, education has spawned cultural illiterates and moral idiots. Schools and universities have been swamped with intellectual laziness bred from the modern doctrine that everything is relative and all values are equal.

Liberal education and knowledge of the Classics, which were the hallmarks of higher education when I was at college, have almost disappeared. The same phenomenon has marked higher education in other countries also.

Professor George Stiegler was one of the most eminent educationists of our times. His special subject was Economics in which he got the Nobel Prize. He thought highly of the ability of modern students but he also realized their shortcomings. Shall I say that his view of the typical modern boy and girl was not exactly idealized. Once, referring to the classic vision of the student and the teacher in perpetual dialogue sitting on opposite seats on a log, he noted that 'It was found more useful to sit on the student and talk to the log'.

Even in the USA where more Indian students go for higher education than to any other country, the professors have remarked on the reluctance of young minds to go in for a liberal education which is not aimed at equipping you for a financially lucrative career. Professor Allan Bloom has written a masterpiece on this topic. No one was more surprised than Professor Allan Bloom when his book *The Closing of the American Mind* shot to the top of the bestseller list in 1987. The subtitle of the book 'How Higher Education Has Failed Democracy and Impoverished the Souls of Today's Students' gives you an idea of what the book dealt with. Originally, the book had trouble in finding a publisher. Luckily, the publishers, Simon and Schuster, who are the American counterparts of Ganesh Ramrao Bhatkal, decided to take a chance. The book has sold more than one million copies. Professor Allan Bloom unfortunately died in October 1992, but not before he had the satisfaction of seeing his book hit with the approximate force and effect of electric shock therapy.

The fatal flaw in Indian democracy has been that we are so wedded to equality that we have reduced this great country to a level where the same degree of equality prevails as in the graveyard. We would rather have uniformity and mediocrity, than meritocracy. It is my unshakable conviction that if Emperor Ashoka or Emperor Akbar were to stand for the office of President, he would have no chance of being elected. Adult franchise in a country without great leadership is virtually an unfailing prescription for backwardness. The only hope for Indian democracy having a rebirth is to produce a strong man of exceptional calibre who can give the right leadership to the people instead of being led by the people. We must bury fifty fathoms deep the notion that decisions must be taken by seeking a consensus.

Technically, we have over fifty per cent literacy (52.1 per cent to be exact). In fact, as we all know, even this disgraceful figure is fudged because anyone who can scrawl his name legibly on a piece of paper is considered literate in our benighted country. According to the statistics published in a knowledgeable journal, only seven countries are more illiterate than us—Pakistan, Bangladesh, Afghanistan, Bhutan, Nepal, Cambodia and Egypt.

I am a great champion of universal education. I have no doubt that every child should be given a chance of developing himself and doing the best he can for his country and himself. But at the same time I do believe that the cleverest and brainiest stratum of the children, who are diligent and endowed with exceptional talent, should be taken special care of and given the environment in which their outstanding ability and character can come to full fruition. The state should spare no money in giving the best possible education to boys and girls who have the capacity to become leaders in their fields.

I know a number of Indians who have settled abroad, not because they can make more money. (In fact, it is easier these days to make a large fortune in India than in foreign countries.) But they have settled abroad because they think that there is no recognition of talent in India.

I now come to the other topic of my talk—The Art of Reading.

I do *not* propose to deal with the art of reading speedily. Mrs Evelyn Wood, who died just four weeks ago, was a great expert in the field of rapid reading and taught millions how to read speedily. The average reader has a reading rate of 250 to 300 words per minute. In years of research Mrs Wood found people from all walks of life who could read from 1500 to 6000 words a minute, and sometimes more. Mrs Wood who could herself read 2700 words a minute discovered that the technique of rapid reading involved the following:

> 'You read down the page rather than left to right; you read groups of words or complete thoughts rather than one word at a time. You avoid involuntary re-reading of material.'

However, I shall say no more about this technique which I think is more useful when reading newspapers which you throw into the dustbin the next day, rather than books which are meant to be your lifetime companions. If you want to read and absorb an immortal thought, e.g.,

> 'You will never enjoy the world aright till the sea itself floweth in your veins, till you are clothed with the heavens and crowned with the stars',

you cannot possibly resort to the technique of speedy reading.

It was said of Leonardo da Vinci, who flourished five centuries ago, that he had mastered all existing knowledge. At the present rate of scientific and technological development when human knowledge doubles itself every nine years, it is impossible for any person to master even one millionth of one per cent of existing knowledge. Naturally, you have to be selective in your reading. More books have been published in the last twenty years than in the preceding five hundred years during which the technique of printing has been in existence. Against knowledge, you may have, as the cynic observed of a certain lady's past, only one serious objection—there is so much of it.

Sir Arthur Quiller-Couch, one of the most distinguished professors at Cambridge, wrote *On The Art of Reading*. The book was published in 1920 and was reprinted several times. I bought from the Popular Book Depot the edition reprinted in 1939, and still have the copy.

Sir Arthur Quiller-Couch summed up the art of reading for examinations in the following three propositions.

First, having regard to the shortness of human life and the mass of printed matter already loaded and still being shot upon this planet, the student must make a selection. There is no other way.

Secondly, you must select the books that are best for you and take them *absolutely,* not frittering your time upon books written about and around the best. The best books come first, and you may have no time left for the secondary second.

Thirdly, if your subject is imaginative literature, you have to absorb and assimilate into your own personality what you read. To the students studying *Hamlet,* Sir Arthur Quiller-Couch's advice is as follows:

> 'To be Hamlet—to feel yourself Hamlet—is more important than killing a king or even knowing all there is to be known about a text. Now most of us have been Hamlet, more or less: while few of us, I trust, have ever murdered a monarch: and still fewer, perhaps, can hope to know all that is to be known of the text of the play. But for value, gentlemen, let us not rank these three achievements by order of their rarity. Shakespeare means us to feel—to *be*—Hamlet. That is all, and from the play it is the best we can get.'

For general reading, the most perceptive comment was that of G.M. Trevelyan, the great grand-nephew of Lord Macaulay, who said, 'Education has produced a vast population able to read but unable to distinguish what is worth reading'.

There is—and there can be—no such thing as the Hundred Best Books. There is in fact no positive hierarchy among the Classics.

I may conclude by relating one small incident.

A certain distinguished astronomer once declared at a scientific meeting:

> 'To an astronomer, man is nothing more than an insignificant dot in the infinite universe'.

Einstein, who was present at the meeting, is reported to have observed:

> 'I have often felt that, but then I realize that the insignificant dot, who is man, is also the astronomer'.

For a nation nothing is more rewarding than education in human values; and, likewise, for an individual nothing is more satisfying than general reading in human values.

VIII

PERSONALITIES

ADI SANKARACHARYA: BUILDER OF THE EMPIRE OF THE SPIRIT

◆

MOST HISTORIANS ARE agreed that if a count were taken of the twelve greatest men who ever lived in any country in any age, Adi Sankaracharya would be one of them. I would call him the Universal Man. He deserves to be called the Universal Man in more senses than one.

He was a poet of the first order and also a philosopher *par excellence.* He was a savant and a saint, a mystic and a religious reformer. He was a *karma yogi, bhakti yogi* and *jnana yogi,* and was in the forefront of each category.

As a man of action he achieved as much as persons who have attained world renown only as 'doers'. He did not propound a religion but propounded *the* religion which underlies all religions. He was a man of infinite faith and infinite compassion. Nothing human was alien to his nature. His knowledge was truly profound. He went to the heart of the *Upanishads,* the Vedas, and the *Bhagavad Gita* and could expound these scriptures in a manner which has been rarely equalled.

What was his aim in having *mutts* in different corners of India? One of his main ideas was that this is one single country. We may have different faiths, different sects, different creeds. Different communities may flourish here, and they have flourished through the centuries, but we are all members of one single family. And his objective in going round the country was to ensure that the message that we have a common and indivisible destiny and a unified culture got across this great nation.

Adi Sankara was universal in his outlook. Swami Vivekananda and Sri Aurobindo must have been thinking of him when both of them said that the destiny of India is to be the spiritual leader and moral teacher of the world.

Adi Sankaracharya did all his phenomenal work in the short span of thirty-two years; bearing out, as Bacon said, that a man may be young in years but old in hours if he has lost no time; and Sankaracharya never lost any time.

Every moment of his life was filled up with thought and action. And the great *mutts* which he founded 1,200 years ago, are still continuing, still imparting the type of guidance which this country so badly needs today.

It is amazing how close Sankaracharya's teachings are to the latest conclusions reached by scientists. The human spirit can, merely by means of meditation and introspection, come to the right conclusion about the ultimate reality, which hundreds of years of scientific research might finally lead to. The main message of modern scientists like Sir James Jeans, Sir Arthur Eddington, Albert Einstein, and Max Planck (one of the authors of *Atom and Atomic Research)* is that although the universe exists, the appearance is different from the reality. The reality, the only reality, is the spirit, the infinite spirit. Dr C.P. Ramaswamy Aiyar believed that the essence of the theory of relativity propounded in the twentieth century was known to ancient India 3,000 years ago.

In any of our greatest scientists' meetings today or in meetings held twenty years ago when some of the most eminent scientists who are now dead were alive, Adi Sankaracharya would have found himself quite at home. He would have discussed, on a level of equality, the ultimate theories of science which he intuitively knew to be right.

His main contribution, summed up by the different people who have written on him, is his synthesis of all religions. It must be remembered that in his time there were already quite a few different sects, sub-sects and castes and creeds. There was the question of Buddhism as against old Hinduism and the question arose to what extent you could reconcile the different philosophies and beliefs.

Adi Sankaracharya not only synthesized the different philosophies and ideals, but he purified them. As any creed or religion or language goes down the centuries, it gathers a crust of useless, immaterial accretions, and those trappings are mistaken for the essence of religion. He broke that crust and went to the essence of all those religions and showed how they all could be synthesized, how they could all be made to fall into one pattern. That gives his philosophy a certain completeness, a certain wholeness. You don't need to supplement Sankaracharya. As for his hymns, they are amazingly beautiful. He composed them in Sanskrit, one of the greatest languages that the human mind has ever evolved. They embody his profound vision.

It has been said in the *Bhagavad Gita* by the Lord, 'When things get very bad, I reappear to re-establish *dharma.*' It seems that we have sunk to such a depth now that that day is at hand.

To Sankaracharya, philosophy was not an intellectual exercise—it was the fruit of the dedication of a life. Sankaracharya looked upon every human life as the embodiment of the Ultimate Reality. And he said that human life which is vouchsafed to us is available for transmuting ourselves into an instrument of the Divine Will.

The four essences of his philosophy, as summarized by both Eastern and Western thinkers, are the following:

First, he says that you must discriminate between what is eternal and what is ephemeral. The One remains, the many change and pass; so do not get attached to what changes and passes, but get attached to the eternal, because that alone is the Ultimate Reality.

He was not against family life. He was sensible enough to realize that if there was no family life, the human race would come to an end. But his message was, 'Realize that everything around you, including your wealth and your family, are all ephemeral things.' Too much attachment would result in diverting your mind from what is timeless to what is evanescent.

His second message was that each one of us has to learn to renounce the thought of reward for what we are doing. Your attitude must be that you are not interested in the reward for what you are doing. I doubt whether Sankaracharya in his own lifetime got full recognition for what he did. But he knew that ages and ages hence, people would realize the importance of his message.

Men do not recompense their greatest benefactors. Christ was crucified by the majority vote of the people around him. Socrates was put to death by his own fellowmen. That again was by a majority vote. So much for democracy. Never mistake the majority vote for a vote in favour of reason or for a vote in favour of what is right. What is right is often quite different from what the majority believes in.

The third message of Sankaracharya was moral preparation. He believed that each life has to be so lived that you are prepared to meet the Maker at the time of 'crossing the bar', and to present a clean record, when the final call comes, of what you have accomplished with whatever you have been endowed with. So, you hold your talent, as much as your wealth, in trust for your fellowmen. He believed that universal compassion and universal love are essential ingredients of the moral preparation.

I would like to quote a few words which are from one of his hymns. 'In you and in me and everywhere else, there is but one Vishnu.' See yourself in all things, give up the false sense of difference from other human beings everywhere. This is his message of universality; the brotherhood of the entire human race.

And his last message was the longing for liberation, what St. Luke in his Epistle calls the 'longing for the Eternal Life'. Adi Sankaracharya said that this world is just a preparatory ground, a school where we are trying to prepare ourselves, educate ourselves, for the life everlasting.

About his year of birth and death, there is no certainty. Max Mueller believed that he was born in 788 and so we celebrated the 1,200 anniversary last year. We are also not sure in which year he died, though the general consensus is that he was perhaps thirty-two years old when he passed away. But whatever might have been the exact year of his birth or death, it is his message which counts, more than his own personal life.

He established what I would call the Empire of the Spirit. Whole generations have come and gone, empires have flourished and vanished, but Sankaracharya's Empire of the Spirit survives. And so long as his great Spirit abides with our people, there is hope for the future greatness of our country.

THE RELEVANCE OF SRI AUROBINDO'S PHILOSOPHY TODAY

◆

15 AUGUST IS the birthday of free India. It is also the birthday of Sri Aurobindo, one of the greatest men that ever lived. He combined an intellect of the highest order with a rarely equalled spiritual force and a vision that transcended the limits of time and space.

He had an unshakable faith in the future of this great country. Having predicted the eventual independence of India three decades before the event, he wrote a Declaration on 15 August 1947, which is of momentous significance. After stating that the coincidence between the birthday of free India and his own was not a fortuitous accident, but represented the sanction and seal of the Divine Force that guided his steps in all his life-work, he dealt with the evolution of mankind and India's role in the unfolding future. World movements had begun in which free India might well play a large part and take a leading position. Deploring the fact that the old communal division into Hindus and Muslims seemed to have hardened, he predicted that in the years ahead, India and Pakistan would ultimately come closer together and stand united. In his own words, 'Unity may finally come about under whatever form—the exact form may have a pragmatic but not a fundamental importance. But by whatever means, in whatever way, the division must go; unity must and will be achieved, for it is necessary for the greatness of India's future.'

The ideal of human unity

Sri Aurobindo in the same Declaration on Independence Day gave expression to his vision of the ideal of human unity. 'Nature is slow and patient in her methods. She takes up ideas and half-carries them out, then drops them by the wayside to resume them in some future era with a better combination. She tempts humanity, her thinking instrument, and tests how far it is ready for the harmony she has imagined: she allows and incites man to attempt and fail, so that he may learn and succeed better another time.'

He foresaw a world union providing a fairer, brighter and nobler life for all mankind. That unification of the human world is under way, the momentum is there and it must inevitably increase and conquer. 'A catastrophe may intervene, and interrupt or destroy what is being done, but even then the final result is sure. For, unification is a necessity of Nature, an inevitable movement. Its necessity for the nations is also clear, for without it the freedom of the small nations may be at any moment in peril and the life even of the large and powerful nations insecure.'

He wanted developments such as dual or multilateral citizenship, interchange or fusion of culture. Nationalism, having fulfilled itself, must lose its militancy and should no longer find the international outlook incompatible with self-preservation. The European Common Market today seems to be a partial fulfilment of Sri Aurobindo's prediction.

Message to students

Sri Aurobindo's philosophy was expressed in words which are within the comprehension of any thinking man. His message to students was memorable: 'There are times in a nation's history when Providence places before it one work, one aim, to which everything else, however high and noble in itself, has to be sacrificed. Such a time has now arrived for our Motherland when nothing is dearer than her service, when everything else is to be directed to that end. If you will study, study for her sake; train yourselves, body and mind and soul, for her service. You will earn your living that you may live for her sake. You will go abroad to foreign lands that you may bring back knowledge with which you may do service to her. Work that she may prosper. Suffer that she may rejoice. All is contained in that one single advice.'

According to Sri Aurobindo, the task free India has set before herself is moral and spiritual. He believed in *dharma** as a mighty law of life, a great principle of human evolution, a body of spiritual knowledge and experience of which India has to be the guardian, exemplar and missionary. He wanted the spirit of dharma to enter into and mould our society, our politics, our literature, our science, our individual character and aspirations.

At the same time, he wanted India to benefit from the developments in the West. 'India can best develop herself and serve humanity by being herself and following the law of her own nature. This does not mean, as some narrowly and blindly suppose, the rejection of everything new that comes to us in the stream of Time or happens to have been first developed or powerfully expressed by the West. Such an attitude would be intellectually absurd, physically impossible and, above all, unspiritual; true spirituality rejects no new light, no added means or materials of our human self-development.'

The role of the State

The core of Sri Aurobindo's political philosophy is that the State exists for the individual and not the individual for the State.

Sri Aurobindo expressed his views about the ideal form of government in the following words: 'The government is for the people. It must provide for stability as well as progress. Stability may be achieved by unity and cooperative action, and progress by free individual growth. The government should be run by people who are selfless, unegoistic, scrupulously honest and capable. Their allegiance should be to the whole country; they should serve the interests of the whole country and not of any party. If the present Constitution does not permit such men, irrespective of parties, to be in the government, then the Constitution should be changed.'

He further observed that it is the energy of the individual which is the really effective agent of collective progress.

**Righteousness: sense of public duty or virtue*

The falsehood of modern political life

Sri Aurobindo believed that the State failed in its duties because the ruling class did not represent 'the best minds of the nation or its noblest aims or its highest instincts'. His portrait of the average politician is incisive and devastating:

> 'The modern politician in any part of the world does not represent the soul of a people or its aspirations. What he does usually represent is all the average pettiness, selfishness, egoism, self-deception that is about him and these he represents well enough as well as a great deal of mental incompetence and moral conventionality, timidity and pretence. Great issues often come to him for decision, but he does not deal with them greatly; high words and noble ideas are on his lips, but they become rapidly the claptrap of a party. The disease and falsehood of modern political life is patent in every country of the world and only the hypnotized acquiescence of all, even of the intellectual classes, in the great organized sham, cloaks and prolongs the malady, the acquiescence that men yield to everything that is habitual and makes the present atmosphere of their lives. Yet it is by such minds that the good of all has to be decided, to such hands that it has to be entrusted, to such an agency calling itself the State that the individual is being more and more called upon to give up the government of his activities. As a matter of fact, it is in no way the largest good of all that is thus secured, but a great deal of organized blundering and evil with a certain amount of good which makes for real progress, because Nature moves forward always in the midst of all stumblings and secures her aims in the end more often in spite of man's imperfect mentality than by its means.'

National education

His philosophy regarding the ideal system of education may be summed up as follows.

First, it is essential that society should refuse to give exclusive importance to success, career and money, and that it should insist instead on the paramount need of the full and real development of the student by contact with the Spirit and the growth and manifestation of the Truth of Being in the body, life and mind.

Secondly, the country must give top priority to the needs of education, and organize the whole life of the nation as a perpetual process of education.

Thirdly, the country must make full and wise use of all the modern techniques of communication such as cinema, television, books, pictures and magazines for spreading the ideal of perfection.

Fourthly, permanent exhibitions and museums should be planned all over the country, even in villages, which could be the centres of stimulating knowledge, including the inner significance and goal of evolution.

Fifthly, teachers must grow into real examples of the perfection that is aimed at.

Finally, the country as a whole should engage itself in the activity of the discovery and realization of its true mission.

Above all, Sri Aurobindo believed that if India is to survive and do her appointed work in the world, the first necessity is that the youth of India should learn to think—to think on all subjects, to think independently, fruitfully, going to the heart of things, not stopped by their surface, free of prejudgements, shearing sophism and prejudice asunder as with a sharp sword, smiting down obscurantism of all kinds as with the mace of Bhima.*

The supramental

The greatest contribution of Sri Aurobindo to philosophy is the vast body of his writings which deal with the adventure of consciousness, man's striving to reach the supramental. He believed that the next step in evolution would raise man to a higher and larger consciousness which would offer the solution for the problems which have perplexed and vexed him since he first began to think and to dream of individual perfection and a perfect society.

Sri Aurobindo knew that the difficulties in the way of attaining the Supermind are more formidable than in any other field of endeavour; but difficulties were made to be overcome, and if the Supreme Will is there, they will be overcome. He further believed that this evolution must proceed through a growth of the spirit

---

**A warrior of ancient India*

and the inner consciousness. The initiative here can come from India and, although the scope must be universal, the central movement would have to be in our country.

Sri Aurobindo said that this transformation of the human race would come about in an iridescent moment which will look like a miracle. Even when the first decisive change is reached, it is certain that all humanity will not be able to rise to that level. This endeavour to be in the supramental sphere will be a supreme and difficult labour even for the individual, but much more for the human race generally. Nevertheless, it would be a transformation and a beginning far beyond anything yet attained.

It is a measure of the distressing apathy of our nation that the works of Sri Aurobindo are not studied throughout the length and breadth of India. The words of wisdom from the writings of this great spirit deserve to be taught in every school and college.

No other thinker of modern times has seen so vividly the pattern of the human cycle down the ages and in the aeons of existence that lie ahead. His life-work will always remain a feasting presence, full of light.

A TREMENDOUS MORAL FORCE

◆

THE PARAMACHARYA OF Kanchi is one of the jewels of modern India. His is not a life to be described in words or to be measured in years. He represents some elemental force of a type which, luckily enough, even if we say it ourselves, only India can produce and has produced over the centuries.

A tremendous moral force, and a linguist—he knows Tamil, Telugu, Hindi and Marathi and I don't know how many other languages—he is a man of utmost humility and total simplicity—not a self-styled Rishi or Maharshi, but a quiet man, a frail man. But this frail human being pits his personality against the brute force which rules over the world today.

Adi Sankaracharya was once asked, 'Who is the true Guru?' His answer was that the true Guru is the man who has realized the truth and who is intent all the time upon the good of his disciples. That definition is totally fulfilled by the Acharya of Kanchi.

He became the Pontiff of Kanchi at the age of thirteen in the year 1907 and since then he has fulfilled his mission as the Guru with a sense of dedication which has never been surpassed. He made a tour of India for twenty-one years mostly on foot between 1919 and 1939, and has been still going on foot around the length and breadth of this country.

He represents the highest aspirations of mankind. He embodies the noblest instincts of the human race. He is, of course beyond all honours and titles. It would not make the slightest difference to him even if the 700 million all together celebrated his birthday. It is precisely because the man is beyond all honours and titles that we do ourselves the great honour of trying to revive and bring to the surface of our mind the memories of a man who has devoted his entire life totally, absolutely, for the good of the country and for the good, in fact, of mankind.

Gandhiji met him in 1927 and started talking with him. As Gandhiji always had his sparse supper before sunset, Rajaji who was present at the meeting reminded the Mahatma that the sun would be setting soon. Gandhiji said, 'I don't need any food today, my food has been conversation with this great sage.'

Spiritual force

I had the honour of calling on him at Kanchi before I went to Washington as the Indian ambassador in 1977. I went to his little hut at Kanchi where he resides, a hut that would not be occupied perhaps by any labourer who is a member of a trade union. He eats food which contains nothing comparable to the calories which are supposed to be essential for a man's life and health.

And as the man came out dressed as sparsely as possible, he was a picture of sincerity, humility and spiritual force which leaves an indelible impression on anyone with some sensitivity. I thought that here was a man who was in total harmony with the elements around him, with nature, with the silence that is in the starry skies, the sleep that is among the lonely hills.

A great thinker once said that the higher a man is in grace, the lower he will be in his own esteem. And if that truth were ever vindicated and demonstrated by a living person today, it is by the sage of Kanchi. His total humility and his utter simplicity are just incredible. You have to meet the man yourself to realize how he personifies these great ancient virtues of our wonderful motherland.

When Rudyard Kipling was once speaking to the students of a university, he said, 'One day, my young friends, you will meet a man who cares nothing for wealth or comfort or fame or glory and then you will know how poor you are.' Everyone who has met the sage of Kanchi knows how poor he is, i.e. the man who has met the sage.

Inward transformation

Once Paul Brunton, a famous English writer and journalist, called on the sage before he wrote his book called *A Search In Secret India* and at that time a conversation took place between Brunton and the sage of Kanchi. The sage told Brunton that the inward transformation of man was the precondition for a better world. You must have transformation from within.

Those who have read Sri Aurobindo's works would know that this is the main thesis of his philosophy. The transformation must come from within; unless it comes from within there is just no hope for the survival, the well-being, the betterment of the human race.

And the sage of Kanchi told Brunton, 'If you scrap your battleships, and let your cannon rust, that will not stop war. People will continue to fight even if they have to use sticks.'

This is a very, very wise and far-sighted observation. If you say we shall have no nuclear weapons, no nuclear bombs, no atomic bombs, even then it is not going to stop war unless the transformation comes from within.

To quote further the words of the Acharya: 'Nothing but spiritual understanding between one nation and another and between the rich and the poor will produce goodwill and thus bring real peace and prosperity.'

Then he was asked by Brunton, 'Is it your opinion then, Swamiji, that men are becoming more degraded?'

Swamiji replied, 'No, I do not think so. There is an indwelling divine soul in men, which in the end must bring him back to God. Do not blame people so much; you have to blame the environment into which they are born. Their surroundings and circumstances force them to become worse than they really are. This is true of both the East and the West. Society must be brought into tune with the higher purpose.'

There is no doubt whatever about the extraordinary spiritual powers of the sage of Kanchi. The most well-known example of that is the event which occurred on 14 June 1932 when a messenger brought a telegram to the sage of Kanchi and the sage asked whether it was from such-and-such a village where his mother was living, and when the messenger said, 'Yes', he asked him to go away and told his disciples: 'What can a sanyasi do or say when his mother is dead?' And the telegram was about the death of his mother.

Even when he looks at a man you can see that he looks through the individual. He is able to see some aura or some light around you which tells him what kind of a man you are and what kind of assistance he can possibly give you as a Guru. His great merit is that to him the entire human race is one family. Not only that he makes no distinction between a Hindu and a Muslim or a Parsi and a Christian, indeed, he makes no distinction between an Indian and a non-Indian; to him the entire human race is one single family.

Let me quote his own words, 'Among us there is the concept of the Ishta Devata or the particular form of God which one chooses for his worship and meditation. To get at the One Supreme, you must start from some manifestation of it and you choose that as your Ishta Devata. Another man may choose some other manifestation. As each progresses in his devotion and concentration, he will be led on to the One where the differences disappear. This is the experience of all the great sages and saints.'

All professionals disagree on various matters within the field of their professional study. But there is one class of human beings who never disagree, and they are the mystics, the seers, whether they lived 5,000 years ago or they live in the twentieth century, whether they live in the West or in the East and whatever language they speak. These mystics will have exactly the same experiences and will have the same lessons to teach. To my mind this is the final and ultimate vindication of the fact that there is a spiritual force behind this universe which is available to human beings, provided they are willing to search for it and imbibe the lessons which it has to teach.

When India became independent in 1947, that was when the Acharya was forty years in the seat at Kanchi, this is the message which he gave to India: 'At this moment when our Bharathvarsha has gained freedom, all the people of this ancient land should with one mind and heart pray to the Lord to vouchsafe to us increasing mental strength and power for making spiritual progress.'

Mind you, he was not asking greater wealth for the country. Look at what he was asking for: 'increasing mental strength and power for making spiritual progress'. It is only by His grace that we can preserve the freedom we have gained and help all beings in the world to attain the ideal of true happiness.

The Acharya's golden jubilee was celebrated in 1957. At that time, he said, 'For fifty years I have been installed in this office.

The race is practically over but the work is never done, while the power to work remains. There are years ahead of men, when the toil must continue.'

The toil never ceases and that is why you will find this great saint going on foot from Tamil Nadu to Satara in order that he can get in touch with the people and give blessings to those who seek them. This is the sense of dedication and duty which the Acharya possesses.

His main message has been the message of love.

'O love that will not let me go,
I yield my weary heart to thee;
I give thee back the life I owe,
That in thine ocean depths its flow
May richer, purer be.'

SWAMI VIVEKANANDA

◆

WE ARE TODAY celebrating the hundredth anniversary of Swami Vivekananda's return to India with a small group of western disciples. That return was in 1897 after he had made his historic appearance as a spokesman for universal ethics at the World Parliament of Religions in Chicago in 1893. The world had not heard a comparable orator before, and has not heard one since then. Vivekananda was rightly described by a reporter as 'an orator by divine right'.

After his return to India, Vivekananda founded the Ramakrishna Mission which has produced a scholar of the eminence of Swami Ranganathananda whom we have the good fortune to have with us today.

In his famous book, *Karma Yogi,* Swami Vivekananda describes the scope of Vedanta so as to include also all seekers of truth who are outside the pale of formal religion:

> '*Karma yoga* is a system of ethics and religion intended to attain freedom through unselfishness and by good works. The *karma yogi* need not believe in any doctrine whatever. He may not believe even in God.'

I doubt whether any religion has taught a greater sense of values than that of Swami Vivekananda whose religion was, 'Glory to God in the Highest and Service to Man.'

He believed that the great destiny of India is to lead mankind to the place where the Vedas, the Koran and the Bible are harmonized, and again in Swami Vivekananda's words, 'where man has learned that religions are but the varied expressions of THE RELIGION which is Oneness, so that each may choose the path that suits him best.'

Swami Vivekananda wrote in a letter dated 10 June 1898 to Mohammed Sarfarez Husain, 'For our motherland a junction of the two great systems, Hinduism and Islam—Vedanta brain and Islam body—is the only hope . . . The perfect India of the future will arise out of this chaos and strife, glorious and invincible, with Vedanta brain and Islam body.'

Vivekananda joined Brahmo Samaj (Society of Brahma) dedicated to eliminating child marriage and illiteracy, and determined to spread education among women and the lower castes.

He believed that God is not interested in religious labels but in the way we conduct ourselves. God sees us as we are rather than by the labels which we give ourselves.

Swami Vivekananda emphasized the importance of universal ethics and moral conduct. Although a man may not have studied a single system of philosophy, although he may not believe in any God, although he may not have prayed even once in his whole life, if the simple power of good actions has brought him to that state where he is ready to give up his life and all else for others, he would have arrived at the same point to which the religious man will come through prayers and the philosopher through his knowledge. Swami Ranganathananda has written a book on this very subject.

Swami Vivekananda liked to see moral men like Gautama Buddha, who did not believe in a personal God or a personal Soul, never asked about them, but was a perfect agnostic, and yet was ready to lay down his life for anyone, and worked all his life for the good of all, and thought only of the good of all. Well has it been said by his biographer, in describing his birth, that he was born for the good of the many, as a blessing to the many. He did not go to the forest to meditate for his own salvation; he felt that the world was burning, and that he must find a way out. 'Why is there so much misery in the world?' was the one question that dominated his whole life.

In Vivekananda's own words:

> 'India was the home of eternal values [and to him] the vision of free India was the vision of the motherland of philosophy,

> of spirituality and of ethics, of sweetness, gentleness and love . . .
>
> 'This is the ancient land where wisdom made its home before it went into any other country . . .
>
> 'Here is the same India whose soil has been trodden by the feet of the greatest sages that ever lived.
>
> 'Here first sprang up inquiries into the nature of man and into the internal world.
>
> 'Here first arose the doctrines of the immortality of the soul, the existence of a supervising God, an imminent God in nature and in man and here the highest ideals of religion and philosophy have attained their culminating points.
>
> 'This is the land whence, like the tidal waves, spirituality and philosophy have again and again rushed out and deluged the world.
>
> 'And this is the land from whence, once more such tides must proceed in order to bring life and vigour into the decaying races of mankind.
>
> 'It is the same India which has withstood the shocks of centuries, of hundreds of foreign invasions, of hundreds of upheavals of manners and customs.
>
> 'It is the same land which stands firmer than any rock in the world, with its undying valour, indestructible life. Its life is of the same nature as the soul, without beginning and without end, immortal.'

You cannot see any greater destiny for India than that which Swami Vivekananda envisaged. Today the country is passing through a time which is the exact opposite of what he envisioned for India. In Vivekananda's own words:

> 'There have been periods of decay and degradation; I do not attach much importance to them; we all know that. Such periods have been necessary. A mighty tree produces a beautiful ripe fruit. That fruit falls on the ground, it decays and rots and out of that decay springs the root and the future tree, perhaps mightier than the first one. This period of decay through which we have passed was all the more necessary.

> Out of this decay is coming the India of the future. It is sprouting; the first leaves are already out; and a mighty, gigantic tree is here, already beginning to appear.'

Such fervour and love for the motherland cannot but stir the emotion of any true Indian. I hope our younger generation will have the occasion to go through Swami Vivekananda's philosophy and feel the exhilaration it produces in their mind, and capture the scientific and humanist impulse to implement his vision of free India.

Coming to individuals, Swami Vivekananda held that the theory of karma and rebirth is the nearest that humankind has come to offering a reasonably plausible explanation for the inequalities of life. He says that the theory is unequivocal in its assertion that, since every present will in the future be a past, our actions today will directly determine how we live in the future. Therefore, we must take full responsibility for what we are and what we will be.

DADAJI AND INDIRA DEVI

◆

IT IS WITH a great sense of honour and happiness that I speak at the inauguration of the centenary celebrations of Dilip Kumar Roy, the greatest man I ever came in contact with. I knew Dilip Kumar Roy as Dadaji over a period of years, and called him by that name with great affection and reverence.

Dadaji was one of the most interesting personalities whom Bengal, ever fertile in men of genius, has produced. This city, Calcutta, had the honour of having given birth to Dadaji on 22 January 1897. Dadaji was a born mystic, a great singer, a fine composer and poet, and a prolific writer. He was the author of more than 125 books in Bengali and twenty-five in English. His books are the precious lifeblood of a Master Spirit. Dadaji lived a life of child-like innocence and angel-like sublimity.

Mahatma Gandhi said of him: 'I may make bold to claim that very few persons in India—or rather in the world—have a voice like his—so rich, sweet and so intense'. In another place, in a letter written by Mahatma Gandhi to Dadaji, the Mahatma said: 'I may forget Uma, the nightingale, though that seems improbable, but how can I forget you?'

Professor D.P. Mukerji called Dadaji 'the supreme missionary of music'. Dadaji sang not only with his golden voice, but with every fibre of his being. I have no doubt that history will rank him as one of the greatest Indians of this century.

Dadaji was a most remarkable human being who spread light and joy wherever he went. Dadaji strove to make the earth a world of harmony, beauty and love. He was a profound seer, philosopher, thinker and poet; but all his life he remained simple as a child—

unspoilt by the veneration and reverence in which he was universally held. He had transparent sincerity and unswerving regard for truth.

Sri Aurobindo had many disciples, and Dadaji was the most outstanding of them all. He met Sri Aurobindo for the first time in 1924. Despite all his greatness and scholarship, Dadaji had unfailing modesty and humility. His work was an offering of love to his Creator.

Dr S. Radhakrishnan, the former President of India, wrote the introduction to Dilip Kumar Roy's book, Among The Great. In that introduction, Dr Radhakrishnan says: 'What is greatness? There does not seem to be any measurable quality of it and yet we recognize it when we meet it. The high minds and brave hearts that press onward to their goal, never doubting, never yielding, have the quality of greatness in them'. Rabindranath Tagore says: 'In every land of every clime, a few men have crystallized into a nucleus of light, men who have made bold to proclaim that, though isolated, they fear none. You may deride them, persecute them, even kill them, but never will they return blow for blow. For they are pledged in everlasting loyalty and love, to the voice of the Lord seated in the Heart.'

All the writings of Dadaji are ennobled by a deep moral concern for the good of humanity. If out of all the books of Dadaji, I have to select one, I would cast my vote for Among The Great. The outstanding men, conversations with whom are reproduced in that book, with the exception of Bertrand Russell who was an agnostic, believed in a Godhead who is the unmanifested principle of all manifestations, and the capacity of human being to love, know and become assimilated to the Divine nature. All of them taught that to achieve this contact is the final end and purpose of human existence. All of them held that man is an unfinished creature and is only a caricature of man to be. It is only progressively that man will attain the level of a supramental creature. Humanity is in the making, and requires to be made. This means that a new discipline, a new law or dharma must be followed, and the way is the main theme of the volume *Among The Great.*

As Dadaji said, 'Grace involves responsibility', and he discharged that responsibility by ceaseless work. To Dadaji work was sadhana. He wrote books which ranked only next to Sri

Aurobindo's in their sweep of thought, spiritual insight and beauty of expression.

Sri Aurobindo did not have any disciple closer to him than Dadaji, and he wrote to him more than 4,000 letters over the years till he passed away in 1950. There is no doubt that Dadaji's years of discipleship under Sri Aurobindo helped to shape and mould his entire life. As Sri Aurobindo himself wrote in a personal letter to Dadaji, whom he regarded as 'a friend and a son': 'Even before I met you for the first time, I knew of you and felt at once the contact of one with whom I had that relation which declared itself constantly through many lives . . . It is a feeling which is never mistaken and gives the impression of one not only close to one but a part of one's existence . . . Go on in the path of yoga without doubt of the ultimate success: surely you cannot fail'.

The one lesson which Dadaji learnt from Sri Aurobindo was that however dark and gloomy the future may seem, one must always have hope that the dawn will break. Sri Aurobindo wrote to Dadaji—in April 1947—about the world conditions: 'All that, however acute, is a temporary phenomenon for which those who know anything about the workings of the world-energy and the Spirit were prepared. I myself foresaw that this worst would come, the darkness of night before the dawn; therefore, I am not discouraged. I know what is preparing behind the darkness and can see and feel the first signs of its coming. Those who seek for the Divine have to stand firm and persist in their seeking, after a time the darkness will disappear and the Light will come'.

In another letter, dated 20 October 1946, Sri Aurobindo wrote to Dadaji: 'But I have not been discouraged by what is happening, because I know and have experienced hundreds of times that beyond the blackest darkness there lies for one, who is a divine instrument, the light of God's victory'.

One of the most memorable books of Dadaji on Sri Aurobindo is entitled *Sri Aurobindo Came To Me.* Dr K.R. Srinivasa Iyengar said: 'Whatever else is read, Dilip's *Sri Aurobindo Came To Me* must also be read. Dilip was to Sri Aurobindo as St. John was in the bosom of Christ; and *Sri Aurobindo Came To Me* is the Aurobindonian Gospel according to Dilip-St. John. It is accordingly an indispensable book to all admirers of Sri Aurobindo; all students of Yoga; all lovers of poetry; and all serious practitioners of the creative art of Life'.

On 8 October 1946, came to Dadaji a most remarkable lady, Indira Devi, known to countless followers of Dadaji as Didi. It was for the first time that Sri Aurobindo and the Mother went out of their way to suggest that this exceptionally gifted lady should join them in the Ashram. She insisted on holding on to Dadaji as her guru, and Dadaji was the first to admit that she had been of the utmost assistance to him both on her own account as sishya and for having invoked the full grace of the Divine. It would seem that a chance is now being given for the chosen aspirants to progress on the path of spirituality, which the world now needs so much. Dadaji and Indira Devi started and maintained the Hari Krishna Mandir in Poona to the great benefit and rejoicing of that intellectual capital of Maharashtra. The people of Maharashtra esteemed Dadaji's Sunday bhajans which were imbued at once with the sweetness of his soul and his honeyed voice and Divine love. Those bhajans tended perceptibly to soothe and elevate their hearts. Dadaji's calm, cheerful countenance and kindly eyes, coupled with the silent, unobtrusive background influence of his daugher-disciple, Indira Devi, created a unique holy atmosphere. Luckily, the task of looking after the Pilgrims of the Stars is continued even today at the Hari Krishna Mandir under the noble guidance of Indira Devi.*

The greatest thing about Dadaji's music was its spiritual appeal which aroused in the receptive listener a wistful longing for the Divine, an aspiration for God. Dadaji used to say that music, to realize its highest possibilities, must be spiritual, that the artist's soul must sing out its apprehension of the beauty and mysterious distance and nearness of God; that music must express one's appreciation, or the seeking of Truth, Beauty and Goodness. Anybody who had the opportunity of listening to Dadaji singing one of his matchless devotional songs had to acknowledge that his art was a revelation, that his voice got something of the music of the spheres and gave utterance to the eternal world itself.

Dadaji was one of the few persons in the world who was equally well-equipped in Indian and Western music, and his various cultural attainments eminently qualified him for the task

---

**She passed away on 31 December 1997.*

of interpreting the East to the West through music and other means. A man who won the admiration and friendship of such diverse personalities as Pandit Nehru and Mahatma Gandhi, Bertrand Russell and Romain Rolland, Tagore and S. Radhakrishnan and, above all, won the love and blessings of Sri Aurobindo—Dadaji was undoubtedly a world citizen.

Dadaji shared with his innumerable admirers the songs conceived by Indira Devi. He set them to tune, translated them and sang them every Sunday morning before a large spell-bound audience. Every evening there was Arti and Meditation. All these were intensely appreciated. He and Indira Devi stressed the necessity of change and transformation of one's nature as did the great master Sri Aurobindo. One must be gentle with others but with oneself one must be utterly ruthless. One must be sincere with oneself before one can be sincere with the world.

Indira Devi wrote *Fragrant Memories* of happenings and Dadaji's sayings which would have been otherwise lost to posterity. Indira Devi was to Dadaji what the Mother was to Sri Aurobindo. There was between them a relationship of ineffable beauty, enriched and ennobled by their spiritual impulse. In Indira Devi's own words, it was a relationship not only of guru and disciple, father and daughter, a teacher and pupil, but the relationship between two friends, two fellow pilgrims of eternity with one goal and one path. Dadaji and Indira Devi were both exceptional souls. In the luminous pages of *Fragrant Memories,* we have memorable glimpses of their eternal quest for Brahma, endless seeking after endless truth.

Indira Devi had a consciousness raised to a higher plane which was in the realm of clairvoyance. She could see events before they manifested themselves and see things at a distance which the physical eye could not reach. On a number of occasions she heard music and songs of Mirabai which she was able to reproduce later after she came out of the trance. Sometimes the songs came to her one at a time; sometimes they came in a torrent. Undoubtedly, there are more things in heaven and earth than are dreamt of in the rationalist's philosophy.

Dadaji had a soul saturated and dripping with music, and the devotion of Indira Devi to music was no less intense. Truly, both were music incarnate. For Dadaji the musical inspiration is a gift of God. 'All truly artistic creation', he says, 'is a gift from the

High. We may call this source the Muse or we may call it God' Indira Devi authored hundreds of songs which Dadaji set to music.

Reading *Fragrant Memories*, I found one of the passages in the book having a bearing on the need for harmony between Hindus and Muslims, and it is so poignantly appropriate today that I should like to refer to it specifically. Our people must be spiritually dead if they are not moved by the fact that according to Dadaji one of the best translations of the *Gita* is by Professor Dil Mohammed, the Principal of the Islamic College, Lahore. In his preface, Professor Dil Mohammed writes in Urdu, '*Gita* is one of the greatest spiritual books in the world. It explains to us what man is, what God is, what Love is, what knowledge is, what is the way to work.'

On his last day on earth, 6 January 1980, Dadaji was his usual, cheerful self, though aware of the impending end. Dadaji said, 'Wash my hands. I have to touch the Lord's feet'. A few hours later, the life of the Illuminate came to an end.

INDIA HAS LOST HER SOUL

◆

THE WORLD'S GREATEST peacemaker has paid the price for peace.

Mahatma Gandhi is dead, killed by one of the very people to whose salvation he devoted his entire life. Only a few days ago we were going through the most anxious time because of the fast unto death he had undertaken so that sanity may be restored in the country. The nation begged of him to change his mind, and gave him no end of assurances that it would live in peace. The Mahatma submitted to the will of the people. There was universal relief—prayers of joy and services of thanksgiving. Barely a fortnight passed. Then comes the most tragic day in the history of India, when her noblest son lies riddled with an assassin's bullets. The heart which bled at the sight of the misery of others has today bled to death with three death-dealing slugs buried deep in it.

Stunned into incomprehension, we are unable to understand why anyone—anyone at all in the whole wide world, however malicious or evil, however revengeful or perverted—would want to lay hands on the one man who sought so much for peace and suffered so much for it. And yet such a one was found among us, who has perpetrated the most heinous of crimes.

The Mahatma has gone the way of all saints. India has lost her soul. But his spirit lives—and that spirit will live among us, as long as India survives.

MAHATMA — THE PILGRIM OF ETERNITY

◆

THE SECOND OF October has again come by, and our hearts and minds go back to the pilgrim of eternity. Smt Kamala, the director of this Gandhi Memorial Centre, gave us a beautiful thought when she said that a part of all the great spirits of the past might have found a place within the soul of Mahatma Gandhi.

Gandhiji's impact on those who came in contact with him was almost magical. Rabindranath Tagore said:

> 'At Gandhiji's call India blossomed forth to new greatness, just as once before in earlier times when Buddha proclaimed the truth of fellow-feeling and compassion among all living creatures.'

Even so hard-headed a man as George Bernard Shaw, to whom praise of others did not come very naturally, when asked for his impression upon meeting Mahatma Gandhi, said: 'You might as well ask for someone's impression of the Himalayas!' Romain Rolland, the great French writer and Nobel prize-winner, said that Mahatma Gandhi 'had introduced into human politics the strongest religious impetus of the last two hundred years'. If instead of two hundred years, he had said twelve hundred years, he would have been still right.

The Mahatma met Charlie Chaplin, confessed to him frankly that he had not seen his pictures, and expounded to him his theory about the disastrous effects of the machine on human life.

Their conversation led Charlie Chaplin to produce *Modem Times.*

In our own times, Anwar Sadat of Egypt has publicly spoken about the tremendous influence Mahatma Gandhi's writings had on him.

Gandhiji gave a decisive new direction to history. What was it about this man which held the human race in thrall? Who was this individual? And how did he come to wield such influence over the rest of mankind? He himself said that he was a very strange individual. He confessed that he was not intellectually brilliant, but he added that while there are limitations to the development of the mind, there are no limitations to the development of the heart.

If one were to denote in a word what the Mahatma had, it is the Sanskrit word, *buddhi*—the capacity *inter alia* to perceive the Truth. This is a capacity which few individuals have, and you can develop it only by deep self-study, by profound devotion. He was able, as a result of his *buddhi,* to propound solutions which went far beyond the insights of any academic studies of politics or economics or science. Let me tell you what he said about himself:

> 'What I want to achieve—what I have been striving and pining to achieve these thirty years—is self-realization, to see God face to face, to attain *Moksha**. I live and move and have my being in pursuit of this goal. All that I do by way of speaking and writing, and all my ventures in the political field, are directed to this same end. I am but a weak aspirant, ever failing, ever trying. My failures make me more vigilant than before and intensify my faith. I can see with the eye of faith that the observance of the twin doctrine of Truth and Non-violence has possibilities of which we have but very inadequate conception.'

The pregnant phrase 'the eye of faith' reminds you of the lines of George Santayana:

> 'Columbus found a world, and had no chart,
> Save one that faith deciphered in the skies;
> To trust the soul's invincible surmise
> Was all his science and his only art.'

**Ultimate salvation upon merger into the Supreme Being*

It was the only science and the only art of Mahatma Gandhi—to trust the soul's invincible surmise.

Before I go further into some of the ideas which the Mahatma propagated, I would like to mention one interesting point. There seems to be a mystic—*karmic*—bond between the United States and India, and you see this link in the case of Mahatma Gandhi. When he was in South Africa (he went there in 1893), the two foreigners who befriended him were both Americans. They gave him succour and shelter. After he came back to India, the first foreigner to spot his incredible spiritual strength was an American. On 10 April 1922, Reverend John Haynes Holmes delivered a speech in an American Church on 'Who is the Greatest Man in the World?' Reverend Holmes declared that he had no doubt that the greatest man alive was Mahatma Gandhi. He compared the Mahatma to Christ. In 1922 no other foreigner had the conception of the Mahatma as the prophet of the twentieth century.

Then came the great years of Mahatma Gandhi in India. There he started his civil disobedience movement, which he implemented with phenomenal success. The one person who influenced him the most in his thinking on civil disobedience was again an American—Henry David Thoreau. He had read Thoreau in the year 1907 when he was in South Africa. He had reproduced extracts from Thoreau's writings in *Young India* which he was editing at the time in South Africa.

The last man to be the disciple of the Mahatma was an American—Vincent Sheean. He met the Mahatma in Delhi on 27 January 1948, three days before the Mahatma was assassinated, and offered himself as a disciple. The Mahatma talked to him at some length on that day on a variety of subjects, and quoted to him the lines from the *Upanishads*: 'The whole world is the garment of God; renounce it then and receive it back as the gift of God.' Sheean was most impressed and met him again on the 28th. They were to meet again in the evening of the 30th, but that was not to be.

The last interview which the Mahatma gave was in the early afternoon on 30 January, and it was to an American. She was Margaret Bourke-White who came to interview him for *Life* magazine. She asked him the question: would he persist in his theory of non-violence in the event of a nuclear attack on a city? The Mahatma's reply was that if the defenceless citizens died in a spirit of non-violence, their sacrifices would not be in vain; they might well pray for the soul of the pilot who thoughtlessly sprayed death on the city. This was his last message of compassion to mankind.

In our times his influence on America has been of the most significant character. It was his influence which led Martin Luther King to start a civil disobedience campaign on non-violent lines. Vice-President Mondale has publicly stated how deeply influenced he was as a young man by Mahatma Gandhi's teachings.

President Carter is another great admirer of the Mahatma. When Hubert Humphrey died, there was one quotation in President Carter's tribute to the eminent Senator and that was what the President had read at the Gandhi Samadhi in New Delhi. The words quoted enumerate what Gandhiji regarded as the Seven Deadly Sins:

> 'Commerce without ethics;
> Pleasure without conscience;
> Politics without principle;
> Knowledge without character;
> Science without humanity;
> Wealth without work;
> Worship without sacrifice.'

Let me now say a few words about the Mahatma's ideas which have changed the course of human history. His main emphasis, as we all know, was on truth and non-violence. A thinker has said that truth is a scarce commodity, but its supply has always outstripped the demand. While truth does not seem to be triumphing all round us—somehow, somewhere, in some way, something is working which is bringing the human race closer to truth.

This is what the Mahatma has to say about truth and non-violence:

> 'I may be a despicable person; but when Truth speaks through me, I am invincible.'
>
> 'Truth alone will endure; all the rest will be swept away before the tide of Time.'
>
> 'Non-violence is the law of our species, as violence is the law of the brute.'

'Non-violence is the greatest force at the disposal of mankind. It is mightier than the mightiest weapon of destruction devised by the ingenuity of man.'

'I do not believe in short cuts which involve violence. However much I may sympathize with and admire worthy motives, I am an uncompromising opponent of violent methods even to serve the noblest of causes. There is, therefore, really no meeting-ground between the school of violence and myself.'

It was not a personal God that the Mahatma believed in. He had the very, very deep and profound Hindu concept of *Brahma*—the all-prevading Reality, which is God in its various manifestations. It is that God that he believed in. To quote his own words:

'To me God is Truth and Love; God is Ethics and Morality; God is fearlessness; God is the source of Light and Life, and yet He is above and beyond all these. He is even the atheism of the atheist; he transcends speech and reason.'

Ralph Waldo Emerson, who was well-versed in Indian culture, has written a poem called 'Brahma', where this very idea is memorably expressed:

'They reckon ill who leave me out;
When me they fly, I am the wings;
I am the doubter and the doubt,
And I the hymn the Brahmin sings.'

God is the doubter and the doubt, and God is the atheist and his atheism. In other words, there is just no escape from Him. The same thought was expressed by Francis Thompson in *The Hound of Heaven*. Ultimately the sceptic realizes that God has been by his side all the time.

Another sentence from Gandhiji: 'Scriptures cannot transcend reason and truth; they are intended to purify reason and illuminate the truth.' He tried to synthesize the essentials of all religions: 'Indeed religion should pervade every one of our actions. Here religion does not mean sectarianism. It means a belief in ordered moral government of the universe. It is not less real because it is unseen. *This religion transcends Hinduism, Islam, Christianity, etc.* It does not supersede them. It harmonizes them and gives them reality.'

He identified himself completely with the common man. He spoke and he worked not for the ruler

> 'but the ranker, the tramp of the road,
> The slave with the sack on his shoulders
> pricked on with the goad,
> The man with too weighty a burden,
> too weary a load.'

As regards the need of identifying oneself with the masses, he observed—

> 'We must first come in living touch with them by working for them and in their midst. We must share their sorrows, understand their difficulties and anticipate their wants. With the pariahs we must be pariahs and see how we feel to clean the closets of the upper classes and have the remains of their table thrown at us. We must see how we like being in the boxes, miscalled houses, of the labourers of Bombay. We must identify ourselves with the villagers who toil under the hot sun beating on their bent backs and see how we would like to drink water from the pool in which the villagers bathe, wash their clothes and pots, and in which their cattle drink and roll. Then and not till then shall we truly represent the masses and they will, as surely as I am writing this, respond to every call.'

The Indian masses responded to the Mahatma's call in a spirit of total surrender.

The Mahatma dealt with problems which are timeless and universal, because they spring from enduring weaknesses of human nature and human society. Since the solutions he found for them were based on eternal verities, his influence and his relevance are also timeless and universal.

On this second day of October, we can have no better wish for India than that the great spirit of the Mahatma may always abide with our people.

RAJAJI—A MAN FOR ALL SEASONS

◆

IT WAS WINSTON Churchill who said that one mark of a great man is the power of making lasting impressions upon people he meets; and another is so to have handled matters that the course of after-events is continually affected by what he did. C. Rajagopalachari—loved and respected by millions as Rajaji—fulfilled both these hard tests.

If greatness consists in the combination of character and intellect of the highest order and if it is to be measured by the lasting value of solid work done in the fields of thought and action, Rajaji was beyond question one of the outstanding men in world history.

Rajaji played many parts with great distinction and ran through the gamut of high public offices, including the highest. He was close to the heart of power for decades, but the corroding power of power left his inborn simplicity and humbleness untouched.

The bane of India is the plethora of politicians and the paucity of statesmen. Rajaji was a true statesman. He had been sometimes wrong; but no other public figure had been so often right and on so many diverse matters.

As chief minister of Tamil Nadu and as a cabinet minister at the Centre, Rajaji practised and preached true socialism. He felt deeply for the poor, without, to use his own phrase, 'the condescension of aristocracy or the sense of extraordinary virtue'.

Rajaji had a mind like a razor. His mental processes worked for decades with incredible speed and incisiveness. His towering intellect cut sharply into the heart of a matter and then with the lift and power of imagination he offered solutions for the troubled subcontinent. The sweep of his mind was matched only by the range of his readings. His vision was almost uncanny. Gandhiji once said, 'Rajaji sees at least six months ahead of me.' John F. Kennedy described the impact of Rajaji on him as 'one of the most civilizing influences since I became President'.

No problem was ever too big for his capacity or too small for his attention. He was a perfectionist in everything that he did.

He had the rare gift of being able to speak to different men at different levels. He could carry conviction to intellectuals with his power of deep thought and precise expression; he could address the masses equally effectively in terms which could stir their minds and hearts.

In an age when 'leaders' do not lead the masses but are led by the masses, when the clamour is for the false, glittering political popularity which like faerie gold vanishes even at the touch, Rajaji stood firmly by his beliefs. His intellectual integrity, his indomitable courage and his absolute simplicity became proverbial. However winds might veer or currents shift, Rajaji always steered by the same star, and that star was his conscience and his inner conviction. During the six decades that he was in public life, none was ever able to overcome his iron will or rupture his sense of public duty.

Seldom has so much been packed into one human life. Rajaji's English translations of Sanskrit classics and his Tamil books on European classics are among the finest in the field. What made him tower over the stormy scene for so long was the fact that he, the man of thought, was also a dynamic man of action. He has rarely been equalled as an administrator. He had that unfailing, uplifted mental and moral vision, combined with the art of adroit and practical management of men and affairs, which is so essential for those who guide the footsteps of nations.

Generations later, Rajaji will be remembered and revered when most of those who dominate the political scene today are totally forgotten. He carried the story of Indian independence forward into a new chapter—freedom from subjugation of Indians by Indians—the full significance of which will be realized only in the years to come.

Not for Rajaji was the satisfaction of enjoying in placid quiet the autumn years of his life. In him, even at the age of ninety-three, there was the intense, unrelenting fervour to carry on with the task that could never end.

Of all his great achievements, perhaps Clio will regard his achievement after the age of eighty as his greatest. Surrounded by politicians whose minds were shrouded in opaque ignorance, he once more decided to do what he had so often done in the past—blaze a new trail. At a time when, despite a Constitution which enshrined the highest ideals of liberty and freedom, the citizens' basic freedoms were stifled by an all-powerful bureaucracy, when a permit-quota-licence raj laid its steel claws upon the nation's economy, and corruption enveloped the land, this frail man of eighty rose once again at the centre of the national scene, and campaigned in support of true freedom.

The old world of culture and *dharma**, of values and decorum in public life, seemed to be doomed; but it did not lack its standard-bearer. He started a new political party. Pithy, trenchant thoughts and phrases poured from his mind week after week. His articles in *Swarajya* and his speeches in various states acted as a solvent of fear and despondency. In the crowded story of freedom and democracy there is no parallel to what Rajaji attempted during his last thirteen years.

Perhaps no other figure in world history, at Rajaji's age and against such overwhelming odds, tried so much, dared so much, toiled so much and gave so much to his people. This man, cast in a heroic mould, sought to bring back to India the Spirit of Liberty, to whose defence he summoned every resource of oratory and dialectic, character and action.

The spirit knows no youth or age, no fatigue or death. Only a man nourished by deep spiritual sustenance and by an abiding faith could think and labour as Rajaji did in his last years. His innate modesty made him conscious that he was only the humble instrument for carrying out the design of the Higher Forces that shape the destinies of men and nations.

Rajaji personified the courage never to submit or yield. You could truthfully apply to him the great words of Milton:

'. . . unmoved.
Unshaken, unseduced, unterrified,
His loyalty he kept, his love, his zeal;
Nor number, nor example with him wrought
To swerve from truth or change his constant mind.'

**Righteousness: sense of public duty or uirtue*

THE ENDURING RELEVANCE OF SARDAR VALLABHBHAI PATEL

◆

I FEEL PRIVILEGED and honoured to be asked to deliver the Sardar Vallabhbhai Patel Memorial Lecture this year. The series started in 1955, and eminent men have spoken in the past decades on various matters of vital importance and significance.

Looking to the state of our democracy today, I thought no topic would be of greater importance than the enduring relevance of Sardar Patel. More than ever before, we need to recall what he stood for and tirelessly strove to create. 'My life is my message,' said Mahatma Gandhi, and Sardar Patel could have said the same.

To question the enduring relevance of Sardar Vallabhbhai Patel to India today is like questioning the relevance of the sun to the solar system. You cannot conceive of a solar system without the sun, and you cannot conceive of modern India without Sardar Vallabhbhai Patel.

In recent world history, two events have thrown up a striking galaxy of talent. The first was when the thirteen colonies in America were fighting for their independence. From 1776 to 1783 the United States of America (as it came to be known later) produced an extraordinary cluster of outstanding men who were the founders of the great republic. In the twenty-five years between 1922 and 1947, India had a comparable galaxy of talent—no inferior to that which America produced—and our leaders combined talent with sterling character. Undoubtedly Sardar Patel was in the top rank.

Sardar Patel was one of the founders of our Constitution.

Luckily, the Constitution was drafted by the Constituent Assembly which was *not* elected on the basis of adult franchise. First-rate minds were handpicked from all parts of India—for their knowledge, vision and dedication. After three years of laborious and painful toil, they completed the drafting of the Constitution which a former chief justice rightly described as 'sublime'. It was the longest Constitution in the world, till the new Constitution of Yugoslavia came into force a few years before the dismemberment of that ill-starred country.

Consider the sharp contrast between India in 1947 and the British Colonies in America after their successful war of independence. They started with every conceivable disadvantage. They were just a loose alliance of thirteen sovereign states bound only by articles of confederation. The thirteen Colonies had no unified nationality, no head of state, no central government, no central judiciary, no national currency, no common system of taxation. In the summer of 1787, the delegates in Philadelphia drafted a document only seven Articles long, which, with its twenty-seven amendments, has lasted more than two centuries and continues to be the fundamental law of the world's most powerful democracy.

The story of Sardar Patel's life is easily told. The traditional date of his birth is 31 October 1875. But really speaking, nobody knows the exact day on which he was born. The traditional date is what he gave for his matriculation examination and he never changed it—rather typical of the constancy which characterized his mental make-up.

Sardar Patel was born to parents who were deeply religious. It is remarkable how frequently the children of deeply religious parents fare well in life. Vallabhbhai himself became the architect of modern India, while his brother, Vithalbhai, was the first Speaker of the Central Legislature. Vallabhbhai was a very affectionate man, though there were not many occasions when he displayed his affectionate nature. He had a very fine sense of humour. Mahatma Gandhi has gone on record to say that during the sixteen months when he was in jail, he was kept in peals of laughter by Vallabhbhai who was a co-inmate.

Vallabhbhai never courted publicity. He never projected himself anywhere but quietly did his work. He was a true *karma yogi*. After he became a widower at the age of thirty-three, the only love in his life was his motherland to which he was passionately devoted.

He had three great ambitions. First of all, he wanted to consolidate India. In the 5,000 years of its history, India was never united: it had always been a group of different states. Vallabhbhai wanted to bring into existence a united, homogeneous India when it became a republic in 1950.

The Times (of London) said that Vallabhbhai's achievement of the integration of the Indian states would rank with that of Bismarck and probably higher. *The Manchester Guardian* rightly said:

> 'Without Patel, Gandhiji's idea would have had less practical influence and Nehru's idealism less scope. Patel was not only the organizer of the fight for freedom but also the architect of the new State when the fight was over. The same man is seldom successful as rebel and statesman. Sardar Patel was the exception.'

While launching the PEPSU Union at Patiala, Sardar Patel said:

> 'This is the first time in history, after centuries that India can call itself an integrated whole in the real sense of the term . . . We must work with unity. If we falter or fail, we shall consign ourselves to eternal shame and disgrace.'

His second ambition was to ensure the survival of a united country through the instrument of a strong civil service. He conceived of the Indian Administrative Service (IAS) in place of the Indian Civil Service (ICS), and it was he who also conceived of the Indian Police Service (IPS). Both these services are very much extant today and have enabled India to survive as a democratic state, while the fortunes of political parties keep changing.

His third ambition was to make India economically strong, prosperous and progressive. This ambition was not fulfilled. After the death of Sardar Vallabhbhai Patel on 15 December 1950, the government consciously discarded the economic policies of the Sardar and adopted a sterile form of socialism which was the bane of India till the present government started its new policy of liberalization.

The nation has not realized the greatness of Vallabhbhai as it should have done. If Vallabhbhai had not lived, India would not be what it is today. He aimed at integration in two ways—not only territorial integration, but the integration of the different communities by developing a sense of national identity. There were 554 Indian States which comprised two-thirds of India, while only one-third was British India. He brought all of them together, while continuing to remain on terms of mutual affection and respect with the former rulers. When the Russian leader Khrushchev visited India in 1956, he expressed his surprise that India had managed to liquidate the princely states without liquidating the princes.

Sardar Patel was also the chairman of the Minorities Sub-Committee of the Constituent Assembly. He sought to forge communal integration. He made different communities give up their claim for separate electorates. Even the spokesman of the Parsis had in mind a separate electorate. But Vallabhbhai merely smiled at the ridiculous idea and the matter was not discussed again. The Parsis were a microscopic minority, but the Muslims, the Sikhs and the Christians were in substantial numbers. Even in those days the Sikhs demanded Khalistan. Sardar Patel dealt with the problem with great understanding. He went to the heart of the Sikh hinterland. He talked to the Sikhs in Amritsar and impressed upon them how we all have to live together as brothers and sisters. The passionate plea of Sardar Patel worked. In a powerful speech he made at Patiala in October 1947 he said that we should not involve ourselves in endless disputes and that we could not afford to follow the mirage of 'stans' like Khalistan, Sikhistan or Jatistan. He pointed out that such separatism could only turn India into 'Pagalistan', a land of lunatics.

He was a true leader, in the sense that he did not flatter the people but plainly told them where they were wrong. In August 1947 he said again in ringing words how and why India could not be divided. India, he said, is one and indivisible. You cannot divide the sea or split the running waters of a river. He said this not merely to the Muslims and the Sikhs but also to the Hindus when the RSS made a strong plea that India should become a Hindu state. His words were:

> 'We in the government have been dealing with the RSS movement. They want that Hindu Rajya or Hindu culture

> should be imposed by force. No government can tolerate this.'

Vallabhbhai was not against anybody except the fanatic. If you were a fanatic he was against you, whether you were a Hindu or a Muslim or a Sikh. It is wrong to portray him as being anti-Muslim. Vallabhbhai, as the home minister, had the courage to ban the RSS. That conclusively shows how totally secular and non-communal Sardar Patel was in his approach. He told the Hindu Mahasabha:

> 'If you think that you are the only custodians of Hinduism, you are mistaken. Hinduism preaches a broader outlook on life. There is much more of tolerance in Hinduism than is supposed.'

In his speech in January 1948 at Calcutta, Sardar Patel warned the country that there could never be any serious talk of a Hindu state. India had elected to be a secular state. He solemnly declared:

> 'If the government could not act as trustees for the entire population irrespective of caste, religion or creed, it does not deserve to continue for a single day.'

In 1947 when people were jubilant that we attained *swaraj,* there were two persons who struck a note of dissent—Mahatma and Sardar Patel. The response of Sardar Patel to independence gained in 1947 was memorable:

> 'What we have is not *swaraj* but only freedom from foreign rule. The people have still to win internal *swaraj,* abolish distinctions of caste or creed, banish untouchability, improve the lot of the hungry masses, and live as one joint family—in short, to create a new way of life and bring about a change of heart and a change of outlook.'

To Sardar Patel, the unity and integrity of India was of paramount importance. He shared the view of the Indian thinker who, when he was told that the British divide and rule, gave the profound response, 'No, it is not the British who divide and rule. It is we who divide and they rule.' That is why he was against the creation of linguistic states. In December 1949, the Working Committee of the Congress directed that a separate Andhra State should be created forthwith. In spite of this directive, Sardar Patel took no action. On the contrary, he criticized openly this directive of his own party. At a public meeting in Trivandrum in May 1950 he said:

> 'Some people say they want provinces on a linguistic basis like Andhra, Tamil and Kerala. What will be its effect in the north or in the west nobody cares to consider. We should cease to think in terms of different states or provinces. Instead we should think that we are Indians and should develop a sense of unity.'

While the unification and integration of India was his greatest achievement, only next in importance was his creation of a strong and independent civil service. He trusted and respected the officers and gained their affection and deep regard. This put the civil servants on their honour to work for him to the limit of their capacity and never, as far as humanly possible, to let him down. H.V.R. Iengar in his *Administration in India—A Historical Review* relates one typical incident:

> 'On one occasion, I took a decision in his absence and reported it to him afterwards. He told me that if he had been consulted he would not have taken that decision. I was very unhappy about this, but he asked me not to worry and said that every human being makes mistakes. When the matter subsequently came before the Cabinet he told them that the decision was his, and there the matter ended.'

In Sardar Patel's words, 'the most dangerous thing in a democracy is to interfere with the Services'. If today the police force is wholly demoralized in most states, it is entirely due to the political interference by ministers and other politicians in the discharge by the police of their professional duties.

The greatest tragedy of India has been that Sardar Patel's economic policies were not implemented. His realism and pragmatism in economic matters were foolishly ignored after his death, as I have said earlier.

Sardar Patel never posed as a socialist. He had no property of his own, except his personal belongings. Once an ardent socialist approached him with an appeal to abolish inequality of wealth and cited as an instance that X was master of several millions. The Sardar let him expatiate on the distribution of surplus wealth. When he had finished, Sardar Patel coolly looked at him and said:

> 'I know the extent of X's wealth. If all of it were distributed equally among the people of India, your share would be about four annas and three pies. I am willing to give it to you from my own pocket if you undertake to talk no more about this.'

He wanted to purge capitalism of its ugly face. But he realized that wealth has to be created first, before it can be distributed.

So long as Sardar Patel was alive, there was no nationalization. He said:

> 'Some people want us to nationalize all industry. How are we to run nationalized industries if we cannot run our ordinary administration? It is easy to take over any industry we want to, but we do not have the resources to run them, enough experienced men, men of expertise and integrity.'

Sardar Patel started the Indian National Trade Union Congress (INTUC) because he wanted a fair deal to be given to labour. But he was not in the popularity contest and he had no patience with people who were. He was against the mindless calls for strikes made by trade union leaders who lived in a thought-free zone. He said in Calcutta in January 1948:

> 'Regarding strikes, I feel that it is deplorable that they have been made so cheap. They are now props of leadership of labour and have ceased to be a legitimate means of redressing grievances of labour . . . The maxim should be 'produce and then distribute equitably'. Instead they fight before even producing wealth. It is to restore sanity and a fair deal between labour and employers and to give a correct lead to labour that we set up the Indian National Trade Union Congress.'

To Sardar Patel, the plighted word was sacred: he never broke his word. He had a sense of honour and good faith which successive governments so sadly lacked. He never dreamt that the promise contained in Article 291 of the Constitution to give privy purses to the Princes would be broken later. The aggregate amount of privy purses guaranteed to the rulers of different states came to an insignificant sum of less than Rs 5 crores. Rulers died in normal course, and the privy purse was reduced when their successors were recognized as rulers. Yet, the then government abolished privy purses disregarding the constitutional mandate. Referring to the guarantee regarding pensions to the covenanted services, which was to be embodied in Article 314, Sardar Patel said in the Constituent Assembly on 10 October 1949:

> 'Have you read history? Or, is it that you do not care for recent history after you have begun to make history? If you do that, then I tell you we have a dark future. Learn to stand upon your pledged word . . . Can you go behind these things? Have morals no place in the new Parliament? Is that how we are going to begin our new freedom? Do not take a *lathi* and say, "Who is to give you a guarantee? We are a Supreme Parliament." Have you supremacy for this kind of thing? To go behind your word? If you do that, that supremacy will go down in a few days.'

Like Article 291, Article 314 was also brazenly deleted after the Sardar's death.

In 1950, the last year of his life, Sardar Patel repeatedly expressed his total disillusionment with the debased standards of politicians and the malfunctioning of Indian democracy. On 27 May 1950 at Porbandar (Gandhiji's home town), in a mood of introspection, he said:

> 'We have not digested Gandhiji's teachings. We are merely imitating. We have adult franchise but do not know how to use it. If we continue to indulge in personal jealousies and power-hunting, we shall turn into poison what Gandhiji had got for us.
>
> 'During the last three years we have worked in a manner which has brought us only shame. We have strayed from the right road and must get back to it and understand Gandhiji's teachings and apply them in life.'

The last Independence Day message which Sardar Patel delivered was on 15 August 1950. His eloquent words deserve to be taught and read in every school and college. They came from the deep anguish in his heart, and require to be quoted in extenso:

> 'Certain tendencies and developments in our administrative and public affairs fill me with some disquiet and sadness of heart. The country can realize the feelings of one who has spent the major part of his public life in witnessing epics of sacrifice and selfless endeavour and feats of discipline and unity and who now finds enacted before him scenes which mock at the past.
>
> 'Our public life seems to be degenerating into a fen of stagnant waters; our conscience is troubled with doubts and despair about the possibilities of improvement. We do not seem to be profiting either from history or experience. We appear helplessly to be watching the sickle of time taking away the rich corn, leaving behind the bare and withered stalks.
>
> 'Yet the tasks that confront us are as complex and taxing as ever. They demand the best in us while we face them with indifferent resources. We seem to devote too much time to things that hardly matter and too little to those that count. We talk, while the paramount need is that of action. We are critical of other people's exertions, but lack the will to contribute our own. We are trying to overtake others by giant strides while we have hardly learnt to walk . . .
>
> 'On this, the third milestone of our career as a free country, I hope my countrymen will forgive me if I have tried to turn the searchlight inwards. In my life, I have now reached a stage when time is of the essence. Age has not diminished the passion which I bear to see my country great and to ensure that the foundations of our freedom are well and securely laid. Bodily infirmity has not dimmed my ardour to exert my utmost for the peace, prosperity and advancement of the Motherland. But "the bird of time has a little way to fly, and lo! it is on the wing".
>
> 'With all the sincerity and earnestness at my command and claiming the privilege of age, I, therefore, appeal to my fellow countrymen on this solemn and auspicious day to reflect on

> what they see in and around themselves and, with the strength and faith that comes from self-introspection, sustain the hope and confidence which an old servant of theirs still has in the future of our country.'

He had the strength to speak out, bluntly and fearlessly, to his own party. At the Nasik session of the Congress on 19 September 1950, he said:

> 'The goal of *Puma Swaraj* must claim our constant attention. The question which every Congressman must ask himself, or herself, is whether we have met this claim or demand. If we are honest with ourselves and true to our conscience, I am afraid, the reply must be in the negative. The greatest danger to the Congress comes from within rather than without.'

Our greatest tragedy is that the lessons taught by this outstanding Indian patriot and statesman who unquestionably ranks in the world class, are so little remembered today.

Winston Churchill said that one of the marks of true greatness is the impact which a man makes on his contemporaries. By this test, Sardar Patel must be regarded as one of the greatest Indians of this century.

'Jawaharlal is a thinker and Sardar is a doer,' said Gandhiji at the Karachi session of the Congress in 1931. The Sardar was also a thinker but not an impractical visionary.

Lord Wavell wrote in his diary that Sardar Patel 'is certainly the most impressive of the Congress leaders and has the best balance'. The Sardar shared Wavell's belief that India can be governed firmly or not at all.

President Rajendra Prasad wrote in May 1959:

> 'That there is today an India to think and talk about, is very largely due to Sardar Patel's statesmanship and firm administration . . . Yet we are apt to ignore him.'

The India of today is certainly not the India of Sardar Patel's dreams. After five and forty years of independence, the picture that emerges is that of a nation potentially great but in a state of moral decay. We suffer from a fatty degeneration of conscience and an unchecked dissolution of values. We have no sense of shame or shock that under a first-class Constitution we run a third-class democracy. The country with the noblest cultural heritage has become the most criminalized and the most violent democracy on earth.

What a transformation could be effected if we relearn the values which Sardar Vallabhbhai Patel stood for! The environment will change beyond recognition when we instal *dharma* on the throne again. The country is crying aloud for moral leadership, fearless and forthright, which will tell the people—as Sardar Patel did—what does not flatter them and what they do not want to hear.

Just as we celebrate 15 August as the Day of Independence, we should celebrate the anniversary of Sardar Patel's birth—31 October—as the Day of Inter-dependence: the dependence of the twenty-six states upon one another, the dependence of our manifold communities upon one another, the dependence of the numerous castes upon one another, in the sure knowledge that we are one nation. A regenerated India, freed from petty squabbles, violence and communal bitterness—and cured of the cancer of divisiveness—would be the greatest monument to the Sardar's memory.

HE IS BEST SUITED TO BECOME PRIME MINISTER

◆

AT FIRST WHEN Shri Atal Bihari Vajpayee as the Foreign Minister asked me to go as the Ambassador to the USA, I declined with great regret saying that my heart was in India and I would like to do whatever I could for my own people. Afterwards Shri Morarji Desai persuaded me to accept Atalji's offer telling me that it was totally wrong on my part to say 'no' when the country needed my services. He reminded me that it was not for me to choose how to serve the country but for the men in power. I saw the force of Shri Morarji's advice and changed my mind.

I recall vividly my first meeting with Atalji. Though he was the Foreign Minister and wanted me to accept the Ambassadorship in the USA, he was humble enough to come to my simple home just to make that request. That humility impressed me tremendously and I said to myself that I could serve under this man who had no false notions of his own dignity and his own importance.

I formed the most favourable impression of Shri Atal Bihari Vajpayee. To me it was clear that he is the person best suited to be the Prime Minister of India. I still think that India would reach the highest degree of development under Atalji. He is totally free from any bias or communalism of any sort. I am convinced that our relations with Pakistan were most cordial when Atalji was the Prime Minister.

Whenever I met Atalji I had no problem being on the same wavelength. He is a very humble man and never puts on airs. I found it very easy to get on with an unassuming man like him

Whenever we met we talked not of politics as understood in our day-to-day affairs, but about the future of the country and what was the best way to revive the past glory of India. I have met him a few times after I came back from the USA, sometimes on the plane, and I have always found it a very enriching experience to meet Atalji anywhere.

I remember vividly that when the Babri Masjid was demolished he expressed his own sorrow that the Hindu community had perpetrated such an act. Such a man is eminently needed to guide the destiny of India at this juncture.

I remember one conversation which I had with Atalji. I met him in Washington and I told him how distressed I was that an employee of the Government of India was treated unjustly and unfairly by the government of our country.

I remonstrated with him and told him that such injustice shocked me to the bone. He corrected me and said that I should not react in that fashion. 'After all, I am here today and will not be there tomorrow; but the government must go on.' As a man who was a minister today and who may not be there tomorrow, he had to take a broad view and put up with any passing injustice which may be done to certain individuals.

I remember the day when we asked Atalji to speak to an audience in Washington. He is a well-known poet and a well-known author of memorable lines in Hindi. And I recall the tremendous applause he drew when he spoke in Hindi in Washington.

In the unlikely event of Atalji asking my advice on becoming Prime Minister again, I would say that his first priority should be to restore cordial relations between Pakistan and India as he so successfully did in 1977-79.

SALUTE TO SOLZHENITSYN

◆

ALEXANDER SOLZHENITSYN is the greatest living Russian writer, and one of the world's greatest in this century. All his life Solzhenitsyn had displayed incredible courage, exemplary patriotism and unbending opposition to communism as practised in Russia. He loved Russia and the Russian people. The old dictatorial regime stripped him of his citizenship and forced him into exile. Only in the last week of May, after twenty years of deportation, he came back to his motherland which, in his own words, had altered beyond recognition. Russia is no doubt free, but Solzhenitsyn is very distressed by what he sees around him—pornography, pop music and pulp literature, the imported 'hamburger culture' of Moscow, and alliance of officials with 'financial sharks' and the *nouveau riche.* He returned to find Russia 'tortured, stunned, altered beyond recognition, convulsively searching for itself, for its own true identity'. His mission is to save the soul of Russia. 'I hope that I can be of some help to my tortured nation.'

Prior to his exile, Solzhenitsyn had been regarded as a national hero; it was roses, roses all the way. But the manner in which the common Russian citizen has reacted to his homecoming exemplifies the truth of what a perceptive thinker said, fame is a vapour, popularity an accident; and those who cheer you today will curse you tomorrow; only one thing endures—character. Some ordinary Russian people were asked by media interviewers for their reaction to the return of Solzhenitsyn. Too many of them virtually suggested that he had outlived his time, and was merely a relic of a bygone age. The youth is unashamedly ignorant of his books which had shaken the world in their time and won him the Nobel Prize.

The same fate has overtaken Gorbachov, the greatest statesman of the century. It was Gorbachov who broke the iron shackles of state tyranny. But he is heard of no more—he is virtually exiled from the minds of his countrymen. General Noriega of Panama developed his theory of 'mass man,' a malleable class of people, unthinking and easily exploited. You recall the poem of Robert Browning where 'The Patriot' is driven to find consolation only in the thought that his reward would be in the next world:

' "Paid by the world,—what dost thou owe
Me?" God might question: now instead,
'Tis God shall repay! I am safer so'.

SIR JAMSHEDJI B. KANGA

◆

DR JOHNSON SAID that if a man were to go by chance at the same time with Burke under a shed to shun a shower, he would say—'this is an extraordinary man.' If a man were to go by chance into the court and hear Sir Jamshedji Kanga argue for a few moments he would say—'this is an extraordinary legal mind.'

A tall commanding figure, by his sheer presence he reduces all around him to less than life-size.

The full biblical span of life has unrolled beneath his feet, leaving him untouched. Black-haired at seventy, he has the irrepressible buoyancy, vigour and agility of life's spring time. The fairies who presided at his birth showered on him a cornucopia of gifts—and one of their choicest was the gift of perpetual youth. 'Whenever you die, William,' said Lady Stanley to her brother, 'you will die young.' To say the same of Sir Jamshedji would only be to err on the side of restraint. If a man is as old as he feels, Sir Jamshedji ought to be still at school.

He has a mind that cuts its way as instantly and easily to the very core of a problem as a hot knife through butter. He thinks in a lightning flash—a flash that illumines the inmost recesses of the case. In quickness of grasp, he has no superior among the legal brains of this country. Before you state your case he has seen the point of it, and before you see the point he has decided it. In court and in conference he is always a mile ahead of all others. He waits for you to arrive and when you at last catch up with him, you find that he has already surveyed the whole area and chosen and lighted the best paths.

The law is the element he has lived in for forty-two years,

taking the judgeship and the advocate-generalship in his stride. In his love of the law he is the first cousin to the great English lawyer, who, after he had fainted, was brought back to consciousness by the smell of an old volume of law reports held against his nose by a ready-witted 'learned friend'.

Sir Jamshedji is saturated with law and has assimilated it to his finger tips. But the law is not the only good thing he has found on this green earth. His keen beaming face reveals that he is still absorbed in the joy and wonder of living.

His memory is phenomenal—some mysterious method of mental card-indexing enables him to recall any case on the instant. The facts of the many briefs before him are carefully stowed away in the innumerable drawers of his memory, and he can shut one drawer and open another within a second without the slightest confusion.

He has intellect enough to succeed without industry and industry enough to succeed without intellect. The combination has carried all before him.

There is no more lovable figure at the Bombay Bar today. The reason is not far to seek. Sunshine is always playing round his heart, and one loves to bask in the sunshine.

M.C. CHAGLA—A GREAT JUDGE

◆

JUSTICE CARDOZO SAID that the work of a judge was in one sense enduring and in another sense ephemeral. What is good in it endures, what is erroneous is pretty sure to perish. The good remains the foundation on which new structures will be built. The bad will be rejected and cast off in the laboratory of years.

There is an immeasurable amount of good in Chief Justice Chagla's long series of judgements, the last of which was delivered a few days ago. They bear the impress of a great and cultured mind—quick in perception, broad in vision, fresh in approach. Justice Chagla knew that reported cases were only 'the small change of legal thought'. The enduring currency is that of first principles, and he liked to rest his judgements on them. He was at his best in dealing with cases where analogies are equivocal and precedents are silent.

The law was to him no lifeless conglomeration of sections and decisions. He illumined justice and humanized the law. He achieved the incredible and humanized even the tax laws.

It is a trite saying that tax and equity are strangers, but he demonstrated that they need not be sworn enemies. His contribution to the growth of income tax law is perhaps the most monumental contribution ever made by an individual judge. Even Justice Rowlatt's work did not cover so wide a field or open up so many fresh avenues for the growth of the law.

His one burning desire was to do real justice. In achieving that aim, he brushed aside the conservatism which fails to conserve and which nurtures the form at the expense of the substance. He went straight for the jugular vein of every matter which came before him—'the hub of the case'. His judgements had no dark nooks or misty crannies.

Daniel Webster used to say that 'the power of clear statement is the great power at the Bar.' It is also the great power on the Bench, and Justice Chagla had it in a pre-eminent degree. He wrote his judgements even as the grass grows—effortlessly, spontaneously. They are tinged with the essential characteristics of his own personality—sweetness and light.

His report in the Life Insurance Corporation Inquiry case is a landmark in the history of public life in this country and bears testimony to his fearless and high-minded nature and his shrewd appraisal of men and human affairs.

To the Romans, Justice was a goddess whose symbols were—a throne that tempests could not shake, a pulse that passion could not stir, eyes that were blind to any feeling of favour or ill-will, and the sword that fell on all offenders with equal certainty and with impartial strength. This goddess brooded over the chief justice's court. But her stern features relented into a compassionate smile and the language of the statue was sometimes subjected to severe strain when one of the parties before the court was of the humble and lowly class.

His incredible open-mindedness has passed into a byword. No case was ever lost or won before him till the last word was spoken. His first impressions, his tentative views, were never tenaciously held; he did not allow them to obstruct the light streaming in from even the juniormost member of the Bar.

The man was as great as the judge. For years and years to come, memory will relive the day gone by, and the counsel who had the privilege of appearing before him and others who came in contact with him will recollect with nostalgic pleasure his unfailing courtesy and his innate graciousness.

The country paid him great honour and gave him historic assignments, but at all times he remained the gentle, modest, affectionate man. There are few persons whom the following lines of James Russell Lowell fit better:

'His magic was not far to seek,—
He was so human! Whether strong or weak
Far from his kind he neither sank nor soared,
But sat an equal guest at every board.
No beggar ever felt him condescend,
No prince presume; for still himself he bore,
At manhood's simple level, and where'er
He met a stranger, there he left a friend.'

MINOO MASANI—A HUMANE HUMAN BEING

◆

IN THE PASSING AWAY of Minoo Masani, India has lost one of her noblest sons. He was one of the few surviving members of the Constituent Assembly of India.

Minoo launched his public career as a socialist but was soon disillusioned. He was humble enough to realize how mistaken he was about the notions of socialism which he had believed in. Later in his life he saw the practical wisdom of the policies of Sardar Vallabhbhai Patel and acknowledged how wrong he was in believing that Jawaharlal Nehru's socialism could serve as a panacea for India's poverty.

In the last decades of his life Minoo devoted his enormous energy to free the Indian economy from the shackles of bureaucratic control. He became a great champion of deregulation and economic liberalization. Luckily, in his own lifetime, he witnessed the biggest metamorphosis in the economic climate which came with the enunciation of the New Industrial Policy in July 1991, when the world's fifth largest democracy reached a turning point in its history.

Minoo had great faith in the future of India. He believed that India has a great future because of its reservoir of talented and skilled labour and abundance of capital for new projects.

Minoo had an unsurpassed reputation as a man of total integrity in public life. And this quality by itself was sufficient to disqualify him from being a successful politician—a profession in which success is measured in terms of ministerial positions and the advantages that accompany such positions even at great cost to the larger interests of the country and its teeming millions steeped in poverty.

Minoo was happiest in the company of young people, and felt sad that the country had let down the youth who, if given the right lead, would be able to unleash their true potential and give of their best to the country which gave them birth. He wrote books for the young in the hope that they would be able to draw some inspiration from his writings. In one of his books, *We Indians,* he wrote about the failure of the government's faulty policies and exhorted the young to avoid the mistakes of his generation. His poignant words in that book come to mind.

> 'We, of my generation, have made such a mess of our country's affairs that, in my opinion, we have no right to preach to young folk . . .'

Minoo will be sorely missed, and fondly remembered, by all who came in contact with him and learned to know him as an Indian at heart and a humane human being.

A REMARKABLE SCHOOL TEACHER

◆

SOMETIMES OF AN evening you might chance to see a fraillooking man, short and short-sighted, in a black coat and with a prodigious head, walking along the Oval pathway. He is a nation builder—he has helped to educate two generations. He must still be coming back into the memory of thousands who have forgotten all that they set out to learn at school.

Life has not given Nusserwanji P. Pavri his meed of reward, but that has not dulled the edge of his cheerful debonair spirit. He evidently believes that Dante was right in condemning to the Stygian marsh those who had been sad under the blessed sunlight. With all his sure and enormous erudition, he is Modesty in person. He has not produced any book. The result of his labour is not so many hundred pages, but himself. The issue of his sustained mental effort is not a volume but a man; it could not be embodied in print, it consists in the living word.

Nusserwanji is a quiet man, not to be easily ruffled or rattled. Patience is an instinct with him. He has the simplicity of the man in Dostoevsky's *Brothers Karamazov* who used to ask the birds to forgive him.

He brought the human touch into his lessons—it was always a lesson and never a lecture. When Nusserwanji taught history, facts were brought to life, the dry bones of history stirred, the ages began to masquerade. He conjured up before you the fog at Lutzen and the snow at Towton, the shower of rain that led to the American Revolution, and the severe winter of 1788 that produced the famine of 1789 and thereby the French upheaval. You saw Brutus, the norm of republican virtue, extorting 48 per cent interest from a wretched Cypriote community; you saw the lights burning low in the skies and the stage darkened in the Middle Ages; you heard the din of toppling thrones and the crashing of empires during the first world conflagration. And never did his vision dim, his grasp weaken, or his memory fail.

His learning does not consist merely in the possession of a stock of facts—the merit of a dictionary—but in the discerning spirit, in the power of appreciation and of comparative criticism. Knowledge is to Nusserwanji the bread of life. He reads as if he were to live forever, even as he lives as if he were to die the next day. He inoculated his students with his own thirst for knowledge. He was a precisian and a martinet in discipline. To him knowledge could no more be acquired without high seriousness than a symphony could be rendered upon the flute.

Punctuality was with him a passion. You could set your watch, correct to half a minute, by the time he came into the class. His private library was at the disposal of all his pupils, and so were his time and his learning. There never was a man more generous in encouragement or gentler in reproach. By personal contact with him you not only learnt something, you became something. Contact with him moulded your character and taught you, in the most impressionable years of your life, to beware of ideas half-hatched and convictions reared by accident. Only a thoroughly good man could be so great a teacher as Nusserwanji indubitably was.

He was unerring in his acumen to scent the latent ability in a student. In that great tempest of terror which swept over France in 1793, a certain man who was every hour expecting to be led off to the guillotine, uttered this memorable sentiment: 'Even at this incomprehensible moment, when morality, enlightenment, love of country, all of them only make death at the prison-door or on the scaffold more certain,—yes, on the fatal tumbril itself, with nothing free but my voice, I could still cry *Take care* to a child that should come too near the wheel; perhaps I may save his life, perhaps he may one day save his country.' Nusserwanji had this large and inspiring belief in the potentialities of a boy. He was personally and vitally interested in the progress and career of all his pupils.

Many other things could be related about Nusserwanji from the wide-leaved book of memories. The associations of travel fade, the incidents of life press so closely one upon another that each in turn is trampled under foot, but one's associations with a teacher like Nusserwanji remain forever unchanged. He has now retired but the energy of his educational service remains. This soothing thought must have opened a larger meaning and a higher purpose to his daily work. His personal influence has not fallen silent. His pupils will long feel the presence of his character about them, making them ashamed of what is indolent or selfish and encouraging them to all disinterested labour both in trying to do good and in trying to find out what the good is.

IX

MISCELLANEOUS SUBJECTS

MY EXPERIENCES AS AN AMBASSADOR*

◆

I AM LUCKY enough to be able to come back alive (on a brief holiday) to report my experiences as an emissary to a foreign country. My forerunners in the diplomatic profession, as history records, did not always have the pleasure of returning to their motherland. In the early stages of history when human beings were cannibals, a tribe would send an emissary to another tribe with which it was at war. Frequently the emissary was unable to deliver the message, because he was eaten before he could deliver it. With the passage of time there was an improvement and the message was first allowed to be communicated before the envoy was eaten. But this was not much of an improvement from the viewpoint of the envoy himself.

The qualifications which are today considered essential in a diplomat are different from those which prevailed in earlier times. The mother of Empress Catherine of Russia advised Frederick the Great to choose as his ambassador to St. Petersburg a handsome young man with a good complexion; while a capacity for absorbing large quantities of intoxicating liquor was considered to be a qualification for an envoy to Holland or the German Courts. If such an ambassador had been recounting his experiences to you, I am sure you would find them much more interesting. But I am afraid, having regard to our mores and our prohibition

---

**This speech was taken on the Congressional Record in July 1979 by the unanimous consent of the US Senate.*

policy, you will have to be content with such dry experiences as I am in a position to recount faithfully.

It has been my great good luck to have the honour of representing India in the United States in the crucial year 1978. Since the end of the Second World War in 1945, no other year has been packed with so much historical significance as the year 1978. It witnessed a powerful move in China towards liberalization, and also the Sino-Japan Treaty, and the US-China Joint Communique under which the Government of the mainland of China has been recognized and the Government of Taiwan derecognized by the United States. History alone can decide whether the US played the China card or China played the US card.

Going a little westwards, 1978 saw significant developments in the 'valuable and vulnerable triangle' formed by Kabul, Ankara and Addis Ababa. It saw Afghanistan, Iran and Turkey go through political developments which are likely to change the course of history in the whole region. 1978 was also the year of the Camp David Summit which, while it failed to bring about a peace treaty, at least brought about peace, between Egypt and Israel. The year was marked by changes of great moment in Angola, Ethiopia and Southern Africa. For good measure, it also witnessed the election of the first non-Italian Pope after 450 years, the first Pope ever from a communist country.

1978 was the year of President Carter's visit to India and Prime Minister Morarji Desai's visit to the United States—the trips that have done so much to consolidate friendship between the two democracies.

For the United States itself, 1978 has been a very significant year. One important event was the Panama Canal Treaty whereunder the United States voluntarily relinquished its sovereignty over the Canal. The year saw the distressing decline of the dollar, which resulted in the unassuming Indian rupee becoming a more stable currency in the world markets than the once-almighty dollar. The fall of the dollar is a matter of deep concern for the whole world, because it is still true to some extent that if the United States sneezes the rest of the world catches pneumonia, such being the impact of the giant American economy on financial and industrial trends the world over. The other important domestic event in the United States was the revolt of taxpayers. Howard Jarvis who is seventy-five years old had been treated for the last sixteen years as a right-wing nut who kept on crying in the wilderness for a cut in taxation. But in June last year, Jarvis had his hour of triumph. In the State of California he proposed what has now become world-famous as Proposition 13 which aimed at cutting property tax by 60 per cent. No less than two-thirds of the votes were cast in favour of that Proposition. Sixteen other States of the USA have, on referendum and initiative, put the proposal for tax cut to vote, and twelve out of the sixteen have voted in favour of drastic tax cuts. Jarvis's popular appeal lies in the growing consciousness that while death and taxes are inevitable, being taxed to death is not.

In the political life of India, 1978 confirmed Murphy's Law, 'If anything can go wrong, it will', and exemplified Trotsky's remark about the bad luck of twentieth-century people who wish for quiet lives.

The United States and its citizens

I have been to thirty-four out of the fifty States which comprise the USA. That country is so richly endowed by nature, and varied resources have been so prodigally gifted to it, that after coming here you almost cease to believe that there is justice in heaven. The country has almost three times the area of India and one-third of its population. By and large, the Americans are a very friendly and warm-hearted people and have a great sense of justice and fairness. It is America's basic friendliness which has made the 300,000 Indians who are settled there so happy and comfortable. Naturally, as in any other country, you do have cases of injustice perpetrated in America, but no one is more critical of such injustice than the Americans themselves. And the Americans are large-hearted to a fault. There is a great tradition in the United States of private giving for public purposes. Their universities are the richest in the world. The Americans support all institutions which aim at anything higher or nobler, either in theory or in practice. I have seen Indian ashrams* and yoga centres flourish in the United States to an extent unparalleled anywhere else.

The Americans have a wonderful sense of humour too. The

**Spiritual institutions or schools*

politicians do not exhibit in public any sense of self-importance. In fact, they cannot afford to. They would be lacerated by the press if they start showing any sense of egoism. When I went to visit a Congressman in his Chambers on Capitol Hill, I found the walls of the ante-room covered with cartoons mercilessly making fun of himself. The legislators there can laugh at themselves and at one another. Congressmen never speak of the Congress as supreme. They know that the Congress is a creature of the Constitution and it is only the Constitution that is supreme.

The United States is one colossal monument to the spirit of private initiative. Its pre-eminence is in the field of technology. 40 per cent of the world's research is carried out in the United States, and the rest of the world (including Great Britain, France, Germany and Japan) share the remaining 60 per cent. Ten years ago, as much as 60 per cent of the world's research was conducted in the United States. Every year $29 billion is spent on scientific research conducted by the government, the universities and the business houses. Sixty thousand to 70,000 patents are issued in the United States every year. What we in India have to learn is that in many areas technology does not reduce the number of jobs but merely reduces drudgery.

A typical example of the incredible strides made by technology is provided by the world-famous newspaper *Wall Street Journal.* At Palo Alto pages are set in type, then scanned by an optical scanner and converted into electronic impulses. The impulses are beamed out into space, at a rate of 300,000 bits of information per second, to a satellite which is 22,300 miles above the earth and whose speed of rotation synchronizes with that of the earth. The satellite's transmissions or signals are received in other cities. The whole process takes just three and a half minutes, and then ten minutes to convert the pages from film to metal. The paper is printed in a dozen different cities from the Atlantic to the Pacific.

Technology is, of course, not always to the good. I have delivered speeches in some buildings which did not have a single window; for example, the building of the City College in New York does not have a single aperture for letting light in. These buildings were constructed at a time when oil was cheap and having the building fully lighted and air-conditioned presented no financial problem. I asked the dean at the City College what would happen if electricity failed and the building was plunged into darkness. He said that they would have to give the day off to the students.

Signs of intellectual ferment are writ large all over the United States. Forty-five thousand books are published in that country every year. This means that, leaving aside weekends and holiday seasons, about 200 books are published per day. They range from utter trash to enduring contributions to human thought.

The national sport of America is no longer football, baseball or basketball. It is law and litigation. There are 167,000 lawyers in the United States. The glut of lawyers is partly responsible for the fact that no less than seven million suits were filed last year—suits by all kinds of people for all kinds of redress. A former student is seeking $853,000 in damages from the University of Michigan, in part for the mental anguish he says he suffered after being given a 'D' grade rather than the 'A' he expected in an advanced German course. A young mother seeks $500,000 in damages from officials on Long Island for preventing her from breast-feeding her infant beside a community wading pool. A twenty-four-year-old Colorado man is suing his parents for $350,000, charging that they gave him inhuman treatment and inadequate care as a child, making it impossible for him to fit into society as an adult. A forty-one-year-old California man, upset at a girl's failing to keep an appointment, unsuccessfully sued his would-be companion for $38 to compensate him for sprucing up and driving forty miles for nothing. It was lawyers who encouraged malpractice suits, and now the lawyers are hoist with their own petard. According to a reasonable estimate, one lawyer out of every ten is either sued or threatened with a suit by his client for negligence or malpractice. A delightful cartoon showed a sorely tried father telling his recalcitrant child: 'What? If I make you drink your milk, you'll SUE me?'

Some common problems of India and the United States

Essentially human frailties and weaknesses are the same the world over. Man is the same trousered ape, whether he is in Delhi or in Detroit, whether he trudges barefoot on dusty road or flies at 600 miles an hour. Whichever degree of latitude or longitude you traverse, and whether the man is in *dhoti** or in blue jeans, he is

---

**A loincloth worn by Hindu men*

the same selfish, fallible creature with his irresistible impulse to put his personal or sectional interest above the national interest. No wonder the State has to control the anti-social impulses of its citizens.

Nothing proliferates so rapidly and so inexorably as bureaucracy; and an ever-growing civil service has become a major problem in the United States as it has in India. Dr Moynihan, who was formerly the US ambassador to India, recently described the US bureaucracy as 'a pea-brained dinosaur'. You find on many occasions that the bureaucracy in the United States, as in India, has more information than knowledge, more knowledge than wisdom, and more intelligence than imagination. Washington DC has been called 'the malfunction junction'; and I can name another city which deserves the title equally well.

Having worked with government officials for more than a year, I have no doubt that the government has at its disposal highly-equipped manpower—a larger pool of talent, expertise and dedication than the private sector or any other segment of society. But unfortunately there is something in the structure or system of a bureaucratic set-up which prevents the highly gifted members of the civil service from giving their best to their country. Happy is the nation which can have civil servants without the bureaucracy!

President Harry Truman used to remark wryly that a President has to learn that he could give all the orders he pleased, but the Federal bureaucracy would not budge. When Jimmy Carter was campaigning for presidentship in October 1976, he said that his administration would provide 'incentives to individuals who saved the government money'. He was referring to a dedicated civil servant, Ernest Fitzgerald, who was discharged from service in 1969 after revealing $2 billion in cost overruns associated with the purchase of a certain plane by the government. However, Fitzgerald, who sued successfully to get back his job as a civilian cost-cutting expert for the Air Force, finds it difficult even now to succeed in his fresh endeavours to save the government money. If the Fitzgerald case proves anything, it is that Hyman Rickover was only too right when he said, 'If you must sin, sin against God, not against the bureaucracy. God may forgive you, but the bureaucracy never will.'

In the United States, as in India, you hear constant complaints about excessive regulation and control. A well-researched recent article in *Newsweek* disclosed some mind-boggling facts. There are now no fewer than eighty-seven Federal entities that regulate US business, and to complete the 4,400 different forms they dispense requires 143 million man-hours of executive and clerical effort each year. The regulators are proposing so many new rules that the Federal Register has ballooned in size to nearly 70,000 pages annually. Companies complain that many of the rules are simply unnecessary. One agency often requests information already on file with another, and at times rulings of one regulator conflict with another's. The biggest complaint against regulation, however, is its sheer cost. Murray Weidenbaum of the Center for the Study of American Business at Washington University estimates the total annual bill at $103 billion. At General Motors, for example, more than 20,000 full-time employees work solely on government regulations. Hospitals are hard hit: in New York State, one-fourth of a patient's bill is attributed to the expense of satisfying rules of 164 government agencies. However, President Carter has succeeded in reducing federally mandated paperwork by 12 per cent.

Bureaucracy is the same the world over. Dr Aziz Bindari blames the 'catastrophic situation' in Egypt on the bureaucracy, 'It's the country's fourth great pyramid. It guarantees societal inertia.'

Among American politicians, as among Indian politicians, there are some who are demagogues and some who make impossible promises to the electorate. In the elections held last November one of the candidates campaigning for a legislative seat promised that if he were elected he would establish schools that would produce 'Beethovens and Einsteins.' He did not realize that many parents would be quite content if the children learned to spell Beethoven correctly. Another politician successfully campaigned for the governorship of Wisconsin State on the slogan that the Federal government at Washington has only three duties: 'Deliver the mail, defend the shores, and get the hell out of my life.'

Sometimes when you feel distressed that persons with a proven record of public wrongdoing are elected to our Parliament, you may derive some consolation from the fact that five members, who had been accused or convicted of mail fraud, misappropriation of government funds and other types of public wrongdoing, were re-elected to the US Congress in the elections last November.

However, most of the persons in political life in the United States are hard-working and professionally qualified individuals who would be able to earn a comfortable living for themselves if they were not in politics. Quite a few of them are men of great ability and wide vision. And the other remarkable feature about American politics is that the majority of governors and Congressmen are in their thirties or forties or early fifties.

Indians in America

There are twenty-five million people of Indian origin settled in different foreign countries, some of the most talented having chosen to make the USA their home. Outstanding Indian scientists expressed to me their willingness to come and work in India, even on a fraction of their large emoluments in the USA, provided they would be allowed to work without political interference and bureaucratic control. We have been remiss in not showing due appreciation for the life-work of our great men who reside abroad. They, who have won world renown, should be invited here as state guests and publicly honoured. We have never done enough by way of grateful recognition for those who have brought lustre to our country.

At Austin in Texas, Dr Swadesh Mahajan told me about brilliant Indian scientists working on the problem of fusion who are willing to come from the United States to work in India. Fusion will probably be the most important source of energy in the next century. Dr Mahajan has already submitted a memorandum to the Government of India expressing his and his colleagues' willingness to pursue their research in India under conditions of freedom. They are still awaiting a governmental reaction to their offer.

I have invincible faith in the long-term future of India. There is a close parallel between our history as a republic and the early history of the United States. We are only twenty-nine years old as a republic. And we are going through experiences which the United States went through when it was in its twenties. In the United States the party which was in power and which had suppressed all criticism of the government called for elections in the year 1800. That party was swept out of office by the voters and a new party came to power which restored all the freedoms to the people. We had the same experience in 1977.

India is poor and illiterate. So was the United States in its twenties. The country which counted for little around 1800 triumphed over poverty and illiteracy and is today the most powerful nation on earth. With the genes of our people evolved over 5,000 years of civilization, we are capable of doing no less. All over the United States—from the Boeing workshop in Seattle to Texas Instruments in Dallas, to the Institute of Technology at Massachusetts—Indian talent is employed and the men in charge expressed to me their gratitude to India for giving them such remarkable human resources. Indian physicians, surgeons, scientists, engineers and professors in various disciplines have proved themselves to be as good as those coming from any other country. Viewed from the right perspective, even our poverty can be harnessed as a tremendous driving force in fulfilling great national purposes.

Three conclusions

Many months' stay abroad has made me reach three basic conclusions.

First, the innate intelligence and inborn skills of Indians are so great that India can reach the top—if only we can have *education, organization* and *discipline.* It is no doubt a very big 'if'. India has today the third largest force of scientists and engineers in the world, the first being the United States and the second the Soviet Union. We have this achievement to our credit while two-thirds of our people are still illiterate. Consider what will be the tremendous scientific and industrial strength of this country when education spreads and the populace becomes literate. What height can we not reach when the entire human potential of our country is deployed and each citizen recognizes his duty as a nation-builder!

It is organization which enables any enterprise or nation to put its talent and manpower to the maximum advantage. At the Cessna Aircraft factory at Wichita in Kansas, I met a couple of Indian technicians who have migrated after having been employed in the Hindustan Aeronautics factory at Bangalore. They told me that 10,000 workers are employed in the Cessna factory and they produce 5,000 planes a year; while 35,000 workers are employed in the Hindustan Aeronautics factory and they produce 100 planes a year; and that the level of talent and skill is as high at Bangalore as it is at Wichita and the plant at Bangalore is as good. The difference in output is largely due to the absence of competition at Bangalore and the absence of business organization of the type which prevails in first-class American corporations. Organization is the one facet of business management which is continuously kept under review in the United States. On an average, a significant organizational change takes place once in four years in dynamic US corporations. Most enterprises in India have yet to learn the art and science of management.

The sad feature of the post-Emergency era is the lack of discipline. It is agonizing to read about the acts of violence after the rebirth of freedom. We need to be reminded again and again of the great saying of Mahatma Gandhi that non-violence is the law of human beings, even as violence is the law of the brute. Our fledgling democracy has had a very narrow escape. Let us not tempt the fates again. Good fortune may not come our way as it did in January 1977 when general elections were announced. It is the duty of each citizen not only to observe discipline himself but to inculcate it in the people around him. The citizens of Bombay will remember the visit of the Pope several years ago. There were crowds of more than 100,000 people and yet how totally disciplined they were. Our armed forces are as disciplined as any in the world. This shows that we are as capable of total discipline as any other people, but, as is demonstrated by the traffic on our roads, we have grown accustomed to a sloppy way of behaviour and accept it as a fact of Indian life. This acceptance of indiscipline is even more disastrous than indiscipline itself.

Secondly, we must eschew the fallacy that all problems can be solved by governmental action. It is this fallacy that makes people willingly countenance unlimited extension of state power which, as Mahatma Gandhi repeatedly observed, in fraught with incalculable mischief. The freedom of the subject is the silence of the laws.

Thirdly, as the late Dr E.F. Schumacher pointed out in his posthumous book *A Guide for the Perplexed,* the western man has become rich in means and poor in ends. The ancient wisdom of India has steadfastly maintained that man's happiness is to move higher, to develop his highest faculties, to gain knowledge of the highest things and, if possible, to see God. The modern experiment of living without faith has failed. Goethe said, 'Epochs of faith are epochs of fruitfulness; but epochs of unbelief, however glittering, are barren of all permanent good.' The modern man, despite all his comforts and conveniences, is still perplexed. He cannot call home the heart to quietness, because his spirit is not in tune with the Infinite and he is troubled by

'The restless throbbings and burnings
That hope unsatisfied brings,
The weary longings and yearnings
For the mystical better things.'

The greatest force in the world is love—and there has never been, and never will be, a substitute for it. From a failure to realize this elemental truth, stems the feeling of rootlessness and loneliness in modern society.

Dr Schumacher's thesis is that one must develop the neglected art of learning to know oneself: 'The cultivation of self-knowledge has fallen into virtually total neglect except, that is, where it is the object of active suppression. That you cannot love your neighbour unless you love yourself; that you cannot understand your neighbour unless you understand yourself; that there can be no knowledge of the "invisible person" who is your neighbour except on the basis of self-knowledge—these fundamental truths have been forgotten even by many of the professionals in the established religions.'

'We see all sights from pole to pole
And glance and nod and bustle by,
And never once possess our soul
Before we die.'

In the case of every soul, however troubled, restoration can come only from within. This is the lesson taught by the great Indian sages, from the nameless ones who lived in the twilight of history to Sri Aurobindo. There is still hope for India, and for the world, if we relearn this lesson today.

REDESIGNING INDIA FOR THE TWENTY-FIRST CENTURY

◆

CYNICS MIGHT RIGHTLY remind me that we should bring India into the twentieth century preferably before we redesign it for the twenty-first. Today India lives in a moral vacuum. Bold surgery is needed to treat the diseased heart of a nation which was once great.

It is a vast subject which has to be looked at politically, socially and economically. We may cast a quick glance at what may be called 'The Seven Pillars of Redesigned India'. They are considered below, not necessarily in the order of importance.

The first and foremost of the seven pillars is a sense of national identity. We have not found it even after thirty-eight years of independence. We have millions of Bengalis, millions of Maharashtrians, millions of Northerners and Southerners—but very few Indians. Parochial loyalties and communal fanaticism are the order of the day. They are a sure prescription for national disintegration.

The greatest enemy of India today is not Pakistan or China, but Indians themselves. No enemy can possibly weaken the country so effectively as Indians can. The defences of our democracy may be impregnable from without, but they are dangerously vulnerable from within.

However, hope springs eternal in the human breast. The poets, the patriots, the prophets and the *rishis*—who have loved India deeply and intensely—have predicted that Indians will acquire a sense of national identity and unity in the foreseeable future. Sri Aurobindo said, 'I believe firmly that a great and united future is the destiny of this nation and its peoples. The power that brought us through so much struggle and suffering to freedom, will achieve also, through whatever strife or trouble, [this] aim . . . as it brought us freedom, it will bring us unity. A free and united India will be there and the Mother will gather around her her sons and weld them into a single national strength in the life of a great and united people.'

The second pillar is the maintenance of law and order, which is the basic duty of every government. Law and order has broken down in most parts of India. In some parts, the situation is so serious that the army is in occupation, not in charge. The statistics given to Parliament last year showed that on an average the army was called out in India once every four days to do some job or the other. If you have to call out the army so often, you are likely to put ideas into the heads of military officers, which ideas they had better be without. It is true that the government is on the horns of a dilemma as in a Greek tragedy: whichever way they decide, they would be wrong. If they do not call out the army, they would be unable to cope with disorder and bloodshed. If they do call out the army fairly frequently, the very survival of democracy would be endangered.

The essential point is that while we cannot avoid calling out the army, let us avoid the necessity of calling out the army. We could avoid the necessity, if we have an efficient and honest police force.

In order to have an honest and efficient police force, it is imperative that it should be fully insulated from political domination. But in reality, in most states the professional autonomy of the police force has been completely destroyed by political directives, political influences and political interferences.

The only alternative is to make the police force as autonomous as the judiciary or the auditor-general. The government cannot seek to influence, or give directives to, the High Courts or the Supreme Court, or the auditor-general, and the police are entitled to the same professional independence. Unless the politicization of the police is ended, the frequent resort to the army will be unavoidable.

A professional and honourable police force is valuable in every society, but it is invaluable in a society like ours which is marked by three characteristics—divisiveness, indiscipline and non-cooperation.

Look at our divisiveness. We must have something to divide us—religion, language, caste, or whatever. If we have nothing to divide us, we would invent something which can possibly feed our divisiveness.

Indiscipline is somehow ingrained in Indian character. We are all individuals, and not the citizens of a cohesive society. The way we behave with total carelessness about public property, the propensity to walk on the road rather than on the footpath, the motorist making the maximum noise with the horn in the silence zone—are some of the regular, maddening manifestations of our total lack of discipline. Disorderly and indisciplined conditions are fatal to development.

Non-cooperation is the other distressing feature. People love not to cooperate with the forces of law and order. When we were fighting for our freedom, non-cooperation was a valuable weapon. But the persistence of this habit after we became a republic is most reprehensible, whether it takes the form of non-payment or evasion of taxes or any other form.

The third priority of a redesigned India has to be family planning. India can never make significant progress so long as the population keeps on increasing at the present rate. Family planning is not only desirable but amounts to a moral duty both of the government and the people.

It has been estimated that a couple at the level of subsistence must have an average of 6.3 children in order to have a reasonable chance that one son survives till the father is sixty-five years old. There is also the other unfortunate fact that in parts of India female infanticide is prevalent as a means of restricting the size of the family. There is no gainsaying the fact that the problem is fraught with enormous difficulties. However, methods—humane but firm and effective—have to be found to restrict the rise in our population.

I come to the fourth pillar—education. It is closely linked to the necessity of family planning—the lowest birth rate is in Kerala where the level of education is the highest.

Education is at the heart of the matter. Confucius wrote, 'If you plan for a year, plant a seed. If for ten years, plant a tree. If for one hundred years, teach the people.'

Literacy is not enough. It is good to have a population which is able to read; but infinitely better to have people able to distinguish what is worth reading. Education is a subject included in the Concurrent List; but it is vital that value-based education should become a national preoccupation. In 1983 the Commission for Excellence in Education, appointed by the US government, warned the American people in its report, 'A Nation At Risk', 'The educational foundations of our society are presently being eroded by a rising tide of mediocrity that threatens our very future as a nation and a people.' [*See p. 200*] Our self-complacency is too overpowering to permit us to entertain such a self-critical thought.

Constitutional integrity, which must be sharply distinguished from constitutional fundamentalism, may be named as the fifth pillar. While Pakistan has gone in for religious fundamentalism, India's besetting sin is secular fundamentalism.

We interpret our Constitution as if it were an exercise in grammar. We are intelligent enough to know full well that we are abusing and mocking at the Constitution by merely construing it literally—e.g., when issuing ordinances, or when the Centre dismisses governors or governments of states. But we are so lacking in intellectual integrity that we pretend to have complied with the Constitution.

The sixth column of a redesigned India should be egalitarianism. Fecund egalitarianism is in sharp contrast to the moss-grown, outworn creed of socialism. I wish India would be the first country in the world to call itself not socialist but egalitarian. We are in desperate need of a new route-map. Today India is the poorhouse of Asia; it can, and should, become the powerhouse of the continent. When a country is bumping along the bottom, there are only two ways to make the economy buoyant—change the policy and change the policy. As I have said before, egalitarianism means the investment of human and material resources in an imaginatively planned manner which can contribute to the vitality and progress of the whole nation, keep it in the mainstream of self-generating growth and development, raise the standard of living of the masses, and enhance the quality of life. While ideological socialism is within the reach of any fifth-rate politician, the translation of egalitarianism into action demands intellect and knowledge, character and dedication, of a very high order.

The late Mr G.D. Birla once said, 'I am interested in anything that creates more wealth, more employment. I am a capitalist, but I believe in a socialism which means equal opportunity, more employment and fairer standard of living for everyone. Socialism does not mean socialising poverty but raising the quality of life for one and all.'

'Socially responsible business' may be termed the seventh pillar of a redesigned India. What a transformation one could effect in this country if only business houses were socially responsible!

As Vinoba Bhave pointed out to a group of businessmen some years ago, in ancient Indian society the businessman was looked upon with respect for many centuries. He was considered to be next only to the king. The king was known as Shahenshah while the businessman was known as Shah. People confidently left their property with the businessman, when they went for a *yatra* (pilgrimage). If they died, they were confident that the businessman would make a fair distribution among the heirs. If they returned, they were equally confident that the businessman could be trusted to return safely all their properties.

Today the malpractices of many businessmen have made society hostile to the class. Let the business community try to recapture that image of honour and integrity which made the trader the repository of implicit public confidence in centuries past.

SIX FATAL MISTAKES

◆

THIS YEAR IS of special significance since it marks the Golden Jubilee of India's independence. In less than 900 days we shall reach the year 2000.

Those of us who have lived through the earlier days of free India, when the entire nation was looking forward with zeal and fervour and with a feeling of national pride to the future, cannot but look upon the present times with deep anguish and distress.

Tall men dominated the scene, fifty years ago, in place of the pygmies who strut and fret their hour upon the stage today. After the passing away of those outstanding leaders, India became an orphan. I look upon those fifty years as the lost decades. And at the end of fifty years, we are nowhere near the other Asian countries which started with us at the same level and are today ahead of us economically and politically.

May I enumerate the six fatal mistakes in the past fifty years which have brought us to this sorry state.

First, our greatest initial mistake was to start with adult franchise. No democracy has ever paid, all things considered, a heavier price for adult franchise than India. I am not aware of any great democracy which started as a republic on the basis of adult franchise: all of them started with a more restricted system and then graduated to adult franchise. Two of our greatest statesmen of the earlier years were C. Rajagopalachari and Sardar Vallabhbhai Patel. When the Constituent Assembly was in session, both those stalwarts recommended that we should not start with adult franchise but educate our people first to make them worthy of discharging their duties as citizens of a great democracy; but they were outvoted.

The second fatal mistake was to let the population nearly treble, in the absence of any sensible or sound family planning measures and policies. Today the problem has become so acute that whatever gains we achieve on the economic front are negatived by the unbridled population growth.

Thirdly, our most disastrous mistake was not to educate our burgeoning population and make them worthy of their right to vote. Value-based education has no political sex appeal. Our politicians gave the least importance to education, unlike Lee Kuan Yew who vowed to make education the priority of priorities in Singapore. To my mind, it is an unmitigated disgrace that in the Golden Jubilee year of India's independence, more than half of our population is literally illiterate. Official statistics give a more comforting figure; but that is only because according to the official measure of literacy, any person who can write or sign his name, is considered to be literate. Education can only be a long-term programme for the uplift of our nation. Professor Amartya Sen has bluntly said that India will be the only country in the world to enter the twenty-first century with half her population illiterate; and that successive State governments have demonstrated 'incredible irresponsibility' with regard to primary education.

This is the one area where the Central and State governments have totally failed the people over the five decades despite the injunction of Article 45 of the Constitution that the State shall endeavour to provide, within a period of ten years from the commencement of the Constitution, for free and compulsory education for all children until they complete the age of fourteen years.

The fourth major mistake of our Central and State governments was to completely insulate the people from our ancient culture and keep them totally ignorant of the priceless heritage which has never been equalled by any other country.

The fifth mistake, of which we have yet to face the consequences, was not to inculcate among our people a sense of national identity. Indians find themselves totally rudderless, with the nagging question which will not go away—Is India a collection of communities or is it a nation; or, is India a state without a nation? The greatest curse of India is casteism—the scourge which has spread across the country more dangerously than any plague ever did.

The sixth, and the most unforgivable omission of the politicians, has been to let the people think that they are entitled to freedom without a sense of duty and responsibility. By definition, Indians lack discipline and a sense of national dedication. The reason why the Chinese, despite their huge population, are able to govern themselves admirably, is that they have a sense of order and discipline. Do we need the Emergency to make us realize the paramount importance of discipline? Without such values, can we ever hope to transform India into a great nation?

May I repeat what I said two years ago? Democracy has become so degraded and depraved that people may yearn for a change. The Indian people may lose their freedom again, or, alternatively, the country may suffer disintegration. This is the exact opposite of what I wish but it is a sad apprehension of what can happen if the present decline is allowed to continue.

Concluding remarks

In the more liberalized climate now prevalent, we stand on the threshold of an exciting future—not without its costs, its challenges, and its risks. We must face up to the real world, and measure up to these demanding times if we are to make a crucial contribution.

This aspiration to do more, to achieve greater good—not just for your Company's objectives, but also in pursuit of national goals—makes us conscious of the necessity of raising our sights . . . of building for a future. Your Company's prolific past—of over 60 event-filled years of pioneering work and many breakthrough achievements—fades into the background, as we aspire to fulfil the demands of our nation's aspirations.

LEADERSHIP

◆

A LEADER IS a man with the rare and special faculty which has been diversely defined as charisma or *buddhi,* intuition or the gift of Grace, and this faculty enables a man to communicate and motivate. Leaders are those who are 'movers of people, mobilizers of opinion'. Emperors rule, but leaders motivate. As Disraeli said, 'We govern men by words'.

Leaders help people to believe in themselves and in the possibilities of the future. President Roosevelt used to give his fireside chats which electrified millions. Those talks transformed the mindset of the American people. They made the people feel that they had a great destiny to fulfil. They brought the people out of the mood of the Great Depression.

It is a cruel twist of fate that today during a time of turmoil, the world should be bereft of political figures with the vision, foresight, and determination to lead us to a safer future. A historian wrote in July 1993, 'I cannot think of a period where there have been so few great leaders'. Talking of the Tokyo Economic Summit, he said, 'What we have in Tokyo is a meeting of the world's strongest countries but the world's weakest leaders'. The real worry is that the leaders we have today are as good as we are likely to get in the foreseeable future.

India produced the greatest leader of the century—Mahatma Gandhi. But we have reached now a stage when you can say without fear of contradition that India is more devoid of great leadership than at any time in our history as a republic. It is true that this desideratum is evident in every democracy, both of the East and of the West. The result is that we enter the final years of the millennium with a sense of foreboding, when there should be a spirit of optimism.

Foremost among a good prime minister's qualities of leadership is an unquenchable thirst for action. 'I am certainly not one of those who needs to be prodded,' said Winston Churchill, 'in fact, if anything, I am the prod'. In the words of Charles De Gaulle, the leader 'must aim high, show that he has vision, act on the grand scale, and so establish his authority over the generality of men who splash in the shallow water'. In our own times, Mrs Thatcher showed what a great leader can do to rescue a nation from an overwhelming feeling of drift and despair.

It is true that no democracy in the world has at present great moral leadership. But while it has no perceptible effects in countries like Japan where discipline and dedication are the order of the day, we Indians find ourselves guideless in the absense of these traits.

Lee Kuan Yew, one of the wisest men in the world today, has repeatedly said that India is like a sleeping giant who, if awakened, could make a powerful impact on the global economy. But he found one thing missing in India—a sense of responsibility and dedication to the country, and a sense of order and discipline. Lee Kuan Yew mentioned that these qualities were found among the people of China and that is why that nation, despite the huge population, is able to bring about a total transformation, which is puzzling even to the developed countries. Unfortunately, in our country we have freedom but too little order and no sense of responsibility or duty. We take it as our birthright to do whatever we want even in the performance of our daily routine—driving and walking in any way we want, making a mess of our roads and our surroundings—without any hesitation or realization that our actions stem from the sense of liberty, without any dedication to the goal of national welfare.

Let me come to leadership in the business world.

Here again, leadership does not come merely from training in a school or college. A business leader is born and not made. Nature's gift has to be there. What Nature has withheld, no school or college can ever supply.

Leadership of the market can be achieved through competitive edge. It means leadership through competitive superiority. This leadership can never exist without making quality an obsession. The most famous advertising agency in the world, Satchhi and Satchhi, had the following motto—It is good to be big; it is better to be good; it is best to be both. My late colleague, Mr Sumant Moolgaokar, always insisted that the motto of Telco should be—Major attention to minor details. God is in the details.

The old-fashioned business virtues like hard work still continue to be the *sine qua non* of business leadership. As a wit said, luck is infatuated with effort. It would be impossible to build up business leadership without integrity on the part of the person wanting to give a lead in the business world. One of the most interesting books published in recent years is the *Autobiography of Charles Forte*—the Italian immigrant who set up his first milk bar in Regent Street, London, in May 1930, and then went on to create one of the biggest catering companies in the world. The advice he gave to his son, Rocco, his heir, who accused him of being too old-fashioned is worth recalling: 'Remember this,' he told his son angrily 'five thousand years ago, what I am saying was right. In five thousand years' time, what I am saying now will still be right—cleanliness, honesty, decency, respect for other people, politeness, good manners, integrity—they will never be old-fashioned.'

Let me end with a few pregnant thoughts of Kissinger about national leadership. 'The task of a leader is to get his people from where they are to where they have not been. The public does not fully understand the world into which it is going. Leaders must invoke an alchemy of great vision. Those leaders who do not, are ultimately judged failures, even though they may be popular at the moment . . . The most important quality of a leader is courage. He must act in risky situations on the confidence in his own judgment.' The best a statesman can do is to listen to the rustle of God's mantle through history and try to catch the hem of it for a few steps. We need a great leader to mould us into a single nation instead of a collection of communities.

LESSONS FROM ISRAEL: A VISION OF THE INDIAN SUBCONTINENT

◆

WE ARE LIVING at a most momentous time in human history. Not only is knowledge advancing at an unprecedented pace (doubling itself in several fields every nine years); but sworn enemies have learnt to live together as brothers—the Germans and the French, the whites and the blacks in South Africa, the Israelis and the Palestinians who entered into an agreement for mutual recognition on 13 September 1993. Recently I was in Israel for five days—five of the most educative and rewarding days of my life.

Nations, like individuals, evolve through suffering; and are prodded to do their best by hardship and distress. The Holocaust killed six million Jews—more than the entire present population of Israel.

In 1948 Israel was a barren desert—as a large part still is—and the inhabitants endured for years the trials and tribulations arising from acute scarcity of water. But with hard work and highly developed technology the Israelis have made the arid wasteland now blossom like a garden. They have become past masters in the modern techniques of irrigation, of recycling sewage water, refurbishing pipelines, desalinating and transporting large quantities of water, and expanding practical research of potential water sources. They are producing vegetables and fruits which are sold to the less industrious peoples who inhabit the far more fertile countries of Europe.

Israel estimates that in two decades the population of the Middle East will double, and the demand for water in the region will increase by approximately one billion cubic meters per year. Israel is well geared to meet the challenge. The 'Rio Declaration', ratified by the United Nations Conference on Environment and Development in June 1992, called for a global partnership of governments and nations for the common cause of protecting the environment. The Declaration states that 'peace, development and environmental protection are interdependent and indivisible.' Israel has already started living up to the Declaration. As a nation, it has reached a stage of evolution which holds significant lessons for India.

President Mitterrand said, 'In future a nation's power will depend less on its financial wealth than on its grey matter.' [*See p. 200*] By this test, Israel is admirably equipped to enter the twenty-first century. The tiny country is studded with eight universities for higher learning, and has achieved hundred per cent literacy (barring some recent immigrants).

Let us never forget that constructive self-criticism is the only key to progress. Israel is to India what quality is to quantity. The territory of Israel extends to 27,817 sq.kms.—less than one-hundredth of India's 3.3 million sq.kms; while its population is only 5.3 million (less than half the population of Bombay) as against our 900 million. But its exports for the last year totalled 23 billion US dollars against India's 22 billion.

Israel is a truly egalitarian society, while India continues to proclaim itself to be, and even largely conducts itself as, a socialist state. The kibbutz is a laudable institution unique to Israel. The members of a kibbutz own and enjoy their property jointly and each person gets what he needs from the common property and income of the kibbutz. There are only 125,000 members of the 270 kibbutzim which are in operation today. They represent a very small percentage of Israel's population, but they are responsible for 35 per cent of the agricultural produce and 8 per cent of the manufactured articles. Communism, which is based on the same ideology, has failed hopelessly because it coerces and tyrannizes people into accepting common ownership. By contrast, kibbutzim succeed because their members are voluntary workers and are free to leave at any time.

The Hindu undivided family is no different, in its concept,

from the kibbutz. In a joint family the members own the family property jointly and the *karta* is expected to satisfy the varying needs of the different members. Today, unfortunately, the Hindu undivided family has become merely a device for reducing or avoiding tax; and thus the noble concept has been debased.

The ultimate resource of any state is the character of its citizens, and it is in this resource that Israel is so rich. The dedication of Israelis to their country is exemplary. No other nation, in world history, has been known to defeat so many enemies in just six days against overwhelming odds as Israel did in the 1967 war.

A single Jewish family, the Rothschilds, donated to Israel the total cost of the magnificent building which houses the Supreme Court in Jerusalem. It is one of the most imposing structures in that city and is kept spotlessly clean. An impartial and well-selected Committee chooses the Supreme Court judges with great care and purely on considerations of merit and calibre. No wonder that the judges command the respect and admiration of the entire population, Jewish and Arab alike. The dignity and decorum with which the legal proceedings are conducted make you recall, nostalgically, the atmosphere which used to prevail in our own Supreme Court in the first two decades of our republic.

Nine million Jews live outside Israel. Quite voluntarily and out of a sense of moral duty, a large number of them send a percentage of their income as their annual contributions to Israel. Contrast that with non-resident Indians. Fifteen million of them live outside India, and their accumulated wealth is conservatively estimated at 100 billion US dollars. Have you heard of any of them sending a voluntary contribution to the Indian exchequer? Perhaps the explanation is to be found not in their lack of patriotism but their distrust of our corrupt and inefficient administration.

But the most important lesson which Israel has to teach us is in the field of foreign relations. We have only one state across the border whom we regard as our enemy—Pakistan. The politicians in each of our two countries have a veritable obsession about their neighbour. The relations between the two countries are in as decrepit a condition as Jinnah's house in Bombay, which we will neither use, nor allow anybody else to use, nor have the decency to keep in a proper state of maintenance befitting the founder of a neighbouring country.

Israel has four neighbours who were once upon a time its deadly enemies—Egypt, Jordan, Syria and Lebanon. But wise statesmanship has effected a transformation. Old, unhappy, far-off things and battles long ago have been consigned to the waters of Lethe. The Government of Israel and the PLO have reached a compromise based on a Declaration of Principles. An agreed process of negotiation between Israel and the Kingdom of Jordan will soon bear fruit. The Jews have already started friendly talks with Syria and Lebanon and are firmly advancing towards an era of enduring peace in the Middle East.

The inarticulate major premise on which Israel's foreign policy seems to be based is that the superior power would be well advised to extend the hand of friendship to its neighbours, instead of whining complaints or displaying arrogance.

After all, India and Pakistan are culturally akin, linguistically knit, geographically close, and historically related. Are there no statesmen in India and Pakistan who, instead of misguiding and exploiting 'the mass man', are keen to bring the two benighted countries together for their common development? Are there no statesmen in our region who, taking a leaf out of Israel's book, can initiate the process which will translate into reality Sri Aurobindo's vision of India and Pakistan coming close together and standing united?

General Omar Bradley said, 'Ours is a world of nuclear giants and ethical infants. We know more about war than we know about peace, more about killing then we know about living. We have grasped the mystery of the atom and rejected the Sermon on the Mount.' It would be the greatest day in the history of our republic when India, with its priceless cultural heritage, disproves this dictum, as Israel has already done.

ETERNAL FRIENDS, NATURAL PARTNERS

◆

FINANCIAL AND COMMERCIAL ties are important. But infinitely more important are cultural and spiritual ties which cannot be measured in terms of money. Of all our trading partners, Japan has the closest cultural and spiritual ties with India. Now that India has adopted globalization as its official policy, this is the time to strengthen the bonds between the two countries which are 'eternal friends, natural partners' in the words of Toshio Yamanouchi.

It is remarkable how many common creative wavelengths have been caught over the centuries by Japan and India. Between the two countries we can complete the Story of the Beautiful—hewn in the marbles of the Taj Mahal and embroidered with birds and flowers upon the fan of Hokusai at the foot of Fujiyama.

The Japanese have studied our civilization and absorbed its values. We would be well advised to study their civilization and assimilate its values. What a transformation would take place on the Indian scene if we had the humility to learn and translate into action the priceless lessons which Japan has to teach us. For instance, we should study carefully the Japanese system of partnership between the public and private sectors and between the employer and the employee.

Again, there is no highly-developed country where litigation is so infrequent as it is in Japan. The total number of lawyers in that country being only 14,000, there is no lawyer-stimulated litigation.

Japan has a history, as interesting and variegated as that of India, going back about 2,600 years. In the nineteenth century, Japan effectively abolished feudalism, serfdom, and slavery, as it was abolished in France in 1789, in Russia in 1862, and in the USA in 1863. In India, slavery and untouchability have been abolished only on paper by the Constitution in 1950. The ambition of Japan now is to be transformed from a mere economic powerhouse into a 'lifestyle superpower' by the early twenty-first century.

The two largest democracies of Asia are Japan and India. Unfortunately, neither has great moral leadership at present (for that matter, no democracy in the world has today great moral leadership). But in Japan this desideratum does not have discernible ill-effects because the people are totally disciplined, characterized by exemplary dedication, and there is hundred per cent literacy. By contrast, we Indians, who lack discipline and dedication and have at least half of our population literally illiterate, find ourselves rudderless in the absence of moral leadership.

Some years ago, when the population of India was a little over 600 million and that of Japan 100 million, the then Japanese Ambassador delivered a frank talk in Bombay and invited questions from the audience. A young Indian got up and asked, 'We Indians are no less intelligent than you the Japanese; how is it that you are on top of the world and we are still wallowing in poverty?' The Ambassador gave a very pithy and pregnant answer, 'My young friend, the explanation is simple. In Japan we have 100 million *citizens;* in India you have 600 million *individuals.'*

The Japanese are, by nature, clean, honest and like to remain on the right side of the law. Cleanliness comes as naturally to the Japanese as filth and slovenliness come to large segments of the Indian people. Seven hundred and fifty million Indians live with no access to basic sanitation, according to the latest Human Development Report of the United Nations Development Programme. By temperament the Japanese are law-abiding. A historian wrote some years ago, 'I have lived in districts where no case of theft had occurred for hundreds of years, where the newly-built prisons of Meiji remained empty and useless.'

It can be said without exaggeration that of all the resources with which a nation can be blessed, the most valuable, in fact the invaluable, resource is the character of the people. Among the economically dynamic nations of the world, Japan is tragically the poorest in fuels and minerals which are indispensable to industry. But it more than makes up for this deficiency by the character of the people. Theirs is a homogeneous society with total dedication to their motherland and an unmatched work ethic. They had the good sense to have ethical socialism which inculcates social justice to all strata of society, and they practised ethical socialism during the four decades that India practised ideological socialism which kept us mired in poverty and squalor. As Ambassador Shunji Kobayashi pointed out three years ago, the advantage of a low wage level in India is unfortunately offset by the low productivity level, and an irrational 'exit' policy which results in labour being treated like spoilt children. (Unfortunately, despite verbal assurances to the contrary, the same pernicious exit policy still continues.)

Japanese manners are a model of diplomatic courtesy. In Japan a formal humility clothes a fierce self-respect. As Will Durant points out, the typical Japanese has all the qualities of a warrior—pugnacity and courage, and unrivalled readiness to die; and yet, very often, he has the soul of an artist—sensuous, impressionable and almost instinctively possessed of taste. He is sober and unostentatious, frugal and industrious, curious and studious, loyal and patient. He has a nimble intelligence, not highly creative in the field of thought but capable of quick comprehension, adaptation and practical achievement. He transforms creatively what he absorbs through imitation. Flowers are the religion of the Japanese; they worship them with sacrificial fervour.

Buddhism which originated in India 2,600 years ago, spread through China for five centuries and then, in the sixth century A.D., it made a rapid conquest of Japan. There are over one hundred Buddhists sects and groups in Japan and there are 75,000 Buddhist temples. Out of a total population of 123 million, no less than seventy-five million are Buddhists. Out of ancestral worship came the oldest living religion of Japan—Shinto, the Way of the Gods. The majority of the Japanese believe both in Buddhism and in their ancient religion, Shintoism. They are generally taken by their parents to be blessed in Shinto shrines at birth but are given Buddhist funerals when they die.

If only Indian authorities had any imagination and sensitivity, we would be flooded by a large inflow of Japanese tourists who are keenly interested in visiting places of interest associated with the Buddha. But the sad fact is that out of eleven million Japanese citizens who travel abroad every year, less than one lakh come to India.

I have no doubt that a closer contact with Japan would not only enrich India economically but enrich Indian life. It would serve as a cleansing influence on our polluted environment and filthy public places. It would also uplift our national character and refine our religious sensitivity to the point where we can have religion in place of religiosity. It would also bring home to us the vital difference between socialism and social justice.

MUMBAI, THE MOST EXPENSIVE SLUM IN THE WORLD!

◆

THE TWO THINGS I miss today most in Bombay are beauty and discipline. I have nostalgic memories of the presence of both these qualities in the city prior to the outbreak of the War in 1939, and even during the War, though to a somewhat reduced extent.

As memory holds back the door, I look back on the more than seven decades which have gone by. During those decades, I saw Bombay bloom, then saw it grow, and sadly decay.

Bombay is India's commercial capital and the country's most sophisticated city as well as its richest. But the garbage it generates, which lies in full public view along every street, the main thoroughfares and the bylanes, is in sad contrast with the international image it has carved for itself. Today the accent in Bombay is on generating wealth by any means, foul or fair, while the quality of life has suffered a severe setback.

To my mind, the most accurate comment on Bombay was made by *The Economist* (of London) in an article last year—'Bombay is the most expensive slum in the world!'

Politicians and businessmen have been vying with one another to transform Bombay into another Hong Kong. I have been to Hong Kong quite a few times in the past. But I am afraid one cannot compare Bombay with Hong Kong. The way things are going at present, I do not think Bombay is a city with a future. I feel distressed to say that the quality of life in our city has deteriorated to such an extent, with the filth and squalor all round, that it is not possible to imagine Bombay ever becoming the Hong Kong of Maharashtra. The infrastructure is pathetic, the public transport systems are unable to cope with the increase in the population, and our people have neither the sense of dedication nor the pride in their own city, which are the prerequisites of a great metropolis.

How can there be any sense of pride among the people of Bombay when they themselves are guilty of desecrating and fouling up the city at every step? I have been a frequent traveller to many parts of the world but I have not found people in other cities abroad using the streets for spitting, urinating and defecating as our people have been doing in full public view without a sense of shame or the slightest embarrassment. Spitting knows no class barriers and is as commonplace among the urban elite as among the simple village folk.

The Bombay Municipal Corporation was an august body which did the city proud some decades ago with leading stalwarts of the day at the helm. Today its own internal administration has become unmanageable because of the rowdyism which has crept in, and the drop in standards of the municipal councillors who are supposed to represent the citizens of the various wards. The union leaders adopt strong-arm tactics, and hold the city to ransom at their own whim and fancy. The labour force hardly does the work which is allotted to it. There are so many members of the staff, owing allegiance to the union, who collect their salaries without doing a day's work of cleaning the city or clearing the garbage. And yet, the same labour force will promptly spruce up particular areas within a short time when they are told of the visit of an important government official or a dignitary of the World Bank who has on his itinerary a visit to a slum which may have been a beneficiary of funds from the Bank.

I do not think there is any other country which has such a noble culture as ours. But we have failed miserably on the education front and totally neglected to impart value-based education. We have never bothered to educate our children on the necessity of keeping not only their own homes clean but also their surroundings. After all, the children are going to be the citizens of the future.

Unless the attitude of the citizens changes and they take the initiative of putting greater emphasis on responsibilities and duties and much less stress on rights and liberty, there is no hope for the future. If we are trying to project Bombay on the world map as the financial and commercial capital of India, let the thought perish!

X

SELECTED LETTERS

DR L.M. SINGHVI

◆

Camp: Raj Bhavan
Bombay
5 May 1998

Dear Nani,

What a pleasure and privilege it was to dine with you last evening! The company was convivial and conversation lively. To see you and Mrs Palkhivala and to receive your hospitality warmed my heart. Many thanks for a wonderful evening and for an excellent vegetarian meal. I hope you did not mind my making the suggestion for a *Palkhivala Reader* in the company of others and without a previous consultation with you. Perhaps I acted on an unconscious impulse and on a signal from the subterranean!

If you do approve of the idea, I would very much like you to help in the selection of materials.

With my warmest regards to you both in which Kamalaji joins me with her apologies for her absence last evening,

Affectionately,

Yours ever,
L.M.

Mr N.A. Palkhivala

Bombay House
Fort, Mumbai
6 May 1998

Dear LM,

Many thanks for your gracious note of the 5th instant.

Nargesh and I were very happy to have you come over for dinner the other evening. We missed Kamala though.

I am grateful to you for the generous suggestion you made so spontaneously. You are welcome to make use of my writings in whatever way you think best. Any assistance I can give by way of selection or otherwise, I would be glad to do so.

With affectionate regards, and every good wish to you and your family for the years ahead,

Nani

Dr L.M. Singhvi,
White House,
Bhagwan Das Road,
New Delhi

8 May 1972

My dear Prime Minister,

I was happy to have had the opportunity of meeting you last month, and am grateful to you for the time you spared for me.

It has been said that almost every figure in world history who has had a significant impact on the course of events can have his life-work summed up in a single word. Your most enduring achievement in the history of our country may well be summed up in the word—*integration*.

I enclose a Note (with an extra copy) on the main points I tried to cover in my talk with you. Your unique position affords a rare opportunity of achieving the goal of integration between—

(a) the states;

(b) the public and private sectors;

(c) the religious communities; and

(d) the government and the people.

I have covered the point about a uniform Civil Code on which you had requested for a written Note.

With best wishes and kindest regards,

Yours sincerely,
Nani A. Palkhivala

The Hon'ble Shrimati Indira Gandhi,
Prime Minister of India,
New Delhi

Four Fields Awaiting Integration

I. The states

The states of India are constitutionally integrated, but their economic integration remains to be achieved. There is a much closer economic integration of the independent sovereign states in the European Common Market than is the case with the states of India. Movement of goods from France into Italy presents fewer fiscal problems and entails far fewer formalities and technical halts than the movement of goods from Mysore into Maharashtra.

(a) Taxation: The complexities of state sales tax and inter-state sales tax have resulted in an ever-growing spate of litigation. As regards textiles, sugar and tobacco, sales tax has been abolished and additional excise is levied by the Centre which is equitably distributed among the states. It is necessary to free other basic commodities, e.g., steel and trucks, from the net of sales tax, by letting the Union levy an additional excise which can then be distributed among the states.

Of all fiscal levies, octroi is the greatest waster of time and the worst impediment to the free flow of inter-state commerce. Official committees have branded octroi as wholly outdated. I believe a truck going from Bombay to Nagpur wastes about five hours at the sixty octroi points which it has to negotiate. The Constitution should be amended by deleting octroi from the State List and finding alternative sources of revenue for the local authorities.

(b) Rivers: Interminable river disputes are pending between different states. The River Boards Act, 1956, is on the statute book, but to my knowledge it has never been used. Tribunals are today functioning under the Inter-State Water Disputes Act, 1956, and experience shows that the machinery of the Act is most unsatisfactory for resolving the disputes. The hearing of a dispute goes on for years, while projects which can change the economic picture not only of the river basin but of thousands of square miles around, have to be kept in cold storage. The present opportune moment, when ministries of the same political party are in power in different states, should be availed of to have a quick political settlement of the disputes by agreement between

the ministries of the states concerned. Projects which would be of benefit to two or more riparian states should be undertaken by the Union. They would go a long way in welding the states together,

(c) Joint sector: There should be a much greater number of new enterprises where the Union government, the state government and the public are joint shareholders. This would give the states a sense of participation in industries controlled by the Union, whereas such a sense of participation is today lacking in crucial economic areas.

(d) Greater autonomy in industries and trade: It is not necessary or desirable to amend the Constitution to give greater autonomy to the states. But the time has come to give back some of the industries to the states, over which the Union has assumed jurisdiction under the Industries (Development and Regulation) Act.

The assumption by the Centre of total domination over almost all large-scale industries is contrary to the basic scheme of the Constitution. The State List in the Constitution confers on the states the power to regulate all industries, except those which are necessary for the purpose of defence or for the prosecution of war, or the control of which by the Union is declared by Parliament to be expedient in the public interest. The Industries (Development and Regulation) Act, 1951, enumerates the industries, the control of which by the Union is stated by Parliament to be expedient in the public interest. By the simple expedient of adding, from time to time, various industries in the Schedule to that Act, the Centre has now brought about a situation in which ninety per cent of large-scale industries have been brought directly under the control of the Central government. Even minor items—e.g., razor blades, soaps, cosmetics, any toilet preparations, matches, glue, any rubber goods, footwear and household electrical appliances—have been taken out of the jurisdiction of the states.

Today, there is an exceptionally strong prime minister and moderately weak chief ministers, and therefore there is no danger of disintegration. But quite conceivably, the opposite situation may arise after years. At that time, the process of disintegration may well set in, if the states remain deprived of a reasonable degree of freedom in industrial and economic matters. It would then be too late to arrest fissiparous tendencies. There is no other Union of States in the world where the states have so little freedom in the field of industries, as in India at present.

II. Public and private sectors

(a) Dichotomy between public sector and private sector: The greater the cooperation and understanding between the government and the people, the less the justification for the dichotomy between the public sector and the private sector. In the search for efficiency and expertise, integrity and dedication, the ideological distinction between the two sectors should be eliminated. Every efficient and honest enterprise, whether in the public or private sector, should be encouraged and induced to expand. The party system makes it difficult to have a Government of All the Talents, but we can undoubtedly have an Economy of All the Talents.

(b) The National Sector: The creation of the right atmosphere or climate has a far greater impact on a nation's development than the churning out of more and more laws. There should be a new concept of the National Sector. Just as honours are conferred upon individuals, enterprises should be honoured by being classed in the National Sector. High standards of efficiency and integrity would be preconditions. The same standards would be required of a unit in the public sector, as would be required of a unit in the private sector, to qualify for being included in the National Sector. The recognition may enure for, say, four years and would be renewed if the standards are maintained.

Today, mere ideological preference for the public sector has put efficiency and managerial talent at a low discount in that sector, even as lack of appreciation has put integrity and a sense of dedication at a low discount in the private sector. The concept of the National Sector would give a boost precisely to those qualities which each sector lacks so badly today.

In administration of laws and in the field of executive action—e.g., in dealing with questions pertaining to monopolies, licences for expansion, and financial assistance—it would be natural and proper to encourage the development of any enterprise in the National Sector.

(c) The joint sector: The joint sector is far preferable to nationalization, because

(i) it combines the human and material resources of the government and the people;

(ii) it gives a greater degree of freedom and a better chance to the enterprise of being run on sound commercial lines with reasonable profitability, and thereby helps the public exchequer.

The joint sector may take the form of financial participation by government (Union or state or both) and the public. The government participation in equity capital should not be so small as to make no impact, and not be so large as to be overpowering in the field of control. Between 26 per cent and 51 per cent government participation in equity capital seems to accord with the principle of the Golden Mean.

Pooling of the experience and disciplines of the private sector and the financial resources of the government would provide a very interesting new category of the joint sector. The entire financial outlay may be by the government which would own the enterprise, and the skills and expertise of private enterprises may be put at the disposal of the government in the national interest for constructing and commissioning the plant. For example, the government may start a new plant in one of the basic industries like steel, where the private sector's skills and experience gathered over decades would be made available to the government without any profit motive.

(d) Closer association and common directors between public and private sectors: More men of proven ability and sense of dedication in the private sector should be associated with public sector enterprises as directors or advisors, just as government directors are associated with units in the private sector; and they would devote only a part of their time and attention as a matter of public service to guiding the public sector enterprises, and thus they would be the counterparts of government directors on the Boards of companies in the private sector. This would result in the closer association of the public and private sectors to their mutual benefit and would be conducive to the speedy and harmonious growth of the national economy.

III. The religious communities

With a view to integrating the different communities, a Civil Code should be passed which would deal with—

(a) Adoption;
(b) Power to deal with and dispose of property during the owner's lifetime;
(c) Testate and intestate succession; and
(d) Other allied subjects.

It would be optional to the member of any community to decide to be governed by the provisions of the Civil Code by declaring his option and registering it with the prescribed authority. No community can object to such a law since it would apply to a citizen at his own volition. It is for the government to consider whether it would be politically unwise to offer some incentives, fiscal or otherwise, to attract people to adopt the uniform Civil Code as applicable to themselves.

Today, the specific subjects mentioned above are governed by the personal law. Hindus have the law of adoption, but there is no law of adoption applicable to Muslims, Parsis and other communities. The Civil Code would provide uniformly for the right of adoption for all communities and would specifically provide for adoption of a child of a community different from that of the adopting parents.

IV. The government and the people

The economic miracles of West Germany and Japan are, in a large measure, due to the total understanding and cooperation between the men who create national wealth and those in power who regulate its creation. In India there is one very significant fact which seems to have escaped public attention. At the meetings of the Boards of Directors of various companies, the directors nominated by the government are generally most helpful and understanding. Likewise, at the annual general meetings of shareholders, the tremendous voting power of the government-controlled financial institutions is used wisely and reasonably. It should not be difficult to have the same spirit of understanding and goodwill evinced in other areas where policies are shaped and the laws are administered.

(a) Bureaucratic control: The confluence of all controls in the hands of the civil administration is frustrating to the technocrats and the professional managers in enterprises, both government and private. This further results in interminable delays. Yet, the speed with which decisions are reached in some efficient ministries with able civil servants shows how the frustrating delays can be easily eliminated, by streamlining procedures and creating an atmosphere where a civil servant is encouraged to make prompt and independent decisions.

(b) Special tribunals: Tens of thousands of tax cases are clogging the High Courts and the lower appellate authorities. For instance, under the Income-tax Act the citizen has a right of appeal to the appellate assistant commissioner, a right of second appeal to the Tribunal, a reference to the High Court on a question of law and, in a fit case, a final appeal to the Supreme Court. The law should be amended so as to give the option to the citizen to bypass all these procedures and go before a specially-constituted tribunal whose decision would be final and non-appealable. That tribunal would not write judgements or give reasons but merely state its final decision. If men of proven ability, knowledge, integrity, and capacity to make quick decisions are appointed to constitute such tribunals, thousands of cases which are pending in appeal, reference, etc. could be withdrawn and referred to the tribunals which would be able to dispose of a large number of cases per day, since their time would not be wasted in writing judgements or reasoned orders. Since this procedure would be purely optional, it would be perfectly constitutional. In the final analysis, this procedure would be more satisfactory from the point of view of the revenue as well as the tax-payer. The heavy arrears of work at different levels of appeal and reference could be eliminated in a short time by appointing such tribunals for income tax and other fiscal laws. Article 32, 136 and 226 of the Constitution should be amended to provide that where the tax-payer has himself chosen to adopt this expeditious procedure, no writ petition or special leave application would be available in the High Court or the Supreme Court.

(c) Taxation: The crushing burden of taxation is primarily responsible for black market money which corrupts social life, civil administration and politics. By and large, the joint burden of

income-tax and wealth-tax in India on non-agricultural income and enterprise is the highest in the world. We keep on passing more and more laws with less and less efficiency of administration, and the ever-increasing tax rates apply only to an eroded tax base. The political courage needed to make the tax structure fair and realistic would be amply rewarded. Under the existing confiscatory rates, the income tax law has lost all moral authority, since the belief is widespread that the state is basically unfair in not permitting citizens to keep a reasonable part of the fruits of their own labour and enterprise.

Bombay,
1 August 1990

Dear Prime Minister,

Re: Demand for the establishment of separate Development Boards under Art. 371 of the Constitution for regions of Maharashtra

My mind has been a great deal exercised by the persistent demand for establishing separate Development Boards under Art. 371 of the Constitution for Vidarbha, Marathwada and the rest of Maharashtra.

I fully acknowledge the necessity of redressing regional imbalances and ensuring that regions like Vidarbha and Marathwada are brought up to the level of development reached by some other parts of Maharashtra. The only question is of the procedure by which such an eminently desirable result can be achieved Developmental backlog can and should be removed by efficacious, democratic means. The Constitution can be smoothly worked only by men of goodwill, with a sense of justice and fairness. But the establishment of Development Boards, as envisaged by Art. 371, would be a disastrous substitute for such goodwill and sense of justice and fairness.

There is no Article in the Constitution more vague and unsatisfactory than Art. 371. It is fraught with such formidable ambiguities that though it was enacted thirty-four years ago, it has never been brought into operation. The only time it was invoked was in February 1977 when the President promulgated an Order which envisaged the setting up of a Development Board for Kutch; but the Order was not acted upon and was withdrawn twelve months later.

May I submit that the establishment of such Boards is likely to create more problems than it would resolve? It would aggravate political acrimony, and entail years of protracted litigation to decide several fundamental questions including the following:

(1) Are the provisions of Art. 371 intended to supersede the normal process of free democracy, as in the case of President's rule under Art. 356 upon failure of constitutional machinery in a state?

(2) In respect of matters covered by Art. 371, can the governor

exercise the executive and legislative powers which, but for the President's order under that Article, would fall squarely within the competence of the Council of Ministers and the state legislature?

(3) Can Development Boards be invested with any administrative or executive powers or are they merely to make recommendations and submit reports?

(4) Is the normal machinery for disbursing or dealing with state finances overridden by functions assigned to the governor and the Development Boards under Art. 371?

(5) If an allocation of funds for developmental expenditure over a region is approved by the governor, can it be debated, examined, altered or voted upon by the legislature, or does it become a sum 'charged on the Consolidated Fund of the state'?

My own opinion regarding the correct constitutional position is as follows:

(1) Art. 371, which deals with two of the most important states of India, must be interpreted in harmony with the rest of the Constitution. It must be read not *in vacuo* but in the context of the other provisions of the Constitution which embody the basic scheme of governance of each state by the duly elected representatives of the people. Since the President's order under Art. 371 may provide for nomination and not election of the members of the Development Boards, it is clear that while the reports and recommendations of the Development Boards should be given great weight, the Development Boards cannot be assigned the executive functions of ministers or the legislative functions of the state Assembly.

(2) Art. 371 enables the President to make an order providing for 'special responsibility of the governor' for the three matters mentioned in clause (2) of that Article. These words merely indicate that the governor should exercise his functions in his discretion and is not bound to follow, and may in a fit case override, the advice of the Council of Ministers. But the fact that the governor has 'special responsibility' in certain matters does not mean that he has to make the regular decisions in those matters. Upon

the President's order being made under Art. 371, the governor has only to *ensure* that appropriate Development Boards are established, and to *ensure* that equitable allocation of funds is made for developmental expenditure, and equitable arrangement is made for education and employment opportunities, in different regions—bearing in mind 'the requirements of the state as a whole'. There is a sharp, though subtle, distinction between the special responsibility to ensure that an equitable allocation is made and the power or duty to make the actual allocation.

(3) Art. 371 cannot be read as if it provided for the governor's rule, analogous to the President's rule under Art. 356. It is significant to note that a Proclamation of President's rule under Art. 356 is hedged in by various safeguards and has to enure normally for a period of only six months: whereas under Art. 371 there are no safeguards whatever and the establishment of the Development Boards can be for an indefinite period.

There are cogent reasons to support the view that it is desirable *not* to constitute separate Development Boards but to evolve some other machinery by which the problem of regional imbalances can be resolved:

(a) Politicians, by and large, have an insatiable appetite for the loaves and fishes of ministerial office. Once the Development Boards are constituted, the demand for disintegrating the Maharashtra State and constituting Vidarbha and Marathwada as separate states will increase, and not diminish. The Development Boards, with their vision necessarily confined to the region they represent, will make demands which are disproportionately large and not 'subject to the requirements of the state as a whole' as enjoined by Art. 371; and the non-fulfilment of the demands will only intensify the agitation for separate states.

(b) It would be difficult to resist similar demands by other regions of Maharashtra, which will ask for separate Development Boards. There is already a unanimous resolution of the Maharashtra legislature passed in March 1989, requesting the Government of India to amend Art.

371 (2) with a view to establishing a separate Development Board for the Konkan.

(c) The establishment of Development Boards in Maharashtra is also bound to give rise to demands in other states for at least Development Boards in regions which have been clamouring to be recognized as separate states, e.g., Jharkhand in the state of Bihar and Telangana in Andhra Pradesh.

(d) It will result in constitutional and political conflict between the governor and Development Boards on the one hand, and the Council of Ministers and the state legislature on the other.

(e) It will drag the governor into the political arena and considerably vitiate the normal functioning of the democratic process.

If action is hastily taken under Art. 371 on a certain legal basis and that legal basis is ultimately held by the Supreme Court to be erroneous, it would obviously create enormous political problems—and Heaven knows we have enough already!

In the circumstances, may I suggest that you kindly consider the desirability of advising the President to make a reference to the Supreme Court under Art. 143 of the Constitution so that the government and the public have clear guidance on the baffling questions which arise under Art. 371. An authoritative pronouncement on the legal implications of Art. 371 may induce second thoughts in the minds of the ill-informed who are today agitating for invoking that Article. In any event, if action is taken thereafter under that Article in the light of the legal position elucidated by the Supreme Court, it would then be beyond the pale of controversy.

In view of the urgency and importance of the matter, I have taken the liberty of sending a copy of this letter to the President of India.

With warm regards, and every good wish,

Yours sincerely,
Nani A. Palkhivala

His Excellency Shri Vishwanath Pratap Singh,
The Prime Minister of India,
New Delhi

Bombay,
6 April 1995

My dear Dr Manmohan Singh,

I am taking the liberty of enclosing my article on the Union Budget 1995-96. A copy has also been sent to every Member of Parliament.

Your proposal in Clause 19 of the Finance Bill to amend Section 80-IA of the Income-tax Act—with a view to allowing a tax holiday in respect of profits and gains from industrial undertakings engaged in development of infrastructure—is well-conceived. But entrepreneurs will ask the question—can they be sure that the law proposed by you will be the law of India at the time when the tax holiday begins for them a few years later? That is why I am very keen that a finance minister of your integrity and extraordinary calibre should start the practice of giving an assurance which can operate as promissory estoppel. (Please see pages 4 to 6 of the booklet.) This assurance is of the essence if we wish to ensure whole-hearted participation by industrial houses in the development of our infrastructure. There is a letter on this subject today in *The Times of India* (Bombay edition) of which I enclose a copy. It would be a great pity if India continues to have the sullied reputation of a country without a sense of honour while you are still in charge of the Finance Ministry.

There are three important proposals in the Finance Bill,* which, if I may say so, should not be there at all because Parliament would not have enough time to devote to changes (in the existing substantive law) of a far-reaching effect and controversial nature, embodied in a Finance Bill and not in a separate Income-tax Amendment Bill. Those three proposals are contained in Clauses 14, 31 and 36 of the Finance Bill. (Please see pages 7 to 11 of the booklet.) They must be referred to a Select

---

*1. *Income from business or profession and from other sources to be computed only in accordance with cash or mercantile system of accounting and no other.*

2. *Deduction of tax at source to be made from fees paid for professional or technical services.*

3. *When bonus shares are sold, their cost to be taken at nil.*

Committee of both the Houses before, if at all, they are made the law of India. I find it surprising that the officials in the Finance Ministry did not think it desirable to draw your attention to the far-reaching implications and highly controversial nature of the proposed amendments.

I think our country has reached a stage when a major decision will have to be taken whether laws should be passed by both the Houses of Parliament after full consideration of the pros and cons, or whether the law should be allowed to be made by the barons of bureaucracy by using the instrument of a Finance Bill in order to avoid detailed and careful scrutiny, by Parliament, of the proposed law. This question is of such grave importance to the future of democracy that I have taken the liberty of writing personal letters to some important Members of Parliament seeking their assistance in ensuring that the above-mentioned proposals in the Finance Bill are not passed into law without a reference to a Select Committee. The first necessary step is to ensure that the proposed Clauses are dropped from the Finance Bill before the Bill is taken up for clause-by-clause discussion by each House.

Yours sincerely,
Nani A. Palkhivala

The Hon'ble Dr Manmohan Singh,
Minister for Finance,
Government of India,
New Delhi

Bombay,
26 June 1995

My dear Justice Khanna,

I would like to take this opportunity, on the twentieth anniversary of the Emergency, to thank you profusely not only on my own behalf but on behalf of the entire nation, for the memorable role you played during those dark days of the Emergency. The country owes you a debt of gratitude—which can never be repaid—for the courage and intellectual integrity you displayed even at great personal loss in doing your duty by the citizen.

I have written articles in some of our newspapers wherein I could not help mentioning about the judge who was mainly responsible for preserving the identity and framework of the Constitution. I am enclosing two of the articles in the hope that they might be of interest to you.

I hope you are keeping well.

With warm regards, and wishing you long years of good health and happiness.

Yours sincerely,
Nani A. Palkhivala

The Hon'ble Mr Justice H.R. Khanna,
New Delhi

23 October 1997

My dear Shri Narayanan,

I cannot tell you how proud and happy I am that the President of my country has distinguished himself so honourably and with such moral courage. There is nothing but praise all over the country for what you have done with great confidence and strength in India's darkest hour.

May God bless you with many long years of good health and continued service to the country.

Yours sincerely,
Nani A. Palkhivala

His Excellency Shri K.R. Narayanan,
President of India,
New Delhi

Bombay House,
Fort, Mumbai
8 September 1998

My dear Swami Ranganathanandaji,

I was happy to learn from Sri S. Ramakrishnan of the Bharatiya Vidya Bhavan that you have been appointed the president of the Ramakrishna Mission.

This is just a line to wish you strength, good health and many long years to lead the Mission on its chosen path. You have spent your entire life in the service of the Mission, having joined the Order at the tender age of sixteen years. It is noble souls like you and the inmates of the Mission all over the country who keep India alive and vibrant in spite of all-round corruption and degradation which we are witnessing today.

With my Pranams, affectionate regards, and, once again, wishing you good health, peace and joy in the unfolding future.

Yours sincerely,
Nani A. Palkhivala

Swami Ranganathanandaji,
President,
Ramakrishna Mission Institute of Culture,
Gol Park,
Calcutta

Bombay House,
Fort, Bombay
3 October 1996

My dear Ramakrishnan,

As I told you some time ago, both on the phone and at our personal meetings, it is most imperative that for some time you must set aside the day-to-day administration of the Bhavan and disengage yourself from the ephemeral matters which pertain to the Bhavan but are not of lasting importance. You should engage yourself in setting down on paper your thoughts and your recollections of the facts. This is the best service you can render the Bhavan and the best service you can render to posterity in our country which has no sense of history. For this purpose, you must have a person who will be whole time available for this job and who can assist you in this work intelligently and with a sense of dedication. I shall be happy to bear the expenses of such a person as far as emoluments and other benefits are concerned.

As I told you today in desperation, the meetings and functions of the Bhavan can always be arranged and taken care of. But it is of paramount importance to reduce to writing the facts known to you. You will do it not in a spirit of self-glorification but in a spirit of dedicated service to the Bhavan which you alone can render at this juncture. I feel so strongly on this matter that I would be more than happy to give up my vice-presidentship of the Bhavan if that can induce you to take up the idea as quickly and as speedily as is possible.

With warm regards,

Yours sincerely,
N.A. Palkhivala

Sri S. Ramakrishnan,
Bharatiya Vidya Bhavan,
Bombay

Copy to: Sri C. Subramaniam,
President,
Bharatiya Vidya Bhavan

SOURCES

◆

'Philosophy of Life'; 'Concern for the Poor in Zoroastrianism', *Bhavan's Journal,* 15 March 1999; 'Are We Masters of Our Fate?'; 'The Message of the Prophets'; 'Essential Unity of All Religions'; Bharatiya Vidya Bhavan, Bombay, 1990; 'The Spirit—Supreme and Infinite'; 'Brahman—The All-Pervading Reality'; 'All Matter is Nothing But Energy'; 'Ancient Insights and Modern Man'; all reproduced from *India's Priceless Heritage,* Bharatiya Vidya Bhavan, Bombay 1989.

'The Judiciary and the Legal Profession—Yesterday, Today and Tomorrow, *125th Anniversary Celebrations of the Bombay High Court, Nagpur,* 'Lawyers in the Dock', *The Government Law College, Bombay, 1948;* 'Sentinels of Democracy', *The First Annual Conference of the Bar Association of India, Bombay, 18 November 1972;* 'Female Education—The Priority of Priorities', *Convocation Address, SNDT Women's University, Bombay, 19 December 1992;* 'Adi Shankaracharya: Builder of the Empire of Spirit', *Public Lecture under the Auspices of the Bharatiya Vidya Bhavan, Bombay, 7 April 1989,* 'A Remarkable School Teacher', *A tribute, published in September 1948, to Palkhivala's teacher, Nusserwanji P. Pavri, who taught for almost half a century in high schools in Bombay;* 'Redesigning India for the Twenty-First Century', *K. Santhanam Memorial Lecture, under the auspices of the Bharatiya Vidya Bhavan, 8 August 1985;* all taken from *We, the Nation,* UBS Publishers' Distributors Ltd, New Delhi.

'A Holistic View of the World', *National Science Day Lecture, New Delhi, 29 February 1996;* 'The Ailing Planet: The Green Movement's Role', *The Indian Express, 24 November 1994;* 'Obedience To the Unforceable', *Convocation Address, The Xavier Labour Relations Institute, Jamshedpur, 29 February 1980;* 'The Future of Democracy in India', *Bhai Parmanand Memorial Lecture, New Delhi, 27 November 1979;* 'The Tasks Before a Free People', *Public Address in Bombay, 13 April 1977, and 'Open Letter to the Prime Minister', The Illustrated Weekly of India, 17 April 1977;* 'Has the Constitution Failed?', *The Illustrated Weekly of India, 16 September 1979;* 'Desirable Changes in Constitutional Law', *Convocation Address, The University of Madras, 28 September 1979;* 'Election of the President of India—The Five Cardinal Rules', *The Times of India,* 1 July 1992; 'States Are Not Vassals of the Union', *Seminar on Centre-State Relations, Bangalore, 5-7 August 1983, abridged version, India Today, 31 August 1983;* 'Socialism—Its Kernel and Its Shell', *Public Addresses Delivered in 1972 in New Delhi, Bombay, Bangalore and Goa;* 'The Humanistic Face of Capitalism', *The Indian Merchants Chamber, Bombay, 26 February 1974;* 'The Budget of My Dreams', *The Illustrated Weekly of India, 14 February 1982;* 'India Has Lost Her Soul', *Evening of 30 January 1948;* 'Mahatma—The Pilgrim of Eternity', *The Mahatma Gandhi Memorial Foundation, Washington D.C., 2 October 1978;* 'Rajaji—A Man For All Seasons', *On the 101st birth anniversary of C. Rajagopalachari, 10 December 1979;* 'Sir Jamshedji B. Kanga' *On his 70th birthday, 27 February 1945;* 'M.C. Chagla—A Great Judge', *On his relinquishing the Chief Justiceship of the Bombay High Court in October 1958;* all taken from *'We, the People',* UBS Publishers' Distributors Ltd, Twelfth reprint 1997, New Delhi, Strand Book Stall, Mumbai, 1984.

'The Union Budget 1993-94', Public Talk in Bombay on 3 March 1993, and subsequently in Calcutta, Ahmedabad, Delhi, Pune, Hyderabad, Madras, Bangalore, Muscat and Dubai; 'The Union Budget 1994-95', Public Talk in Bombay on 3 March 1994, and subsequently in Calcutta, Ahmedabad, Delhi, Pune, Hyderabad, Madras, Bangalore, Muscat and Dubai; 'The Union Budget of 1995-96', The Times of India, 21

March 1995 and Financial Express, 27 March 1995; 'Bypassing Parliamentary Select Committee', all from the Forum of Free Enterprise, Mumbai.

'Memories of the Emergency', *The Indian Express, 25 June 1995;* 'Emergency Remembered', *The Times of India, 26 June 1995;* 'Hindutva and State', *Press Statement, 8 March 1996;* 'Corruption in Administration', *Press Statement, 29 June 1994;* 'Electoral Reforms', *Press Statements;* 'Some Suggestions For Accelerating Economic Growth'; 'Asian Values and Economic Development', *Rieter Celebration at St. Andrews, Scotland, 6 May 1995;* 'The Current Economic Situation in India', *The Yeshwantrao Chavan Memorial Lecture, (1996-97), Bombay, 26 November' 1996;* 'Indian Economy—The Shape of Things to Come', *Mashreq Bank, Dubai, 13 March 1997;* 'The Philosophy of Taxation in India'; 'Education for India's Moral and Spiritual Regeneration', *First Convocation Address, Sri Sathya Sai Institute of Higher Learning—Deemed University—Prasanthi Nilayam (A.P.), 22 November 1982;* 'The Treason of the Intellectual', *Convocation Address, The University of Bangalore, 15 January 1972;* 'Education and the Art of Reading', *Ganesh Ramrao Bhatkal Memorial Lecture, Bombay, 20 September 1995;* 'The Relevance of Sri Aurobindo's Philosophy Today' *All India Radio, Bombay, 14 August 1972;* 'A Tremendous Moral Force', *Bhavan's Journal, 1 June 1985;* 'Swami Vivekananda', *Centenary Celebrations of Ramakrishna Mission and Swami Vivekananda's Return from his Spiritual Odyssey to the West, Bombay, 7 January 1997;* 'Dadaji and Indira Devi', *Centenary Oration, Calcutta 22 January 1996;* 'The Enduring Relevance of Sardar Vallabhbhai Patel', *Patel Memorial Lecture, All India Radio, 30 October 1992;* 'He Is Best Suited to Become Prime Minister', *In conversation with a reporter, The Times of India, 25 December 1997;* 'Salute to Solzhenitsyn', *The Times of India, 13 June 1994;* 'Minoo Masani—A Humane Human Being', *Bhavan's Journal, 15 June 1998;* 'My Experiences As An Ambassador', *Indian Council of World Affairs, Bombay, 28 December 1978;* 'Six Fatal Mistakes', *Chairman's Statement at the 61st Annual General Meeting of The Associated Cement Companies Ltd. 3 September 1997;* 'Leadership'

Bombay Samachar, 21 March 1997; 'Lessons From Israel: A Vision of the Indian Subcontinent', *The Times of India, 2 July 1994*; 'Eternal Friends, Natural Partners', *The Times of India, 25 November 1994*; 'Mumbai, The Most Expensive Slum in the World!', *Bombay Times, The Times of India, 14 November 1997*